Teaching School Subjects 11–19: Mathematics

Candia Morgan, Anne Watson and Clare Tikly

 RoutledgeFalmer
Taylor & Francis Group

LONDON AND NEW YORK

First published 2004
by RoutledgeFalmer
2 Park Square, Milton Park, Abingdon, Oxfordshire, OX14 4RN

Simultaneously published in the USA and Canada
by RoutledgeFalmer
29 West 35th Street, New York, NY 10001

RoutledgeFalmer is an imprint of the Taylor & Francis Group

© 2004 Candia Morgan, Anne Watson, Clare Tikly

Typeset in Sabon and Bell Gothic by
Florence Production Ltd, Stoodleigh, Devon
Printed and bound in Great Britain by
TJ International Ltd, Padstow, Cornwall

British Library Cataloguing in Publication Data
A catalogue record for this book is available from the
British Library

Library of Congress Cataloging in Publication Data
A catalog record for this book has been requested

ISBN 0–415–32112–3 (Hb)
ISBN 0–415–32113–1 (Pb)

Contents

Illustrations

FIGURES

TABLES

Preface

When the editors of the Teaching School Subjects series approached us, we were immediately struck by the importance of the theme of the series: the unique role that the subject plays in teaching in the secondary school. As teacher educators involved in working with both beginning and experienced mathematics teachers, we have sometimes been alarmed at how little mathematics itself has featured in teacher education and in guidance for teachers, even in some courses and publications aimed specifically at mathematics teachers. It seems as if teaching mathematics is not really any different from teaching English or science or geography or any other subject – we just have to substitute our curriculum, our textbook, our exercise, our problems into generic templates of teacher knowledge and skills.

Yet in conversations with colleagues from other subject areas we have often found ourselves saying 'but it's different in mathematics'. Writing this book has given us the opportunity to examine this, initially intuitive, claim, to explore how the nature of mathematics influences each aspect of the job of teaching mathematics and to justify our belief that good mathematics teaching is continually informed by thinking about mathematics beyond the confines of the textbook or the examination paper.

We have imagined a reader who is new to teaching, perhaps recently qualified, on a training course or considering embarking on one – and a specialist in mathematics. This is not a textbook that will take you step by step to meet the standards required to enter the profession. It will certainly help you to address all of these standards, but it will, we hope, help you to go further: to build a sound foundation for continuing professional development and, importantly, to become the kind of teacher who inspires young people to learn and to enjoy learning mathematics.

Candia Morgan, Anne Watson
and Clare Tikly
December 2003

Abbreviations

ACME	Advisory Committee on Mathematics Education
APU	Assessment of Performance Unit
ATM	Association of Teachers of Mathematics
BPRS	Best Practice Research Scholarship
CAME	Cognitive Acceleration in Mathematics Education
CSMS	Concepts in Secondary Science and Mathematics Project
EAL	English as an Additional Language
EBD	Emotional and Behavioural Difficulties
GCSE	General Certificate of Secondary Education
HEI	Higher Education Institution
ICT	Information and Communication Technology
IEP	Individual Education Plan
ITE	Initial Teacher Education
JMC	Joint Mathematical Council
LEA	Local Education Authority
MA	Mathematical Association
NC	National Curriculum
NFER	National Foundation for Educational Research
NQT	Newly Qualified Teacher
QCA	Qualifications and Curriculum Authority
QTS	Qualified Teacher Status
SMILE	Secondary Mathematics Individualised Learning Experience
SMT	Senior Management Team

Chapter 1

Introduction

What is special about being a teacher of mathematics? How is it different from 'just' being a teacher or from being a teacher of another school subject? You may respond that you have your specialist knowledge of mathematics, your love of the subject, your desire to help young people share that knowledge and enthusiasm, and to help them to gain some of the skills and qualifications that will be of importance to them and to society in the future. 'I know mathematics, and now I want to learn how to teach.' These are some of the reasons commonly given by people applying for initial teacher training courses. Of course, these are all important prerequisites, but we will argue that there is more to becoming a mathematics teacher than learning how to teach. Crucially, we believe that continuing to learn and re-learn mathematics, and to learn about students learning mathematics are essential factors in your professional development at all stages in your career.

EXAMPLE

One of the first topics Maria was expected to teach was quadratic equations. She prepared carefully for the lesson, refreshing her memory of solution methods, looking at the methods presented in the students' textbook and mentioned in the school's scheme of work, the National Curriculum and the examination syllabus. She also found out what sort of questions about quadratic equations her students were expected to be able to answer in the textbook and in examination questions. In the first lesson, she explained a method of solution by factorisation carefully and clearly, and was pleased to find that most of the class were able to answer correctly most of the questions in the textbook. A successful lesson, she concluded. After the lesson, her mentor, whose class she was teaching, congratulated her and then posed some questions that made her think:

- Some of the students got all the early questions in the exercise right but then gave the answers 8 and 12 to the equation $x^2 + 4x = 12$; how might they be getting these answers? And how might you address this?

- How are you going to respond to the student who asked what the point of quadratic equations is?

- What 'big mathematical ideas' could you use this topic to develop?

- What sort of links could you help the students make with their learning in other areas of mathematics, including number and geometry?

- How are you going to respond to the student who looks up the quadratic formula and brings it to your next lesson?

- How are you going to respond to the student who looks up quadratic equations on the Internet and finds references to cubic, quartic and quintic equations, and the existence (and non-existence) of solution methods?

Maria started her teaching with a perspective (common to many beginning teachers) that took the mathematical content for granted, and assumed that the clarity and completeness of her explanations would be sufficient to communicate her knowledge to her students. Clearly, her personal mathematical knowledge, her research into the curriculum and her excellent communication skills were vitally important and provided a sound foundation for her development as a mathematics teacher. Yet her mentor's questions highlighted other critical factors: the ways in which students may understand or misunderstand mathematical ideas; the ways in which students may or may not be motivated to learn; the image of mathematics as a whole that is communicated to students; the need not only to teach each topic separately but to make links between topics and to build strong foundations for future mathematical learning; variations between students and the need to be aware of these variations, and to value and support the learning of each individual. These are some of the issues that we will address in this book, perhaps not providing direct answers to the mentor's questions, but suggesting ways of thinking about mathematics, about students, and about learning and teaching that will help you to find your own answers.

We imagine that most readers of this book are likely to be in the early years of their career. Yet we believe that more experienced teachers may also find some parts useful and that those working with beginning teachers may use it with those they are mentoring – and find that they are learning in the process. Certainly, in the process of writing the book we have found ourselves restructuring and developing our knowledge of mathematics, our ideas about learning and teaching mathematics, and our ways of working with our own student teachers.

At present, mathematics teaching in England and Wales is regulated by the National Curriculum (DfEE, 1999) and, at Key Stage 3, is guided by the National Strategy and the National Framework for Mathematics (DfES, 2001). Teacher education is regulated by standards that must be met by all teachers in order to achieve Qualified Teacher Status (QTS) (DfES, 2002) and to have this status confirmed at the end of an induction period. The details of these regulations and guidance are available in the documents cited, but these are subject to revision as policies change. Rather than attempt to refer in detail to each curriculum objective or teaching standard, our aim in this book is to provide a more holistic approach to mathematics and to teaching mathematics. We will address all aspects of the standards for QTS and for induction, and will work with examples of mathematical content relevant to the National Curriculum and curricula for post-16 students, but we will not generally give specific references to the official documents. This approach reflects our belief that mathematics is more than a list of discrete topics and that becoming a teacher of mathematics involves more than acquiring a defined set of knowledge and skills.

Similarly, you will find no separate section devoted to the use of information and communication technology (ICT). This is not because we do not think that ICT has an important role to play in the learning and teaching of mathematics (indeed, some types of ICT use have great potential to transform mathematical activity) but because we see it as one set of tools among many others – and one that is changing rapidly with new developments in technology. Reference to the use of various forms of ICT occurs throughout the book, integrated into the context of discussions of mathematics, learning and teaching.

We have included a number of references to the work of researchers and other authors in the field of mathematics education and to research that we have carried out ourselves. This is not just a claim to academic respectability! We believe that research and the accumulated knowledge of other professionals can and should play an important part in informing our thinking about teaching and our practice. For example, in Chapter 8 we cite some results of research about children's understanding of specific mathematical concepts and show how these might affect your design of questions for your own students to assess their prior knowledge before starting to teach a topic. Indeed, in later chapters we suggest that undertaking research into your own teaching and the learning of your students is a powerful way of enhancing your professional development and contributing to the development of the profession itself. At some points we have tried to draw your attention to books and other sources that can be particularly useful to you, providing information and evidence to inform your planning and teaching, or offering further suggestions of lesson ideas.

The chapters in the rest of the book are arranged in three parts (corresponding approximately, but not exclusively, to the main sections of the current *Professional Standards for Qualified Teacher Status* (DfES, 2002): Knowledge and Understanding; Teaching; Professional Values and Practice). The theme of the first part, *Framing the subject*, is mathematics itself: its place in schools and in society; the relationship between the mathematics taught in school and that encountered in the university and in the 'real world'; alternative ways of thinking about the mathematics in the school curriculum. The subject mathematics is not the same in different contexts and, as you prepare to teach it in school, you need to consider its complexity and connectedness, its fundamental ideas, its applications and how these may relate to the beliefs, understandings and motivations of your students. We believe that teachers' knowledge and understanding of mathematics continue to develop throughout their professional career as they prepare and teach their lessons, and as they observe and reflect on the ways in which their students learn. This part does not, therefore, seek to give a complete picture of mathematical subject knowledge for teaching. Rather, it provides examples and ways of thinking about restructuring and recontextualising your own knowledge to enhance this developmental process. The issues, examples and 'big mathematical ideas' introduced here form a basis for thinking about learning and teaching the subject in later parts.

The four chapters in the second part, *Learning and teaching mathematics*, focus on students and the mathematics classroom. We start by thinking about students and the ways in which they may learn and be motivated to learn mathematics. This understanding of learners and learning, together with the understanding of mathematics, underpins the planning process. In Chapters 6 and 7, we address planning for teaching, not by providing a comprehensive guide or framework for lesson planning (these are generally provided by initial training courses and may be found published elsewhere, for example, Johnston-Wilder *et al.*, 1999) but by offering some example lessons and discussing the principles and thought processes behind their design. While the examples may provide some immediately practical ideas for lessons, we hope that the discussion will provide more generally applicable approaches to planning as you develop your own lessons. In the final chapter of this part, we turn to assessment, focusing primarily on the role that assessment plays in the learning and teaching process. We consider what information about students' mathematical understanding may be useful (or, indeed, essential) for teachers and suggest approaches to gathering that information and using it to inform and enhance learning and teaching.

The final part of the book, *Professional values and practice*, takes a broader view of what it means to be a mathematics teacher, considering how teachers can take responsibility for their own practices and for the development of better mathematics education for all. We start by examining some of the assumptions that are commonly made about what kinds of mathematics curriculum and teaching may be offered to various groups of students. Having high expectations of all results in teachers constantly challenging these assumptions, while having the realistic and practical means of providing access to the curriculum for all students.

Entering teaching and developing as a teacher are not just about gaining skills and experience. Becoming a mathematics teacher can be seen as learning to participate in a community of practice that continually evolves as it responds to changes in wider society and as new participants bring with them new perspectives, energy and initiative. We believe that it is important that teachers as professionals neither adopt traditional practices uncritically nor develop their practices only in response to external pressures. Chapter 10 looks at the ways in which teachers may be involved in the processes of curriculum development and in the development of approaches to teaching. This chapter reviews teacher involvement in developments at local and national level, and suggests ways in which individual teachers can play an active role in developing their own practice and contributing to the development of the wider profession.

Continuing professional development is the theme of the final chapter. We see professional development as something that continues throughout a teacher's career, involving a deepening understanding of the processes of learning and teaching mathematics and of mathematics itself, and a developing ambition and vision to improve the learning experience for students of mathematics. For many, it will also lead to career enhancement, taking opportunities to lead a mathematics department, to support the development of new teachers, to develop some aspect of the mathematics curriculum within a school or as part of a local or national project. We discuss ways in which mathematics teachers can actively promote their own professional development. A key to this is working with fellow teachers and other professionals both within the walls of the classroom and the school, and outside the school as part of the broader community of mathematics teachers.

Part I

Framing the subject

What do teachers need to know about mathematics in order to teach it? It seems natural to assume that well-qualified graduates of mathematics or of other highly quantitative disciplines are sure to know enough. Moreover, most programmes of initial teacher education for graduates are too short and crowded to allow much time for developing thinking about the subject matter itself. Yet our experience, and that of many other teachers we have known, is that the knowledge needed to be a successful learner and to pass examinations is only a part of the mathematical knowledge that is needed to be a successful teacher, to communicate effectively with a wide range of learners, to structure their learning experiences, to address their difficulties constructively, to inspire students with enthusiasm for mathematics and with an understanding of its potential use. We hope to prompt you to reflect on mathematics and on the ways in which you and others may know and understand it.

The chapters in this part address the nature of mathematics, its privileged place in the school curriculum and its role in the 'real world'. The mathematics studied at university often seems to be a completely different subject from that found in school, but we would argue that insight into advanced mathematics and its application is an essential basis for teaching. We explore some of the 'big ideas' and connections between mathematical topics and consider how these can be used to inform teaching at secondary school level. The theme of connections within mathematics and to other domains of human experience is important, not only in this part, where we look at mathematics itself, but throughout the book as we try to find ways of helping learners to make sense of mathematics.

Chapter 2

Why teach mathematics?
Why learn mathematics?

KEY QUESTIONS

- What are the aims of mathematics education?
- What reasons may students have for wanting to learn mathematics?
- Why does mathematics hold such a central position in the school curriculum?

Why teach mathematics indeed! With mathematics as a high proportion of your degree studies you have very marketable skills. You may already have been working in industry, commerce or the public services. You may be a recent graduate who has focused for some time on preparing to become a mathematics teacher or you may be 'testing the water' in the classroom, trying to decide if a career in education suits you. Your own education may have been entirely in England or you may have first-hand experience of one or more other national education systems. Mathematics teachers as a group have a diverse range of knowledge, attributes and experiences to contribute to our schools but generally share some common aims. Significantly, you are likely on the one hand to enjoy mathematical activity yourself and on the other hand to enjoy working with children and young people, and to have a desire to contribute to their lives so that they might derive benefit from their mathematics, as you have done. In making a decision to enter mathematics teaching, you have probably already reflected on your personal reasons for wanting to teach and for choosing mathematics as your subject. But why should mathematics be taught? In this chapter we discuss reasons for the place of mathematics in the school curriculum and the ways in which studying mathematics may impact on learners' lives and on society more broadly.

The most recent version of the National Curriculum for England and Wales states some of the ways in which mathematics is important: in everyday life and employment; as a powerful set of reasoning and problem-solving tools for understanding and changing the world; as a creative discipline; as a source of pleasure and wonder (DfEE, 1999: 14). This provides a reassuringly broad set of goals that becomes more difficult to summarise briefly as we realise their complexity and their implications. In fact, we begin to realise that the responsibilities of mathematics teachers are rather awesome. Are the claims made about the potential value of school mathematics valid? Do the programmes of study in the National Curriculum make it possible to design schemes of work that reflect an appropriate balance between the various aims? What is the full extent of teachers' accountability?

The statement of the importance of mathematics goes beyond possible benefits for individual learners to outline how mathematics can contribute to an understanding of the world and the ability to take part in public life. It is likely that most teachers support the notion that an educated individual has a chance to be an asset in society through a constructive career and active citizenship. What type of education is necessary to provide such general benefit to society and to what extent is mathematics a necessary component? Are mathematics teachers able to answer with integrity the most commonly asked question: 'Why do we have to learn this?' In our experience it is not always easy to come up with a satisfactory answer to this question, particularly when faced with a bored teenager who seems unlikely to be convinced by suggestions that he might enjoy solving quadratic equations, or appreciate their beauty, or that this will be useful for him at some point in his future career, or that it will make him a better citizen. Such a situation is less likely to arise, however, if the teenager's general experience of learning mathematics has been purposeful and motivating, and if his teacher's approach to teaching mathematics has taken account of a broad set of goals and provided students with a meaningful insight into the ways that mathematics can have an impact on their present and future lives and on the society of which they are a part.

PURPOSE AND MOTIVATION

When we have asked prospective teachers why they like mathematics, we get a wide range of different answers:

I've always been good at it.

You always know whether your answer is right or wrong.

I like seeing how it can be applied in so many different ways.

You don't have to learn very much because you can work it all out from a few principles.

Doing mathematics is like playing a game.

I like the way that one thing leads to another.

It's a powerful way of thinking about things in the world.

It's challenging.

It's easy.

It's so satisfying to get to a solution after struggling with a problem for a long time.

You may agree with some of these preferences or you may have others of your own. Indeed, you may not even really understand what some of them mean, as they have little connection with your own experience of learning and doing mathematics. It is important to recognise, however, that people have very different reasons for enjoying mathematics and that there are very different ways of experiencing it. This means that, even if your teachers made mathematics enjoyable for you, their teaching approaches may not have suited all your classmates and certainly may not suit all your future students. An important challenge for mathematics teachers is to identify what may motivate their students to learn mathematics and to see it as a purposeful activity – even if they are not 'good at it'.

We are using the terms *motivation* and *purpose* and need to distinguish between them. Students may be motivated to engage in mathematics lessons for all sorts of reasons. They may want to succeed in gaining a qualification or to please their teacher or their parents; these kinds of motivation are sometimes referred to as 'extrinsic' motivation because they have nothing to do with the nature of the learning activity or of the knowledge being acquired. Students whose only motivation is of this kind are unlikely to enjoy the subject or to choose to study it at higher levels. Other students may enjoy certain kinds of activities in their mathematics lessons because they like working in a group or using a computer. While this kind of motivation is more closely related to the activity itself, it is still not directly related to the mathematics being learnt and may not be sustained once the novelty has worn off. Yet others may be interested in finding the answer to an intriguing mathematical problem or enjoy the challenge of solving a puzzle; they may feel satisfaction in knowing that they have achieved a correct answer or generalisation or a convincing proof or they may appreciate the elegance of a neat solution or the power of a method that can be applied in many different contexts. These students are motivated by the mathematical activity itself and, for them, this activity is purposeful in its own right. It is this group of students who are most likely to sustain an interest in the subject and to wish to continue to study mathematics.

What can make mathematics lessons purposeful and motivating for secondary school students? Teachers generally have a feel for when lessons are going well: the happy hum of activity; relaxed comments and questions; no hint of doubt about purpose. It sometimes seems a mystery why one lesson works like this, while students are restless or fail to engage with activities in another lesson. When lessons go well it is worth trying to identify which mathematical objectives and activities are contributing to the higher than usual levels of motivation, and to consider them separately from the numerous other factors that affect classroom ethos. Sometimes the selected approaches to a topic are particularly effective in unlocking pathways to understanding. New insights emerge linked to what has previously been consolidated, with comments like 'Now I've got it!'

In secondary schools it is often, though not always, the case that higher-attaining students are more regularly motivated to work hard at mathematics. Pleasure and excitement in acquiring new knowledge and understanding are sometimes features, but these students too will have a mixture of motivations. These may include focused career aspirations, self-esteem, a sense of responsibility, or a wish to fine-tune skills to apply to other subjects. On the other hand, where higher-attaining students are grouped together in 'top sets', a fast pace of work and pressure to achieve can have a negative effect on some of these students' motivation and self-esteem (Boaler *et al.*, 2000). It may be more difficult to motivate lower-attaining students to learn mathematics if they frequently experience failure or if they think that the qualification they are likely to achieve is not going to help them in the future to which they aspire. For these students, relying on extrinsic motivational factors is unlikely to be successful – but this does not mean that they cannot be motivated to participate in interesting and purposeful mathematics lessons. There are also likely to be cultural differences in the extent to which various factors motivate students, giving rise to differentiated patterns of participation and attainment. These issues are discussed in more detail in Chapter 9. For most students, whatever their level of attainment, to rise to the challenges inherent in learning mathematics, they need to appreciate its power to be useful, and to see that concepts and procedures might have a more general application.

When we talk about making the mathematics that we teach 'relevant' to students and to the 'real world' we need to be careful not to make simplistic assumptions about what young people may find relevant or real. Devising mathematical tasks set in the contexts of football, contemporary music or mobile phones may seem to make connections with important things in the lives of teenagers. While some students may indeed find these relevant and motivating, others will not, preferring to kick a ball, listen to a band or text their friends without thinking about these as topics for studying in the classroom. In fact, contrived tasks about 'popular' contexts run the risk of being seen as patronising by the very students they are intended to motivate. On the other hand, it is important to be aware that the classroom environment itself can be the 'real world' for children, in which they spend a high proportion of their waking hours each week. As such, classroom activities are almost certainly more of a reality than the distant contexts of adult life. If children are to get a glimpse of the possibilities of applying mathematical concepts and techniques outside school mathematics lessons, they must have experienced and talked about how they used mathematics to control and explain some activity that they have made their own. A 'pure' mathematical investigation can be real and relevant when it starts from a puzzling or interesting situation and gives rise to intriguing or aesthetically pleasing results – it can certainly be more real, relevant and purposeful for many teenagers than calculating mortgage repayments.

Although our discussion of teaching and learning mathematics in this book will centre on education in England, we should also set this in the context of a more global perspective. For a child in a country where incomes are low, who has to work to help to pay for the family's water supply, the calculation of quantities lost through leakage is a purposeful activity if it will allow the family to budget more effectively or to put forward arguments to the suppliers to reduce their charges. Taking a broader perspective, designing a more efficient supply system might benefit not only that family but also those of its neighbours. To be able to use mathematics to design a more efficient system, however, such children will have to extend their knowledge beyond the context of the leaking tap; they will need to have a more formal mathematical education. Taking another common situation, in many cities throughout the world are children who work with their parents, designing patterns, weaving fabrics and selling them to tourists. They learn to become adept at currency conversion, at estimating allowable discount as they bargain with customers, at the measurement of length, area and volume, at calculating what transport needs there will be to supply the business. Studying mathematics in school could relate directly to these children's everyday lives, providing them with tools that could make their current ways of living more efficient and comfortable, or help them to participate more effectively in struggles to transform the systems on which they depend. Yet the curriculum and teaching offered to them often makes little connection with their lived experience, being more suited to allowing a small minority of students to gain qualifications to find a way out of this deprived community than to empowering a larger number of students to play a role in improving the local economy and environment. One of the challenges for education in this community – and in others – is to devise and implement a curriculum that will allow mathematical learning to be purposeful both for individuals and for the society in which they live.

QUALIFICATIONS, EDUCATIONAL AND CAREER PATHWAYS

One of the key reasons given by many people for studying mathematics is that it is important to have a qualification in the subject in order to get a good job. Mathematical skills and qualifications have a significant impact on young people's employment prospects. Research has shown that adults who have failed to achieve basic numeracy skills have an increased likelihood of unemployment or employment in low-paid unskilled manual work and that poor numeracy seems to have an even greater negative impact on employability than poor literacy (Bynner and Parsons, 2000). At the same time, those who have studied Advanced level mathematics have been shown to be earning more than the rest of their peer group (Dolton and Vignoles, 2000). These findings do not enable us to say that studying more mathematics will necessarily increase your earning power, but they do suggest that the subject cannot be dismissed as irrelevant to life after school.

Of course, mathematics qualifications are also formally demanded as a prerequisite for numerous jobs and for entry into many courses in higher education. It is not always obvious why this demand is made – you might ask what the relevance of a GCSE in mathematics is for someone who intends to be an art teacher in a secondary school. Sometimes it seems that a mathematics qualification is being used as a general indicator of some kind of 'intelligence' rather than as an indicator of specific neces- sary knowledge and skills. Nevertheless, whatever the reasons, gaining a mathematics qualification at this level is a high priority for many students.

Beyond GCSE level, however, the position of mathematics is not so secure. Students who are striving for a stake in the modern world may perceive that qualifications in mathematics will enable them to achieve stable careers, personal advancement and some choice about where they work and live. Such attitudes are not universal, however, as shown by the unrelenting decrease in the proportions of young people opting for mathematics beyond GCSE level. This may be due in part to the increasing number of subjects available for young people to choose between. Recent investigations, however, suggest that mathematics at Advanced level has a reputation for being one of the harder subjects and that many young people see the subject as boring and irrelevant. This is a serious problem for the subject and for society as the decline in students studying mathematics at degree level is leading to a shortage in the supply of mathematicians to industry (and a shortage of well- qualified mathematics teachers in schools). Solutions to this problem need to be sought at a number of levels. The structure and content of the curriculum are constantly under review by the QCA (Qualifications and Curriculum Authority) and by high-level scientific and professional bodies such as the Royal Society and the JMC (Joint Mathematical Council).[1] There are high-profile attempts to change public attitudes towards mathematics; for example, Maths Year 2000 organised fun events in local shopping centres as well as in schools and on the Internet.[2] Most importantly, perhaps, the experiences that young people have with mathematics in school need to encourage them to enjoy studying mathematics, to appreciate its relevance and to feel that they can learn it successfully. Throughout this book we shall be attempting to suggest ways of thinking about mathematics and about teaching mathematics that should support you in providing these sorts of experiences.

MATHEMATICS AT WORK

As we have said, qualifications in mathematics are frequently required by employers or, if not required, are seen as a strong advantage. They are also required as prerequisites for further study in many other subject areas (although the decline in numbers choosing to study mathematics at Advanced level has led some university departments in subjects such as chemistry and economics to relax this requirement, adapting their courses to take account of lower levels of mathematical knowledge at entry). Public concern about standards of achievement in mathematics is often expressed in terms of the needs of industry and the benefits to the economy of good mathematical education. When we actually look at the mathematics that people use in their work, however, there is not a simple relationship to the mathematics they have been taught in school. In fact, studies of mathematics in work consistently show that people tend not to use the formal generalised mathematical techniques they have been taught, but rather use informal rules-of-thumb and problem-solving methods that are specifically applicable to the context of the job they are doing.

For example, nurses need to be able to work out what doses to give to their patients when a doctor has prescribed a particular quantity of a drug that is provided in solutions with different concentrations or in different standard measures. You might expect this to be a situation for application of the methods of working with ratio and proportion that have been learnt in school (and which are also taught to nurses in training). Studying what nurses actually do in these situations, however, shows that, while they sometimes do pencil-and-paper calculations of the type learnt in school, they often use less formal strategies that employ their expert professional knowledge of particular drugs. Hoyles *et al.* report a number of such strategies, including, for example, the nurse who described her calculation method for one drug that comes prepared in 100 mg per 2 ml vials: 'With the amakicine, whatever the dose is, if you double the dose it's what the mil is' (2002: 19). This combination of mathematical reasoning with contextual knowledge is more appropriate in these circumstances – and may help avoid some of the potentially life-threatening mistakes that the abstract application of school-learnt techniques would risk. Mistakes in converting between units, for example, are very common when operating abstractly, but very unlikely if the resulting dose is obviously ten times bigger than that which the nurse is used to administer. The same study found that nurses were dealing with complex problems involving regulating the amount of a drug in the body of the patient at any point during the day and adjusting the rates of flow and concentration of fluids in drips. Although their school mathematics probably had not included the mathematical modelling of such complex situations, nurses are able to solve the practical problems using a combination of calculation, estimation, rules-of-thumb and contextual knowledge (Noss *et al.*, 2002).

Even where very relevant mathematics has been studied, it may not be easy to transfer it immediately into the workplace context. A study that looked at the mathematics encountered by Advanced level college students on work placements found that students who were successful with the types of routine questions set in examinations nevertheless had difficulty recognising similar problems encountered in the workplace. For example, a student on work placement in a chemistry laboratory experienced significant difficulties as she attempted to make sense of a graph with multiple traces of temperature and pressure, using two different vertical axes. Although the mathematics involved was well within her experience and capabilities, the way in which she encountered it was bafflingly unfamiliar (Williams *et al.*, 2001).

The finding that school mathematics is not often simply applied at work is not a reason for arguing that mathematics does not need to be taught in school or even that learning mathematics in school does not help people cope with the mathematics they need in their work. It does, however, mean that we need to look critically at simplistic assumptions about the 'usefulness' of the mathematics we teach our students and recognise (as most students already do anyway) that the argument that 'you must learn topic X now because you will need it in your future job as a Y' is a weak justification for teaching the topic.

On the other hand, it can be argued that mathematics itself is of increasing importance in today's world and that being able to understand and engage with mathematics is a powerful asset for individuals as well as for employers in industry, business and government. However, what is needed is not just the 'basic skills' of 'numeracy' but the ability to make sense of the mathematics that underlies so much of the world around us and to make reasoned judgements about the solutions that are presented to us. A mathematician working in a major telecommunications company, reflecting on the future shape of mathematics education, writes about the need in an increasingly computerised working environment for employees at all levels to be able to make critical judgements about the systems they are expected to work with, not only making decisions about whether the solutions given by the computer are sensible or not, but also judging whether the systems are effective, efficient and appropriate for the problems faced in the workplace (Clayton, 1999).

At the time of writing this chapter, one of us is engaged in the process of buying a house and is faced with the need to make a decision about what kind of mortgage to apply for. To get beyond the lure of the advertising from a daunting number of possible lenders, it is necessary to take into account and manipulate many variables – not just the competing headline interest rates, but also the risks involved over the term of the mortgage and how those risks might interact with possible changes in national and international economies, and in personal circumstances and lifestyle. Understanding probabilities and handling risk is arguably one of the most important areas in which mathematical thinking can enhance not only personal and business-related financial decision-making, but also participation in reasoned debate about both personal lifestyle decisions and public policies in areas such as investment in health provision for different types of diseases and conditions; protection of the environment, exploitation of natural resources and genetically modified crops; and transport systems and safety regulations. This is not to say that mathematical reasoning by itself can resolve such issues, but rather to say that it can provide a firm base on which to construct ethical, economic and political arguments.

However strongly we may argue that mathematics is useful if not essential in many areas of human endeavour, a recurring theme in this section of the chapter has been the mismatch between this 'applied' mathematics and the way in which school mathematics is most usually defined in terms of discrete skills and techniques. The application of mathematics in important contexts (not just the contrived 'word problems' we find in most textbooks and examination papers) and the use of mathematical reasoning to inform and influence decision-making in a wide range of areas of endeavour do not fit neatly into a curriculum that is defined in terms of learning objectives at eight (or however many) levels. This is not to say that they cannot be addressed in mathematics classrooms. Indeed, teaching based around extended work on purposeful projects, involving applications and decision-making as well as investigations in pure areas of mathematics, has been shown to be just as effective at helping students to achieve conventional examination results as more traditional technique-centred teaching, while also leading to more positive attitudes towards the subject and recognition of its usefulness (Boaler, 1997).

The value of problem-centred teaching and learning is recognised in some recent changes to the post-16 curriculum for those students who do not choose to study mathematics at Advanced level. The need to enhance the level of mathematical knowledge and skills among this group of students has to be met by developing it in ways that are more clearly related to the demands of their other studies and their participation in society. The Key Skill 'Application of Number' is intended to be incorporated into all courses of study, developing mathematical knowledge and skills, while undertaking activities based in other areas of the academic or vocational curriculum. Students may also choose to study 'Free Standing Mathematics Units' which develop fundamental mathematical concepts through working on problems that are embedded in the other subjects they may be studying. For example, students may work on statistical techniques through considering problems in geography or sociology; they may develop a more advanced knowledge of functions and graphs while making connections with their studies in science or economics.[3] This curriculum poses a challenge for teachers who need to develop appropriate teaching methods and to collaborate with their colleagues in other subject areas to ensure that the problems they use are meaningful and relevant to the students' needs in those subjects. For teachers at other levels of schooling, where the curriculum is generally defined in more abstract ways, the challenge of finding ways of teaching that connect with real ways that mathematics is used is even greater. We suggest some examples of such approaches to planning and teaching mathematics in later chapters.

AESTHETIC APPRECIATION, CULTURAL KNOWLEDGE AND CREATIVITY

It is apparent that studying mathematics is of benefit to individuals in terms of career development and that an ability to apply mathematical knowledge and ways of thinking is valuable in workplace contexts. We also believe it has the potential to enrich personal lives in ways that are not immediately utilitarian.

Teachers in primary schools know that young children find pleasure and emotional engagement in the aesthetic outcomes of their observations and activities. For example, they may be fascinated by the arrangements of petals on a flower or by simple number patterns emerging from games. They may be excited when they realise how to position building blocks to make stable structures or when they notice symmetries in decorative patterns. Through their senses they feel stimulated to try out alternatives and, above all, to talk about what they experience. In expressing what they feel, they will develop their use of language, some of which will be mathematical. Their teacher will encourage this as one part of their developing ability to communicate. Later on, they might use intersecting circles to draw petals, shapes might be named and tessellated and the familiar counting numbers will be joined by fractions. Activities with building blocks may evolve into the purposeful construction of solid artefacts, accompanied by talk like 'Place the cylinder up there, at an angle so that it can move around.' Mathematical concepts emerge in the course of such activities and the language needed to talk about them becomes more specialised. Reasoning develops alongside aesthetic appreciation and emotional response, with comments like 'If I make the angle smaller my puppet will look better.'

Later still, during lessons called 'mathematics', young students study number sequences and patterns in shape and space. Games may include discussion of probabilities. New types of numbers come on the scene: integers, irrational numbers, random numbers and constants such as π. Letters used to stand for unknown numbers are succeeded by algebraic expressions and equations. Aesthetic appreciation develops to become rather more intellectual than sensual, focusing, for example, on elegance of abstract structures or economy of forms of reasoning. Similar transitions from the sensual to the intellectual also happen in the arts subjects: visual, literary and musical forms are analysed and re-created by the students in various ways. However, in these contexts appreciation of form and analysis of structure are less likely to become detached from the experiences of the senses. As the mathematics curriculum becomes more analytical, teachers need to remember the importance of retaining an aesthetic dimension, complementing abstract ideas with sensual experience, simultaneously making the ideas more accessible. Examples we have observed include: making explicit links between sequences, such as the Fibonacci sequence and the natural world; initiating a study of polygons through tiling patterns, 3-D symmetry and architecture; and constructing programs in Logo to make fractal designs. Mathematics has much to contribute to the development of aesthetic appreciation, and unlocking this potential can prove to be a rewarding experience for teachers as well as students.

Mathematics can also provide students with ways of understanding cultures of the past and present. In combination with other school subjects, mathematics can contribute to students' abilities and inclinations to inform themselves about ways of living and to make critical choices about lifestyle – to see possibilities that might otherwise not have occurred to them. The secondary school mathematics curriculum has the potential to illuminate many forms of cultural knowledge and every teacher will make selections to suit the students in their classes. In our cities, for example, students are surrounded by brickwork and tiling patterns from Victorian and Edwardian times, and they also see buildings, or photographs of buildings, embellished with complex designs from Islamic cultures. These can provide a rich starting point for the exploration of polygons and tessellations. The theme of architecture can continue in three dimensions with both an aesthetic and a multicultural flavour. What shapes of bricks are needed to make curved walls like the circular one around the tree in the playground or the elliptical perimeter around the ruins of Old Zimbabwe? Historically, craft and design have depended on an appreciation of patterns in shape and space, and on the numerical relationships required to continue them. Nowadays, repeating patterns may be designed and printed using digital technologies. This will seem less removed from traditional cultural experiences if students are given the opportunity to use computers to generate patterns and number sequences of their own.

The study and analysis of patterns in number or in shape and space can act as a starting point for creative engagement in mathematics. As in other areas of endeavour, creativity often starts with familiar patterns, adapting and changing them. In mathematics, one approach to this involves posing and following up the question 'What if . . .?' – changing one or more of the starting conditions of a problem situation and analysing the results. To give a simple example, we are all familiar with Pythagoras' Theorem for right-angled triangles, but what if . . .:

> . . . we construct other regular polygons instead of squares on each of the sides of the triangle?
>
> . . . we look at triangles where the relationship is $c^2 = a^2 + 2b^2$?
>
> . . . we try to find sets of integers satisfying the relationship $z^n = x^n + y^n$?

It is not always easy to predict which of the new problems arising from this process will give rise to new insights and higher levels of generality and which will be less productive. Following them up and evaluating the outcomes is part of the process of developing mathematical reasoning and judgement.

Investigative tasks in which students are encouraged to pose their own problems and to adapt and extend the situations offered them provide an obvious context for creative activity in school mathematics. As we have indicated above, other parts of the mathematics curriculum can also be approached in open-ended ways, providing opportunities for forms of lateral thinking associated with creativity. While we make no claims for mathematics as a uniquely creative subject, we do believe that the processes of mathematical enquiry can be a valuable part of creative endeavour. In later chapters we suggest ways of following the curriculum that can develop creative potential.

DEVELOPING LOGICAL REASONING

It is sometimes claimed that studying mathematics is useful for developing logical reasoning. What does it mean to be reasonable and how might the study of mathematics help individuals to develop this attribute? All subjects aim to enhance students' abilities to reason in a logical and informed manner, to make valid generalisations and to apply and adapt them. For example, through a study of geography, students learn that settlements grew up on sites with particular characteristics and that it can be reasonably predicted that there will be villages, towns or cities in similar places today. However, they also learn that circumstances change and that the model of an ideal place to settle might have to be adapted to different human needs and technologies. Valid generalisation involves the ability to reason and to make conjectures within a structure of available knowledge that includes processes for checking and justification. It must include the expectation that logical argument will reveal the existence of exceptional cases and counter-examples. Reasoning goes beyond logical argument, but it does depend upon it.

School science introduces students to the processes of gathering information through experimentation, making conjectures, testing them and constructing theoretical models. They learn about how scientists work within their accepted models of the universe and how they adapt theory in the light of new and unexpected discoveries. Thus, the indivisible atom became the solid nucleus orbited by electrons and, later still, the nucleus was revealed to be composed of much smaller particles. Sometimes the inconsistencies that lead to models being adapted are revealed mathematically, when observations of phenomena do not fit with expectations consistent with existing accepted patterns. Such was the case when the model of a geocentric universe could no longer support the more closely observed motions of the planets. In this case, mathematical reasoning was able to reveal a flaw in a scientific theory and hence lead to a revision of the theory and to scientific advance. It is hard to argue, however, that mathematics is uniquely placed to develop young people's reasoning skills and problem-solving abilities.

Other areas of the curriculum also expect students to solve problems, to make and test conjectures, to justify their conclusions and to construct and defend arguments. Nevertheless, there are aspects specific to mathematical reasoning that have particular value. One of these is the distinction between deductive and inductive reasoning, and recognition of the difference between the strengths of the certain conclusion of a chain of deductive reasoning and of the provisional conclusion of induction from a wealth of experiential evidence. This distinction and the skills associated with developing deductive reasoning are a major focus of the secondary school mathematics curriculum. Another crucial aspect of mathematical reasoning is the ability to make sense of, use and critique quantitative information. In a world in which quantitative data increasingly informs governmental and commercial decision-making and in which more and more quantitative information is available to the public as well as to policy-makers, active citizenship depends on mathematical competence, especially on the understanding and interpretation of statistical methods and probability, as well as on the exercise

23

of social and moral judgement. Thus mathematics plays an important role in developing the understanding both of classical standards of proof and of informed probabilistic decision making.

CONCLUSION

In this chapter, we have presented a range of ways in which learning mathematics can have an impact on the lives and futures of young people. Some of these, such as the importance of qualifications and the use of mathematics in the workplace, are widely recognised by students, their parents and the wider public, even if there may be some misconceptions about the relationships between school mathematics and the ways that mathematics are used in 'real life'. Other important aspects of mathematics, including the appreciation of its aesthetics, its potential for creativity, its contribution to decision making and active citizenship, are less prominent in the public image of the subject. Yet these aspects, which have as much in common with the arts and humanities side of the curriculum as with the sciences, may prove to be a key to capturing the interest and imagination of those students who are turned off by utilitarianism. As you prepare to teach your diverse students, you will need to consider the various aspects of mathematics that may motivate each of them. You will also need to communicate to them the breadth of mathematics and open their eyes to the ways in which mathematics can be important for them. This breadth is a theme that runs throughout this book as we consider mathematics in the curriculum and approaches to learning and teaching mathematics. In particular, Chapters 6 and 7 will look in a practical way at examples of lessons addressing some of these different purposes for teaching and learning.

THINKING ABOUT PRACTICE

- How can you communicate the importance of learning mathematics to your students?
- What kinds of classroom activities may your students find purposeful and how may this differ for students of different ages and with different motivations?
- What room is there for creativity in the mathematics curriculum of your school?

Chapter 3

From university to school mathematics

KEY QUESTIONS

- How can teachers with knowledge and experience of advanced pure or applied mathematics make use of this in teaching elementary mathematics at secondary school level?
- What new ways of thinking about mathematics may new teachers need to develop?

Looking back on the mathematics you studied at university, whether within a mathematics degree or as part of a degree in another field such as engineering or economics, what did you learn that will help you to teach mathematics to 7-year-olds, 11-year-olds, 15-year-olds or 18-year-olds? Many new teachers find it hard to give a positive answer to this question. After all, where do group theory, fluid dynamics, operational research, etc. appear in the school curriculum? How are they going to help you teach fractions or quadratic equations or the properties of quadrilaterals? Even where a topic such as differential equations is part of the curriculum at university and at school (at least for some of the 18-year-olds), the differences in the types of equations considered and the methods used are enormous. Indeed, on entering teaching, it is common for new teachers to feel less confident about their knowledge of school mathematics than they did before they started their degree courses. Yet a degree with a substantial proportion of mathematics is required for entering mathematics teaching. In this chapter, we will explore the relationship between university mathematics and school mathematics, and

25

identify some fundamental ways in which studying mathematics at a high level can inform your teaching at elementary levels.

Teachers in other subject areas are likely to have rather different experiences of the relationship between their university studies and the subject they are teaching. Teachers of English, for example, are likely to have learnt ways of reading and thinking about texts that enable them to help their own students to appreciate their reading. Teachers of history, even if teaching about a period in history different from those they studied at university themselves, are likely to have learnt research skills that help them to prepare to teach the school curriculum. Why does mathematics seem to be so different?

Not only are the mathematical topics studied at university different, but the type of activity also seems very different. Students starting university mathematics courses often report a feeling of discontinuity from their school experience of mathematics. For some, this is accompanied by a feeling of disappointment or even failure, as the satisfaction and success met at school level are not immediately continued. For others, new challenges, interests and satisfactions appear.

Mathematicians and educators have tried to explain this phenomenon in terms of the nature of mathematics itself and the psychology of learning mathematics. For example, some people argue that mathematical knowledge is arranged hierarchically. In other words, the order in which topics are taught and learnt is determined by the logic of the subject itself. There is some truth in this. For example, it is difficult to imagine learning to solve quadratic equations without previous knowledge of basic arithmetic and the solution of linear equations (though saying 'it is difficult to imagine' does not necessarily mean it is impossible). However, research into learning shows that children often acquire mathematical knowledge in orders that do not match either the apparently logical mathematical hierarchy or the order in which they have been taught (Denvir and Brown, 1986). The introduction of new forms of technology can also change the accessibility of some topics for learners (Noss and Hoyles, 1996) and hence the order in which it may make sense to meet them. For example, the use of graphics calculators or computer graphing programs allows students to work meaningfully with transformations of graphs and relationships between the algebraic forms of a wide range of functions and the properties of their graphs, even while they are still developing skills in plotting simple graphs.

Another explanation for the discontinuities experienced between school and university mathematics argues that there is a progression in learners' development of mathematical reasoning from 'computational' reasoning, carrying out computations and procedures with specific numerical or symbolic objects, through 'descriptive' reasoning, manipulating more general objects and describing classes of objects, to 'deductive' reasoning, thinking in a theoretical domain of definitions and deductions (Barnard, 1995). As with other theories of developmental levels, it is difficult to know whether this is a necessary progression or just a reflection of traditional curricula and expectations. However, it is probably fair to say that the vast majority of school mathematics is at the computational level (focusing on developing students' ability to carry out mathematical procedures but also, of course, on understanding how and why the procedures work), while many university level mathematics curricula move rapidly to the deductive level.

The move from school to university mathematics is widely recognised to be problematic and some attention has been paid to the design of syllabuses and courses at the interface between the two phases in attempting to bridge the gap or ease the transition. Much less attention has been paid to those who make the move in the opposite direction – graduates becoming school teachers (though see Anderson et al., 2000). For some new teachers, returning to school mathematics feels like a comfortable return to the subject they enjoyed at school themselves. But teaching a subject is not the same as studying it and the kind of subject knowledge required for teaching a topic is different from that which is needed to answer an examination question successfully. So what does your university level experience add to your knowledge of school level mathematics?

YOU NEED TO KNOW HOW A TOPIC DEVELOPS AND CONTRIBUTES TO OTHER TOPICS IN ORDER TO TEACH IT IN A WAY THAT WILL SUPPORT LATER LEARNING

We are not suggesting that you should teach your students as if they were all preparing to study mathematics at university level. This is highly unlikely to be either realistic or effective! Indeed, attempts to structure the school mathematics curriculum to match the concerns of university mathematicians such as the 'Modern Mathematics' movement of the 1960s[1] are now generally recognised to have been unsuccessful. It is a mistake to confuse the mathematics that teachers need to know with the mathematics they actually need to teach.

Nevertheless, it is demonstrably true within the school curriculum that approaches to teaching the early stages of a topic need to take into account the later parts of the curriculum that build on those basic ideas. Some of the common 'misconceptions' seem to arise from approaches to topics at lower levels that do not support extension of the topics at higher levels. For example, 'you can't take a larger number from a smaller' or 'multiplication makes things bigger' are ideas that many children hang on to from their early number experiences long after they have started working with negative numbers and fractions. At a higher level, students can successfully complete an Advanced level course (depending on the options they choose) with the idea that quadratic equations have two roots when $b^2 - 4ac > 0$ one root when $b^2 - 4ac = 0$ and no roots when $b^2 - 4ac < 0$. This can make it difficult for them to integrate their knowledge as they are introduced first to complex numbers and then to more general polynomial equations and the idea that an equation of degree n always has n roots. Teachers who have a deeper understanding of the relationships between the sets of natural numbers, integers, rationals, reals and complex numbers, and the operations that are possible within them, can help their students to appreciate the similarities as well as the differences as they progress in their learning. Partial knowledge at a more elementary level must be challenged but does not need to be thrown away. An important part of your role is to help your students to examine their old knowledge, to recognise that it is partially but not completely true, and to adapt and extend it to fit new, more general situations. This describes a fundamental process of learning known as 'accommodation'.[2]

Of course, not all school students will go on to study higher mathematics and these students may never 'need' to know about complex numbers. Nevertheless, sharing your holistic view of numbers with them is likely both to help students at any level to make better sense of what they are learning and also to affect students' attitudes towards the subject. If you know a little of the development of mathematics, it can be useful here to let students know about the historical struggles over the acceptance of negative and imaginary numbers – both to show the 'human' face of a subject that some find it difficult to relate to and to show that 'real' mathematicians have had some of the same problems. There are many accessible sources of such information about the history of mathematics in books and on the Internet. (We return to this issue in Chapter 4.)

ADVANCED STUDY CAN ILLUMINATE ELEMENTARY IDEAS

Mathematics sometimes seems to be a collection of unrelated topics with little in common. An important part of the argument we are making here and in the next chapter is that there are, in fact, strong connections between topics and within mathematics as a whole. Among these connections are fundamental ideas that are encountered across a wide range of areas of mathematics. In this section, we shall look at some of these fundamental ideas as they emerge from abstract algebra, the study of structures such as groups, rings and fields. This is an area that is not generally encountered in the school curriculum and at first sight it may seem to be of little relevance or use to a teacher. However . . .

Important ideas in group theory in relation to school mathematics

Studying group theory provides you with an example of an *axiomatic system*. The definition of a group itself and subsequent definitions of special kinds of groups and of other related structures are stated in terms of conditions that must be fulfilled (see note on p. 31). Developing knowledge in this area involves applying these conditions and deductive reasoning from them. This method of reasoning, making use of formal definitions, is a very important part of doing mathematics at all levels, yet it is not always easy for students. For example, an argument that commonly arises in both primary and secondary classrooms is that of whether a square is a rectangle. This may be resolved in at least four different ways:

- by natural language and common sense: a square is not a rectangle because they have different names;
- by visual intuition: a square is not a rectangle because it doesn't look like a rectangle;
- by authority: a square is a rectangle because I say so;
- by reasoning from a formal definition: a square is a rectangle because it satisfies all the conditions in the definition of a rectangle that we are using.

29

Only one of these resolutions involves a mathematical form of reasoning. It is important that students should be helped to recognise this and to begin to use this form of reasoning themselves – perhaps more important than that they should get the right answer to the original question. When such a question arises during a lesson, it can be useful to spend some time discussing it, allowing these different types of argument to arise and then considering the merits of each of them with the class.

We have already seen above in the discussion about students' progression from working with just the natural numbers (positive integers) to working with the reals and even with complex numbers that the concept of *closure* plays an important part in thinking about the need to introduce new kinds of numbers in order to be able to find solutions to equations. Using the operation of subtraction prompts a move from the natural numbers to integers so that $a - b$ has meaning for all a and b, while using division prompts the extension of the set of numbers to include the rationals. Indeed, these are important ways of thinking about negative numbers and fractions. Similarly, the concepts of *identity* and *inverse* are fundamental to developing understanding of how numbers and number operations work, and of the relationships between different kinds of numbers and different kinds of operations. Some examples:

- Equivalent fractions: how do you justify multiplying the top and bottom of the fraction by the same number?
- Converting a fraction to a percentage: what are you doing when you multiply the fraction by 100 per cent?
- Solving a linear equation: how do you decide what to add to both sides?

All of these rules can be taught and learnt simply as rules to follow. However, students who understand how these and other parts of mathematics are connected not only have less to learn and remember (for example, recognising that converting a fraction to a percentage is the same as finding a particular equivalent fraction means that you have to remember only one rule not two), but are also more likely to appreciate the nature of mathematics itself as a coherent body of knowledge rather than a disconnected collection of arbitrary procedures.

Appreciating that subtraction can be thought of as addition of the additive inverse (and division as multiplication by the multiplicative inverse)

NOTE: REMINDER OF GROUP THEORY

The first type of structure usually dealt with in degree courses is the group.

- A GROUP is a set A together with an operation*. It must satisfy the following axioms:
- CLOSURE: for all elements a and b of A, $a * b$ is also an element of A.
- ASSOCIATIVITY: for all elements of A, $a * (b * c) = (a * b) * c$.
- IDENTITY: the set contains an element e (known as the identity element) for which $e * a = a * e = a$ for all elements a of A.
- INVERSE: for every element a of A, there is an element also in A (the inverse of a, denoted a^{-1}) such that $a * a^{-1} = a^{-1} * a = e$.

We will illustrate the axioms, taking the group consisting of the set {0, 1, 2} with addition modulo 3 as an example. It is often helpful to construct a table such as that in Figure 3.1 (like the familiar multiplication table) to help look at group structure:

$+_{mod3}$	0	1	2
0	0	1	2
1	1	2	0
2	2	0	1

Figure 3.1 *The group consisting of {0, 1, 2} with addition modulo 3*

CLOSURE can be seen by the fact that all the entries in the table are elements of the set.

ASSOCIATIVITY can be checked exhaustively (or you can make an argument based on the properties of ordinary addition).

The IDENTITY element is 0. You can see this from the table, as the first row and the first column in the middle of the table are identical to the top row and outside left column – and these also have identical ordering. Thus, for each element a of the set, $a +_{mod3} 0 = 0 +_{mod3} a = a$.

You can also see from the table that each element of the set has a unique INVERSE element within the set as 0 appears exactly once in each row and each column, and the arrangement of 0s is symmetrical about the leading diagonal of the table. The inverse of 0 is, of course, 0 and the elements 1 and 2 are the inverses of each other.

Other examples of finite groups include:

- the set of symmetry transformations of a square with composition of transformations;
- the set of permutations of the digits 1, 2, 3 with composition of permutations.

The set of integers with addition is an example of an infinite group. However, the integers with multiplication are not a group because they do not satisfy the axiom that every element should have an inverse within the set. (If you extend the set to include the rationals – and exclude zero – it does form a group with multiplication.)

not only gives you insight into why 'two minuses make a plus' (and why 'turn the second fraction upside down and multiply' works) but also, by reducing the number of operations involved, allows more similarities to be seen between arithmetic structures and those arising in other areas of mathematics. As students progress to learning about the combination of functions, combinations of transformation of the plane, matrix multiplication, etc., it becomes more necessary to think in terms of inverse elements rather than inverse operations. Looking at these apparently disparate areas of the curriculum through eyes informed by the study of abstract algebra allows us to see similarities and to highlight significant differences.

Functions – informed by group theory ideas

Let us start by looking at functions as an example. Students generally meet the ideas of combination of functions, the identity function and inverse functions in the upper years of secondary school, usually starting with linear functions. (Note that the set of linear functions $a \mapsto ax + b$ ($a \neq 0$) with combination of functions forms a group. You can check this using the group axioms listed in the box above.) When preparing to teach a topic, it is often helpful to think about the mistakes that students commonly make. Here we will focus on two of these.

Mistake 1

Combination of functions is commutative, i.e. $f \circ g(x) = g \circ f(x)$

It is likely that this mistake arises at least in part from thoroughly ingrained experience with number operations (many students take a long time to be fully aware of the lack of commutativity of subtraction and division). In fact, there are subsets of linear functions for which it is true that combination is commutative. Specifically, the set of functions of the form $x \mapsto x + b$ (b being a real number) is a commutative subgroup of the group of linear functions. In fact, this subgroup is isomorphic to the group formed by the set of real numbers with addition. Similarly, the functions $x \mapsto ax$ ($a \neq 0$) form a commutative subgroup, isomorphic to that formed by the real numbers (excluding 0) with multiplication. However, if you put these two sets of functions together (and of course the functions of the form $x \mapsto ax + b$ created by combination of one of each type) you find that, in general, combining functions is not commutative. For example:

If $f: x \mapsto 2x + 3$ and $g: x \mapsto 3x - 1$, then

$f \circ g: x \mapsto 2(3x - 1) + 3 = 6x + 1$

but

$g \circ f: x \mapsto 3(2x + 3) - 1 = 6x + 8$

Thus the structure of the group formed by real linear functions is very different from that of any arithmetic structure the students will have met before.

When you prepare to teach this topic, you will have to make decisions about the examples of functions you wish your students to work with. At some points you may want to draw their attention to how similar working with functions is to working with numbers (perhaps to help them feel more secure as they are introduced to new concepts), restricting the examples used to either of the two commutative subgroups identified above. At other points, however, you will want to highlight the differences, particularly the general lack of commutativity. You could, for example, set your students the task to collect examples of pairs of functions where $f \circ g = g \circ f$ and examples where $f \circ g \neq g \circ f$, to classify them, and form and test hypotheses about which pairs are commutative and which are not. This sort of investigation can help students to construct robust ideas both about combination of functions and about commutativity. We return in Chapter 5 to consider the usefulness and the risks of focusing students' attention on similarities or on differences between two areas of mathematics.

REMINDER

In general, groups do *not* have to be COMMUTATIVE. Those groups which are commutative are known as ABELIAN groups. The example used earlier, {0, 1, 2} with addition modulo 3, *is* abelian, as can be seen in the symmetry of the group table.

In addition to combination of functions, other examples of non-commutative operations include, of course, subtraction and division of numbers as well as multiplication of matrices, combination of permutations and combination of transformations of the plane (see below).

Mistake 2

The inverse of $x \mapsto 10 - x$ is $x \mapsto 10 + x$ or (when this is found not to work) $x \mapsto x - 10$.

Again, it is likely that this mistake results from overgeneralisation of experience with functions of the form $x \mapsto x - a$, whose inverse is $x \mapsto x + a$. There often seems to be considerable resistance to the idea that a function and its inverse can be identical. Of course, in the domain of numbers, the only number that is its own inverse is the identity element. It is thus hardly surprising that self-inverse functions appear strange. Students are likely to need some concrete experiences in order to establish rich meanings for this new phenomenon, even if they are already able to operate symbolically to construct the inverses of other linear functions. A possible concrete activity would be to use a calculator or computer to see the effect of repeatedly applying functions of this type. It is easy for students to set up a graphics calculator or a spreadsheet to do this.

NOTE

Spreadsheet: enter any number in cell A1. In cell A2, enter the formula $10-A1$. Copy this formula down the column. Change the number in cell A1.

Graphics calculator: enter any number. Enter $10-ANS$. Press EXE repeatedly. (These instructions are for a Casio calculator. Other models will need slightly different instructions.)

Challenge: generate the sequence $^-3, 4, \ ^-3, 4, \ ^-3, 4, \ldots$

Transformation geometry – informed by group theory ideas

The idea of self-inverse elements also appears when students work with transformations of the plane. This is perhaps an easier context in which to be introduced to the idea, as it seems intuitively obvious that reflections and rotation through a half-turn are self-inverse transformations. Here is another topic whose study can be enriched by insights from group theory. Up to GCSE level, it is possible to deal with transformation geometry in a purely computational (or even in many cases intuitive) way. That is, students can solve the problems they are set by constructing the results of individual transformations and sequences of transformations on specific objects. To work only in this way, however, is to miss opportunities to develop students' mathematical reasoning and appreciation by exploring aspects of the topic that connect with more general and powerful ideas. Moreover, for some students, particularly those who do not relate to the visual aspects of transformation geometry, it can appear meaningless or trivial unless seen in a wider context.

Clearly, one of the objectives that has to be achieved when studying this topic is skill in applying specific rotations and reflections and combinations of these to find the image of a given object. Instead of doing a sequence of independent exercises in which various objects are transformed, an investigation organised around the ideas of group structure can achieve the objective of developing skills while simultaneously allowing students to engage in purposeful enquiry and introducing them to some powerful ideas.

Choose a starting object and label its vertices (it is probably a good idea to choose a simple shape such as a square).

Rotate it through 90° anti-clockwise. Rotate the resulting image through 90° again. And again . . . and again . . . and again . . . (See Figure 3.2.)

The first part of this investigation constructs a cyclic group, generated by the rotation through 90°. This group is isomorphic to the group consisting of the digits {0, 1, 2, 3} with addition modulo 4.

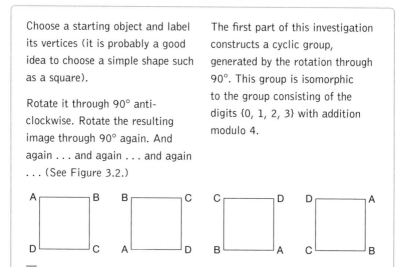

Figure 3.2 *Rotations of a square through 90°, and through 90° again, . . .*

Describe the outcome of each combination of 90° rotations as a single transformation. What is $(R_{90})^2$, $(R_{90})^3$, $(R_{90})^4$, $(R_{90})^7$, . . .?

Make a 'multiplication' table showing the outcomes of combining rotations of 90°, 180°, 270°, 360°. What is the identity transformation? What is the inverse of R_{90} etc.?

(What if you had started with a rotation of 60° or a rotation of 30° or 40° or 50° etc? How many

The introduction of a notation is important here. Not only does it make recording easier but it helps to make the transition from thinking of transformations as procedures to thinking of them as objects that can themselves be operated on – a crucial transition in many areas of mathematics. Even when thinking about integers, we need to be able to shift between thinking about them as points on a number line (objects) and as movements along it (processes).

different rotations would you have in your table?)

Now introduce a reflection in the horizontal axis (y = 0).

What happens when you reflect in y = 0, then rotate the image by 90°, 180°, 270°, 360°? Describe the outcome of each combination as a single transformation.

What happens if you rotate, then reflect? When does it matter what order you combine transformations?

Add all these extra transformations to your table and fill in the gaps. What is the identity? What is the inverse of each transformation?

By including one reflection, others also have to be defined in order to achieve closure. This emphasises the point that a reflection combined with a rotation forms a reflection, while the combination of two reflections or of two rotations result in a rotation.

The 'multiplication' table is an extension of a familiar recording device that makes the structure of the situation visible and allows the identity element, inverses and commutativity to be identified easily.

We have mentioned the notion of *isomorphism* several times while discussing the two examples above. While its formal definition may not be appropriate at secondary school level, the idea that two domains can have identical structure is accessible and, used in a relatively informal way, can help students to see that mathematics is not just a collection of unconnected topics. Other places where it can be useful to draw attention to similarity of structure – and to consider the differences – include:

■ multiplication of numbers with several digits and multiplication of algebraic expressions;
■ the arithmetic of surds and of complex numbers, for example, the processes of dividing expressions involving surds,

$$\frac{1}{3 + \sqrt{2}} = \frac{1}{3 + \sqrt{2}} \cdot \frac{3 - \sqrt{2}}{3 - \sqrt{2}} = \ldots$$

37

and dividing complex numbers,

$$\frac{1}{3+i} = \frac{1}{3+i} \cdot \frac{3-i}{3-i} = \ldots;$$

- symmetries of a square and permutations of a set with four elements (and symmetries of an equilateral triangle and permutations of a set with three elements and . . .).

The realisation that facts that have been established in one domain are therefore true in another not only reduces the number of facts you have to learn, but can also be a source of appreciation of the beauty of mathematics.

Although we have argued that ideas encountered in group theory are important to teaching at school level, we are not suggesting that every mathematics teacher must have studied abstract algebra (though we wouldn't want to stop you!). In fact, the important ideas we have highlighted are important precisely because they play a role in many mathematical fields at all levels and because they are fundamental to mathematical reasoning across different areas. We chose to use group theory as an illustration because these ideas emerge explicitly at an elementary level. You should be able to see these ideas at work in other topics you studied as part of your own degree course.

DOING 'REAL' MATHEMATICS – NOT JUST 'SCHOOL' MATHEMATICS

In Chapter 2, we discussed various reasons for studying mathematics at school. Among these was the claim that mathematics is 'useful'. However, when asked to identify where they actually use the mathematics they learnt at school, very few adults can identify more than a little arithmetic. Without a broader view of mathematics and its applicability, the rest of school mathematics seems to become just an end in itself, resulting in students who believe that the subject is abstract and irrelevant. 'Applications' found in school level textbooks are often artificial, either simply dressing up standard exercises in a context or using mathematical techniques to address problems that, in reality, would be solved in alternative ways. However, reflecting on your experience of doing mathematics beyond school level can inform your teaching in ways that will give your students a much fuller insight into mathematics and its place in the world.

Many new mathematics teachers bring with them knowledge and experience of important applications of mathematics from studying 'applied' topics within a mathematics degree, from studying and then using mathematics within a degree in engineering, economics or another quantitative subject, and from using mathematics in work. Working with 'real' problems, however, often seems to involve using mathematical techniques that are a long way beyond the school curriculum. How can mathematics be applied in concrete, meaningful ways that are accessible to your students? In order to answer this question it is useful to think about the contribution that professional mathematicians, both academic and non-academic, make to solving real world problems.

One obvious contribution is in establishing techniques, methods of calculation and analysis that can be applied in specific situations and that the users of mathematics – engineers, financiers, architects, etc. – can rely on to give valid results. Much of school mathematics involves students becoming users of mathematics. That is, they learn techniques that have been established by mathematicians and learn to recognise some of the situations in which they can be applied. For example, young students learn reliable methods for adding numbers with several digits and come to understand that these techniques may be applied in order to find the total cost of the items in their shopping basket; older students learn formulae for calculating the arithmetic mean and the standard deviation of a set of numbers and apply these formulae to compare the test scores of two groups of students. (It is not always the case that learning the technique comes before its application. Attempting to find the solution to a problem can be a powerful way of learning a technique and knowing what sort of problems an application will be able to solve can be an important motivation for learning.)

Another important contribution made by mathematicians is in the construction of mathematical models of real world processes or objects. Such models may be used to improve efficiency or profit, to simulate the outcomes of experiments that would be too difficult, expensive or dangerous to carry out in reality, to analyse where problems are likely to arise in a process or what will happen in exceptional cases. They may involve gathering and analysing data or constructing a theoretical relationship between relevant variables. The outcome may be in many forms: a formula, a graph fitted to data, a spreadsheet embodying the relationships, a diagram, a physical model. Whereas 'pure' mathematics is often characterised by an emphasis on certainty and precision, the modelling process, as a way of dealing with the complexities and uncertainties of the real world, is marked by approximation and by practical choices and judgements about alternative valid solutions. Applied mathematics is not just an academic discipline, it is an approach to addressing problems that arise in the real world: a set of tools and a characteristic way of thinking about the world. The set of tools available to school students is limited, but students can still be introduced to characteristically mathematical ways of thinking.

MAKING SCHOOL MATHEMATICS MORE 'REAL'

An important insight that we can gain from looking at how mathematics is used in the real world is the realisation of how different it is from much of what is offered to children as mathematics in school. It is often suggested that students can be motivated to learn mathematics by the realisation that it is 'useful'. It is hardly surprising, however, that such motivation is lacking when we look at some of the applications of mathematics that they are asked to make. (We return to the issue of motivation in later chapters.) In most of the textbooks used in secondary schools you will find problems set in contexts that have the appearance of applications of mathematics. For example, in a chapter entitled 'Adding and subtracting decimals' the first question for students to do poses a number of context-free calculations with whole numbers (presumably for revision purposes) such as $395 + 403$ and $266 - 108$. Immediately after this are the following questions:

a   The attendance at four football matches were

   3 503, 8 271, 12 643, 6 487

   What was the actual attendance at these matches?

b   A car is due for its service at 90 000 miles. It has currently travelled 82 643 miles. How many more miles is it until its service is due?

c   A theatre has 1 484 seats. On Monday 637 seats were taken. How many seats were empty?

(Capewell *et al.*, 2002)

These questions provide students with further opportunities to practise the addition and subtraction skills already used in the context-free
questions. In addition, they have the task of deciding which of the two
operations is required. (Other exercises may remove even this amount
of decision-making by dealing with only one type of calculation.)
Researchers (for example, Nesher and Teubal, 1975) have shown that
some children develop 'tricks' for answering questions such as these that
allow them to ignore the majority of the context, like taking the word
'more' in question b as a sign that a subtraction is required or using
the fact that there are four numbers in question a as a cue to add.
In practice, these are not in any way questions about anything outside
school mathematics but are exercises in decoding 'word problems'.

THINK POINT

You may ask yourself:

■ In what 'real' circumstances might it make sense to ask these ques-
tions?
■ What sort of methods might actually be used in such circumstances?
■ What degree of accuracy would be appropriate?

Rather more complex problems, requiring students to choose and
combine a number of different concepts and skills, tend to have rather
more apparent connection to real applications of mathematics. For
example, when learning about area, students are often given exercises
asking them to work out how much carpet they will need for a room
and how much it will cost (see Figure 3.3). In order to get the answer
given in the back of the book, students are expected to calculate the area
of the given shape in m² and to multiply this by a specified price per m²
of carpet. In practice, however, this method is not likely to give you a
useful answer. In fact, it is most likely to underestimate the actual cost
of the carpet – an unhelpful outcome for anyone with a tight budget.
Carpet comes in fixed widths and has to be cut to shape and size; when
deciding how to fit the carpet, it is important to avoid having small
pieces, too many joins, joins near a door, and so on. It is thus very
unlikely that the householder could get away without paying for an area
of carpet greater than the area of the room. Students who have been

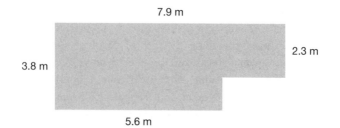

Figure 3.3 *Find the cost of carpeting a room with the dimensions shown in the diagram using carpet costing £7.99 per m²*

involved in their families' DIY efforts are likely to be aware that such exact calculations are not generally used.

Of course, this exercise is primarily intended to give students practice in calculating areas. We are not attempting to train them in the techniques used by carpet layers or to teach them the models and rules-of-thumb used by experts to work out how much carpet actually ought to be purchased. On the other hand, reflecting on the ways in which mathematical methods might more realistically be used in this situation may help students to see a little more of the power and relevance of mathematics. (In Chapter 4, we look again at practical, 'informal' methods of area calculation and consider their role in the classroom.)

Let us consider this situation as an example of mathematical modelling rather than an exercise in applying area formulae and multiplication of decimals. There are a number of aspects of the modelling process that are relevant here.

- *Identify the relevant variables and procedures.* Clearly the dimensions of the room and the price of the carpet are relevant, but what about the width in which the carpet comes? Will we adopt an approach based on calculation only or might we use diagrams or cut up pieces of paper to create a physical model of the carpet-laying process? How much attention shall we pay to issues such as the size of pieces of carpet and joins between pieces?

- *Identify the assumptions behind the model.* Any decisions about what variables to take into account will be based on different sets of assumptions. For example, in the 'standard' (area calculation) approach it is assumed that it is possible to buy the exact amount of carpet required, that there will be no waste and that no allowance needs to be made for mistakes in measuring or cutting the carpet.

- *Consider the degree of accuracy required.* The measurements of the room were given in metres to one decimal place. Is this a reasonable degree of accuracy? What would be the practical effect of the maximum error in these measurements? (How would you cope with a gap of 5 cm between the carpet and the wall?) How important is it in practice that your calculation of the cost of the carpet is accurate to the nearest penny and how much under-estimation could your budget tolerate?

- *Evaluate the effectiveness of the model.* Are you satisfied that your method will give you an answer that is good enough for your purposes? Depending on your personal circumstances, you may need to consider the amount of time it takes, the risks involved (for example, the likelihood of miscalculation and the consequences of under- or over-estimation) and the tightness of your budget. If you have several rooms to carpet, is this method going to be easily transferable to other sizes and shapes of room?

- *Consider alternatives.* How about going to the carpet shop with your sketch of the room and asking them to do the calculations for you? What might be the advantages and disadvantages of this solution?

We are not suggesting that every question set in a context needs to be treated as a substantial exercise in modelling; there is a role for making a direct connection between skills that are being taught and contexts to which they might be applicable. Moreover, students need to be prepared to answer the types of questions that appear in examination papers without asking too many questions about the reality of the contexts in which they are apparently set (we return to this point in Chapter 8). Our job as teachers of mathematics, however, goes beyond preparing students for the next examination. We are also responsible for communicating with students, their parents and other teachers about the nature of mathematics itself. Utility is one of the bases for arguing for a privileged place for mathematics in the curriculum, so we must be able to demonstrate that mathematical thinking really is useful and meaningful. One way of addressing this might be to use the type of exercises provided in the textbook, devoting part of the lesson to a discussion of how real the questions and answers are, drawing on students' personal real world experience and perhaps using some of the questions related to the modelling process identified above. Another approach is to immerse the students in a real or imagined situation in which they can act as mathematical consultants, producing a solution to a problem and arguing for its viability. An example of such an exercise is presented in the following case study.

DOING REAL MATHEMATICS IN SCHOOL

We will outline a possible class activity and then discuss how it illustrates important aspects of the use of mathematics in the 'real world'.

EXAMPLE

Your school senior management team (SMT) is concerned about potentially dangerous overcrowding in corridors and on staircases at some times of day. They propose instigating a one-way system around the school and have asked your class to act as consultants.

You might start by considering the question 'Is there a problem?', calling for some initial gathering of data. Have there been any accidents (and are these due to overcrowding)? Do people (students and teachers) feel unsafe? What are the current safety regulations relevant to the situation? However, you have been given the task by the SMT with the assumption that there is a problem and that it is about overcrowding, so you take this as your starting point.

You and your class discuss the problem, using knowledge and experience of the school to raise some more questions:

- Where and when is the worst overcrowding? Is it the same on all days of the week and at different times of the day?
- What routes are people taking and why are they choosing these routes?
- Which corridors and staircases might be made one-way and what difference would this make to numbers of people using them?
- What constraints are there on the design of the one-way system? For example, will the headteacher be happy to have a route taking large numbers of students down the corridor outside their office?

 44

These questions require different kinds of investigation, so groups within the class take on responsibility for various tasks, including:

- going back to the SMT to check their expectations and establish the constraints on any solution;
- establishing the numbers of people passing through overcrowded areas at critical times during the day;
- questioning a sample of those people to find out where they are coming from, where they are going to and why they have chosen their route;
- constructing a map of corridors and staircases;
- using the map to design several different one-way systems.

Each of the groups reports back on their results to the class. The whole class then works to consider which of the proposed systems would be best, testing each using the data gathered from asking people about their starting points and destinations. They come to a decision after a debate between groups advocating different proposals, using arguments based on the data.

Finally, the class puts together a report of the work of all the groups to present to the SMT, giving several possible solutions and the arguments for and against them, concluding with the recommendation for their favoured one-way system. In addition, they decide to append some alternative suggestions arising from the investigations into the journeys actually being made. These include suggestions about allowing more time for moving between lessons and avoiding timetabling any year group for consecutive English and geography lessons as movement between these two subject areas seemed to be a significant source of congestion.

Apart from the (non-trivial) spatial aspects of drawing and interpreting maps and testing routes around these networks, the 'school mathematics' that students would use as they work on this problem would mostly be related to the 'handling data' part of the curriculum. This would include specifying the problem, deciding what data to collect and how to collect it, and analysing and presenting their conclusions in appropriate forms. There are other features of the process of solving this problem, however, that can be seen to have a lot in common with the ways in which people who have been trained as mathematicians or engineers may find themselves working in industrial, commercial or public service settings:

- The initial problem is underspecified, requiring further clarification and knowledge of the context.
- Different approaches could be taken to the problem, for example, using information drawn from the school timetable instead of questioning a sample of students about their routes.
- Teamwork and communication are important aspects of the work.
- There may be several equally valid alternative solutions. This is one of the crucial ways in which real applied mathematics differs from the sort of exercise commonly found in school textbooks.

This example might be enhanced by collaborating with the geography department. Again, professional mathematicians often work in interdisciplinary teams in which the different disciplinary priorities can contribute alternative perspectives and insights as well as complementary skills. There are also, of course, many opportunities for mathematical modelling that arise within the science and technology curricula and that could be fruitful for cross-curricular collaboration within the school.

MATHEMATICS TEACHER AS SUBJECT SPECIALIST

It sometimes looks as if mathematics teachers have little choice about what they teach. The National Curriculum lists the content of the curriculum. The National Framework for Mathematics details and illustrates learning objectives and recommends teaching methods. Examination syllabuses and papers specify what kinds of things students must do in order to get the qualifications they need. Textbooks, some of which are even published by the examination boards, claim to provide the information students need and the learning activities that will enable them to meet the objectives of the curriculum (although they tend to lack sufficient opportunities for developing problem-solving, investigation and application skills). Surely all the teacher has to do is 'deliver' the curriculum as it has been defined by the experts in the government, the examination boards and the publishing houses? From this perspective, there does not seem to be much role for specialist mathematicians in the classroom.

As should be clear by now from what we have written in this chapter, we do not believe that this is a valid, or even viable, perspective. Mathematics is more than a list of discrete topics. It is a richly connected body of knowledge with important common ideas and themes that run through its various parts. It provides rigorous ways of thinking about the world and of approaching problems that may be abstract or of immediate practical significance. Its complexity and connectedness cannot easily be represented in a list of topics or a set of exercises. This is where the subject specialist is needed: to help students to see the connections; to highlight the themes such as identity, inverse or isomorphism; to model the ways that mathematicians, whether pure or applied, approach problems; to guide students into thinking mathematically about real world problems. In this chapter, we have illustrated ways in which the kind of mathematics done in the university and in non-academic settings can inform the mathematics done in the secondary school. Many of the important mathematical ideas discussed here will be met again in later chapters as we turn to thinking more directly about learning, planning and teaching mathematics.

THINKING ABOUT PRACTICE

■ When preparing to teach a topic, what 'big mathematical ideas' might be developed while working on this topic?

■ When planning to give students 'problems' to solve by applying recently learnt techniques, how might one or more problems be developed to give students insight into the modelling process?

■ What real problems are there in your students' direct experience that they could tackle mathematically?

Chapter 4

Making sense of school mathematics

KEY QUESTIONS

■ Can school mathematics be seen as a coherent subject rather than a collection of separate topics?

■ In what ways can school mathematics be seen to be connected to other meaningful domains of human experience?

The title of this chapter can be interpreted in at least three ways:

■ making school mathematics sensible, coherent and reasonable;
■ presenting school mathematics to learners in such a way that they will understand it;
■ understanding school mathematics (that is, developing your understanding of it).

These interpretations are, of course, closely related. Our aim in this chapter is to address all of them through focusing primarily on the first – the coherence and reasonableness of mathematics itself.

Mathematics is sometimes taught and learnt as a set of discrete facts and procedures, each of which is encountered and memorised separately. This is an inefficient process, putting unreasonable demands on the memory and providing many opportunities for forgetting or mis-remembering. Many of the errors that learners make result from incomplete, muddled or slightly inaccurate remembering of facts and procedures they have been taught. Some examples:

■ **48**

- add a list of whole numbers by lining up the left-hand side
- $-(x - y) = -x - y$
- $\frac{1}{3} = 0.3$ and $\frac{1}{4} = 0.4$

Such dependence on disconnected memorising is not only an inefficient process but actually misrepresents the nature of the subject. It can also prove a demoralising and demotivating experience for students who wish to make coherent sense of what they are learning. The best teachers not only help their students to construct connections between the various topics they are studying – for example, emphasising the similarities between fractions, decimals, percentages and ratios as well as their differences – but also draw out 'big ideas' that play important roles in many areas of mathematics and that are fundamental to mathematical thinking. Some common ideas about the nature of mathematics and learning mathematics include:

- mathematics is the same now as it has always been;
- mathematics is dry and abstract;
- mathematics isn't meant to make sense – just learn the rules by heart.

In this chapter, we hope to challenge these ideas and to show, by working with examples of topics from different areas of the school curriculum, how these ideas can be turned upside down, demonstrating that:

- mathematics is historically situated and has been different for different people at different times;
- mathematics can connect with people's lives and the 'real world';
- the rules of mathematics are not arbitrary but work because mathematics is a coherent body of knowledge.

NEGATIVE NUMBERS

Let us start by looking at the case of negative numbers. This is often perceived as a dull topic, taught to children in the early years of the secondary school because it is necessary for performing the arithmetic and algebraic manipulations needed for later parts of the curriculum.

While the notation of negative numbers is encountered in use in everyday life, especially in the context of the Celsius temperature scale, it is difficult to use such contexts as motivation for learning how to perform calculations with them. For many learners, then, this is an abstract and largely pointless area of mathematics, notable mainly for the poorly understood and often misapplied rule 'minus and minus makes plus'.

Historical experience of negative numbers

NOTE

The earliest known representation of negative numbers was in China, where red (positive) and black (negative) rods were manipulated to perform calculations, including, for example, solving systems of simultaneous equations. However, negative solutions were ignored, primarily because the calculations arose as a means of solving practical problems in which negative answers were not useful. (See Joseph, 1991.)

It is not only children who find negative numbers hard. The history of mathematics shows that, although negative numbers have been used in some form since the early years of the last millennium, it was not until very recently that they have been fully accepted as numbers with the same status as their positive counterparts. While they have been represented in iconic or symbolic form so that they could be manipulated while solving problems, solutions involving negative quantities have often been ignored or rejected as meaningless. We can only hypothesise about how the early Chinese and Indian mathematicians understood what they were doing when they worked with their representations of negative numbers. Within the more recent Western tradition, however, we have plenty of evidence of the feelings of discomfort and even hostility towards negative numbers experienced by mathematicians as late as the eighteenth century. Anne Boye cites a number of mathematicians through the ages, including one Francis Maseres in 1759:

They are useful only, in so far as I am able to judge, to darken the very whole doctrines of the equations and to make dark of the things that are in their nature excessively obvious and simple. It would have been desirable in consequence that the negative roots were never allowed in algebra or that they were discarded.

(Boye, 2002)

Connecting negative numbers with the 'real world': using metaphors

The 'real world' contexts in which children are most likely to first encounter negative numbers tend to use them as a means of representing quantities below zero, but do not on the whole give rise to an extensive use of them in calculations. Addition can make sense when dealing with changes in temperature (a rise or fall of a given positive number of degrees) and multiplication or division of a negative by a positive number can make sense in the context of debts (the consequence of repeatedly spending the same amount or of reducing a debt by a factor). However, knowing how to calculate with negative numbers is not really necessary in order to solve problems in these contexts, which are often more efficiently addressed using informal methods. When we use them during the introductory stages of teaching the topic, it is not to show learners a practical application of this new concept. Rather, we are using the context as a metaphor to help learners construct meaning for negative numbers by making connections with everyday ideas that are more familiar to them.

NOTE

A *metaphor* is a way of thinking and talking about one domain as if it were another. The objects and relationships within one domain are mapped on to objects and relationships in the other. Thinking about the domain of directed numbers as if it were the domain of temperature means creating a mapping between: positive numbers and high temperatures; negative numbers and low temperatures; adding a positive number and a rise in temperature; adding a negative number and a fall in temperature.

As we have said above, the temperature and debt metaphors are not very helpful when it comes to dealing with subtraction and with multiplication and division by negative numbers. Teachers have long recognised these limitations and the pages of textbooks and teachers' professional journals bear witness to the ongoing search for a concrete situation that will give learners a consistent metaphorical model for operations with positive and negative numbers. Some examples:

- A physical representation using black counters for positive, red for negative (good for subtraction, not so good for multiplication) or using the two parts of the Yin-Yang sign. (See Figure 4.1.) A useful feature of this model is the visual image it provides of pairing up each number with its additive inverse to make zero.

Figure 4.1 *A Yin-Yang sign can serve as a model of positive and negative numbers*

- Walking along a number line: forward for positive, backward for negative and turn around through 180° in order to subtract – if you start by facing in the positive direction then subtract ⁻3, you turn around and walk three paces backwards. This has the same effect as adding +3 (i.e. walking forward three paces without turning). With this model, the idea of changing sign as changing direction is stressed – an idea that recurs in several mathematical topics encountered later in the curriculum, such as rotation, velocity, etc.

The number line is a particularly strong metaphor that most learners will have experienced extensively since the early years of primary school and which continues to provide support for conceptualising extensions of the number system up to and including the real numbers. Even beyond the level of school mathematics, the number line appears as a useful image in addressing issues to do with continuity and completeness, providing visualisations of the notions of *neighbourhood* and *cut*. Although subtraction of negative numbers as described above may seem complicated, addition is dealt with relatively easily by treating integers as shifts along the number line in the positive and negative directions and addition as a simple concatenation of these shifts. Even here, however, it is necessary to conceptualise numbers in two different ways: both as a position on the number line and as a shift along it. Thus, for example, to add $^-4 + {^-6} + 8$: start at $^-4$ (a position), go down 6 (a shift) to $^-10$ (a position), then go up 8 (a shift) to $^-2$ (a position).

A similar dualism is needed to deal with combining vectors, thus

$$\begin{pmatrix} 2 \\ -1 \end{pmatrix}$$

may need at different times to be considered both as the vector joining the origin to the point with coordinates $(2, {^-1})$ and as a movement with a horizontal component of 2 (or 2 to the right) and a vertical component of $^-1$ (or 1 down). In the case of numbers, it may not be necessary for teachers to draw this dualism to the attention of their students. However, it is important to be aware of it and to be ready to address it if it arises as a problem for some learners.

NOTE

The metaphor of vectors as journeys also involves the need to shift between thinking of a vector as the process of making a journey and as the outcome of completing the journey. Thus in Figure 4.2, a + b is both different from and equal to c + d.

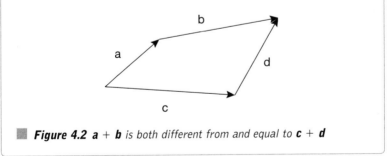

Figure 4.2 *a + b is both different from and equal to **c** + **d***

Different metaphorical models stress different important aspects of the situation. Working with several of the models may help learners to construct rich and connected conceptions of operations with negative numbers – although we need to be careful to avoid confusion by presenting too many alternatives at the same time, unless the relationships between them are carefully structured. The point is not that learners should continue to think of negative numbers as low temperatures or debts or red counters or walking backwards, but that they may find these metaphors helpful as supports for their thinking until they are able to operate fluently and confidently with the abstract symbols.

Negative numbers as part of a broader coherent system

One of the ways in which negative numbers became an essential part of the Western mathematics tradition was as solutions to apparently well-formed equations. To take a simple example, linear equations of the form $x + a = b$ are clearly meaningful and have easy-to-find solutions when b is greater than a. But what about when b is less than a? If you can think about mathematics as an abstract system rather than (or as well as) a representation of concrete objects, it is possible to see all such equations as essentially similar and to extend the number system to make it possible to find solutions for them in consistent ways. Negative numbers are thus conceptualised as the solutions of equations such as $x + 4 = 2$. This opens up some important concepts and processes of doing and creating mathematics. Mathematicians can extend the universe of mathematical objects by constructing a coherent and consistent set in which this equation, and others similar to it, do have solutions. A similar process can be used to extend the universe of numbers to allow solutions for equations such as $x^2 = 2$ (algebraic irrational numbers) and $x^2 = {}^-1$ (imaginary numbers).

The idea that mathematics should be consistent and coherent provides us with some ways of helping learners to make sense of operations with negative numbers by appealing to their sense of pattern. For example, the patterns in the subtraction table (see Table 4.1) can help to convince learners that subtracting $^-2$ is the same as adding 2. Like some of the metaphors discussed above, this pattern has some additional useful features. In particular, it stresses the important fact that the result of subtracting any number from itself is zero.

The 'minus and minus makes a plus' rule for multiplication can be justified similarly by appeal to patterns in an extension of the familiar

Table 4.1 *Subtraction table for integers*

				second number			
−	**3**	**2**	**1**	**0**	**⁻1**	**⁻2**	**⁻3**
3	0	1	2	3	4	5	6
2	⁻1	0	1	2	3	4	5
1	⁻2	⁻1	0	1	2	3	4
0	⁻3	⁻2	⁻1	0	1	2	3
⁻1	⁻4	⁻3	⁻2	⁻1	0	1	2
⁻2	⁻5	⁻4	⁻3	⁻2	⁻1	0	1
⁻3	⁻6	⁻5	⁻4	⁻3	⁻2	⁻1	0

(first number — row labels at left)

Table 4.2 *Multiplication table for integers*

×	**⁻3**	**⁻2**	**⁻1**	**0**	**1**	**2**	**3**
3	⁻9	⁻6	⁻3	0	3	6	9
2	⁻6	⁻4	⁻2	0	2	4	6
1	⁻3	⁻2	⁻1	0	1	2	3
0	0	0	0	0	0	0	0
⁻1	3	2	1	0	⁻1	⁻2	⁻3
⁻2	6	4	2	0	⁻2	⁻4	⁻6
⁻3	9	6	3	0	⁻3	⁻6	⁻9

multiplication table as in Table 4.2. It is relatively easy to extend into the second and fourth quadrant by conceptualising a product such as $3 \times {}^-4$ using repeated addition, as $^-4 + {}^-4 + {}^-4 = {}^-12$ and to complete the third quadrant by continuing patterns downwards or across.

The appeal to regularity and pattern is an important characteristic of much creative thinking in mathematics – new types of object and operations on them are often constructed deliberately in ways that will make them consistent with existing structures. Similar patterning approaches can also be an effective way of developing meaning for negative indices.

Another approach that appeals to the idea that number systems should be consistent makes use of the distributive law – assuming that it works for negative numbers too. The argument in Figure 4.3, though not fully rigorous, makes use of mathematical forms of deductive argument, starting from previously established facts or assumed axioms. (In this case we have at least four of these: a and its additive inverse ^-a add to zero; the product of any number and zero is zero; the distributive law; the implication that $x + y = y + z \Rightarrow x = z$.)

$(a + -a) \times b = 0$		$(3 + -3) \times 4 = 0$
$a \times b + -a \times b = 0$ [1]	or, using	$3 \times 4 + -3 \times 4 = 0$ [1]
similarly:	specific	similarly:
$-a \times (b + -b) = 0$	numbers,	$-3 \times (4 + -4) = 0$
$-a \times b + -a \times -b = 0$ [2]		$-3 \times 4 + -3 \times -4 = 0$ [2]
From [1] and [2] $a \times b = -a \times -b$		From [1] and [2] $3 \times 4 = -3 \times -4$

Figure 4.3 *A deductive argument for 'a minus times a minus makes a plus'*

Of course, there is no guarantee that introducing learners to these ways of thinking about negative numbers will prevent all their difficulties with the topic! It may, however, succeed in helping them to see that mathematics is not just a disjointed collection of arbitrary rules that have to be memorised.

QUADRILATERALS

Unlike the negative numbers whose notation and use appear briefly in the curriculum in the upper primary and lower secondary school before being assumed as prerequisite knowledge in later years, learning about quadrilaterals starts in the earliest years of schooling and continues to appear in the curriculum in various forms throughout the primary and secondary school. Though seldom named as a separate topic in a scheme of work, they play a central role in the teaching and learning of many geometrical topics and, because of their familiarity and relative simplicity, can be used to provide an introduction to general geometrical principles, methods and forms of reasoning.

Perhaps more clearly than any other area of mathematics, geometry illustrates the multiple purposes that we may have for studying mathematics (see Chapter 2). Its origins as 'earth measure' point clearly to practical utility; the axiomatic deductive method of the Greek geometric tradition has customarily been seen as a high point of abstract rational thought, while the more recent development of algebraic approaches to geometry illustrates the power of symbolisation as a problem-solving tool; the use of geometrically based decorative designs in many cultures across the world shows the wide aesthetic appeal of mathematics as well as, in some cases, its spiritual significance. In many of these aspects of geometric activity, the study and use of quadrilaterals have played a central role.

The human origins of geometry

For agricultural communities, measuring the land has long had practical significance: for planning and estimating quantities of seed and of crops; for determining taxes; for settling disputes between neighbours. George Joseph cites Herodotus, the fifth-century BC Greek historian, who wrote:

> Sesostris [Pharaoh Ramses II, c. 1300 BC] divided the land into lots and gave a square piece of equal size, from the produce of which he exacted an annual tax. [If] any man's holding was damaged by the encroachment of the river ... The King ... would send inspectors to measure the extent of the loss, in order that he may pay in future a fair proportion of the tax at which his property had been assessed. Perhaps this was the way in which geometry was invented, and passed afterwards to Greece.
>
> (Joseph, 1991: 39)

Evidence of the construction of square plots of land in early civilizations and calculation of their areas (and of areas of much more difficult shapes) is widespread, as well as the geometrical design and calculations required for the precise construction of edifices such as the pyramids. The Egyptian 'rope-stretchers' seem to have known and used constructions similar to those we now teach to school students as straight edge and compasses constructions.

As is suggested in the quotation above, Greek mathematicians inherited much from the Egyptian tradition. The Greeks' unique contribution was the development of geometry as an axiomatic deductive system, undertaken primarily for its own sake rather than in order to solve practical problems. At some periods in the past, geometry has been taught

57

in a very abstract way, focusing solely on the reproduction of formal deductive proofs. Many students have not found this a productive way to learn, and more recent curriculum developments have introduced a more practical orientation. However, deductive proof is a fundamental part of mathematical activity as a means of validating results and as a means of deriving new results and making connections. For example, the standard (Euclidean) definition of a rectangle as a quadrilateral with right angles and parallel sides is logically equivalent to the implicit definition used by home-builders in Mozambique who use two ropes of equal length tied at their centre points to construct rectangular foundations (see Figure 4.4) (Gerdes, 1988). Deriving one from the other (in either direction) can help learners to appreciate that mathematical facts are not arbitrary and that practical methods can be justified by theoretical reasoning and can contribute to its development.

Looking at the place of quadrilaterals and other geometrical shapes in historically, geographically, ethnically and religiously diverse cultures can also develop insight into aesthetic and spiritual dimensions of mathematical activity. Tessellations, friezes and other designs that are constructed using geometrical properties have been widely used for decorative and ritual purposes. See Metz (1991) for examples of the use of Islamic patterns as a source of classroom activities.

(a)

(b)

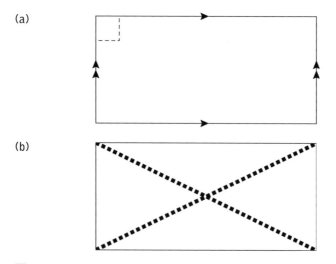

Figure 4.4 (a) A rectangle defined as a quadrilateral with right angles and two pairs of parallel sides; (b) a rectangle constructed by stretching two ropes of equal length, tied at their mid-points

The geometry of quadrilaterals and the real world

The everyday activity of architects, bricklayers, builders, carpenters, designers, draughtsmen, dressmakers, engineers, scaffolders, surveyors and others involved in design and construction in a variety of media makes use of the properties of quadrilaterals, symmetry, similarity, rigidity of structures, tessellation, measurement of length and angle, calculation of area, perimeter and volume, and so on. However, this activity often bears very little resemblance to anything found in the school curriculum. The argument that young people should be taught the mathematics that they will use in the adult world of work, while appealing, is not very strong. There is plenty of evidence that, in almost all occupations, very little recognisable school mathematics is directly relevant and, even where it is relevant, workers in the field are likely to use idiosyncratic, context-dependent methods that are more efficient and effective for them than the abstract general methods taught in school (see, for example, Nunes *et al.*, 1993). Much of the mathematics is hidden within technological devices or frozen in traditional procedures, algorithms or rules-of-thumb. Nevertheless, working on tasks arising from real problems that occur in the world of work can motivate learners by using problems faced by people they know or can relate to. It can also help them to gain insight into the power that mathematics has outside the classroom.

The field of 'ethnomathematics' – the study of the mathematics used by identifiable cultural groups – is one source of real world problems that may be used in the classroom. The example discussed here is taken from work done by Gelsa Knijnik with workers and their children in an agricultural community in southern Brazil (Knijnik, 2000). Three of the local workers describe the methods they used to find the area of a four-sided melon field:

Jorge's method: First we add together all the sides. Next we divide the answer by 4. Then we multiply the number we have found by itself.

Adão's method: First we add two opposite sides and divide by 2. Next we add the other two sides and divide them by 2 also. Then we multiply one number by the other.

Sérgio's method: We put a tractor on the land. Working with it for 3 hours ploughs up one hectare.

(Knijnik, 2000: 53–4, translation by Candia Morgan)

Knijnik notes that Adão's method is also used in other communities in Brazil and Chile and, moreover, is found in ancient Egyptian papyri as a method used for calculating taxes on land. She describes her use of these methods with students within the community, comparing them with standard methods of the calculation of area and discussing their advantages and disadvantages, relating them to the contexts of their practical use. In particular, she argues that it is important to address the question of whose interests might be served by using a particular method. At the time of her project, a disastrous hailstorm had just destroyed the melon crop, making the approximate measurement of the size of the fields and the crop an immediate source of conflict of interest between the farmers and their insurance companies. Similarly, it seems likely that the Egyptian authorities were quite aware that the method they used for calculating land for taxation generally resulted in an approximation greater than the actual area.

The greatest value in this example lies in its use within a community in which the learners have a sense of the social, cultural, political and economic context. The comparison and discussion of the various methods is thus not only meaningful for them but also empowering, as it enables them and their families to make informed decisions about important aspects of their lives.

For learners elsewhere, such an example would have very different meanings and, while possibly an interesting and motivating context for the investigation of geometry and area calculations (and an opportunity for learning about the experience of living in a community in the developing world), would be unlikely to be as empowering as an example situated in their own cultural context. Ole Skovsmose proposes some examples that may be more effective in industrialised urban communities: students might consider different ways of distributing the money available for child benefit or financial support for families; they might study the production of different kinds of food or energy and consider the social, economic and ecological costs of consumer choices (Skovsmose, 1994).

Working with problems like these not only addresses a range of aspects of the mathematics curriculum, but also contributes to learners' awareness and ability to deal with social and citizenship issues.

NOTE

The question of when Jorge's and Adão's methods would yield 'good' approximations can provide opportunities for learners to engage with: methods for finding areas of irregular shapes; relationships between perimeter and area, leading to the recognition that a square field would have the maximum area; the derivation of area formulae for different quadrilaterals and consideration of connections between them; judgements about the quality of approximate answers and the choice of degrees of accuracy appropriate to a context.

Quadrilaterals as part of a coherent mathematical system

Proof and reasoning

We have discussed above the importance of deductive proof in geometry and in mathematics as a whole. Engaging in proving is one of the most obvious ways in which learners' experience of working with quadrilaterals can be integrated into their understanding of mathematics as a coherent system. It can connect knowledge about quadrilaterals not only with other areas of the geometry curriculum, but also with ways of reasoning and arguing that are used in many different areas of mathematics. We offer two examples here of specific aspects of mathematical thinking with particular relevance to work with quadrilaterals.

The use of inclusive definitions: a general tendency in present-day mathematics is to use inclusive definitions (i.e. definitions that imply that a square is a rectangle; a rhombus is a kite). These differ from much everyday usage but provide more potential for the logical derivation of further properties. Thus, anything that you know is true in the case of a rhombus must also be true of a square. Examples from other areas of mathematics include the way in which the number system is constructed: integers are rational; rational numbers are real. Similarly, linear and quadratic functions are polynomials. Many learners find these definitions strange and will need to work explicitly with them.

Alternative perspectives on the same object: in spite of the apparent lack of ambiguity provided by formal mathematical definitions, many mathematical concepts can, in fact, be understood in multiple ways, all of which are valid and useful. For example, mathematician William Thurston lists eight different ways of thinking about the derivative of a function and suggests that the list could be continued indefinitely with new insights and mental images (Thurston, 1995). Unambiguous, complete definitions play a central role in deductive reasoning and formal proof, but personal and partial insights are crucial for creative thinking and problem-solving.

One way of appreciating the richness of mathematical concepts and extending your personal list of insights and images is by using different media to investigate the same object. Take, for example, the task of drawing a square. If you use just a pencil, you will probably focus mostly on the appearance of the shape you draw – if it looks more or less like a square you will be happy. If you have a ruler as well, you are likely to pay attention to making the lengths equal. If you are making a grid or tessellation of squares, you are likely to concentrate on making sets of parallel lines. Making a Logo procedure for drawing a square might emphasise the 'fourness' of the square (repeat 4 [forward 100, right 90]) while also demanding an explicit declaration of its properties in a formal language. Constructing the square using straight edge and compasses or a dynamic geometry package would involve using additional knowledge about the construction of perpendicular lines and the use of circular arcs in order to make equal distances. A square can also be constructed by using two ropes or sticks of equal length, crossing

NOTE

Perks and Prestage consider the different aspects of area (Perks *et al.*, 2002) and of constructing a rhombus (Perks and Prestage, 2002) that are emphasised by tasks set to learners using different kinds of computer software (including a graphing package, a spreadsheet, Logo and dynamic geometry). They present a fuller account of their approach to designing purposeful mathematical tasks for learners – and plenty of examples – in their earlier book (Prestage and Perks, 2001).

at right angles (geo-strips, which are widely available in schools, are a suitable apparatus to use for this). This method focuses attention on the properties of the diagonals. These are all important aspects of 'squareness' but, when planning tasks for learners, you will need to consider which aspects to prioritise and what type of media and task will help your students to attend to these aspects.

Approximation and limits

In the early stages of learning about area, counting the number of square units inside a shape is often used as a method of finding areas of both regular and irregular shapes. This provides a stepping-stone on the way to knowing and using the formula for the area of a rectangle and subsequently to deriving other area formulae. However, it can be useful for us to think of it as a method of approximation that is returned to and refined at later stages. Dividing up areas into rectangular or trapezoidal strips is the basis of both algebraic and numerical approaches to integration. The finite sum of areas of trapezoid strips given by the trapezium rule $\int_a^b f(x) \, dx \approx \frac{1}{2} d(y_0 + 2y_1 + \ldots + 2y_{n-2} + y_{n-1})$ (where d is the width of each strip and y_{r-1} is the y-coordinate of the left side of the rth strip) yields an approximate answer for the area under a curve whose accuracy is improved by narrowing and increasing the number of trapezia, while the exact integral function is conceived as the limit of a process of summing ever narrower rectangular strips. The increasing importance of numerical methods at higher levels of mathematics, enabled by new technologies, needs to be supported by understanding created at school level of the role of approximation, its strengths and limitations, and an ability to judge degrees of accuracy. It is possible for learners to engage with these ideas before encountering calculus by considering the accuracy of various approximations of areas of irregular shapes made by counting, using different sorts of grids.

Moving from geometry to number and algebra – the case of 'square'

Geometry and algebra at secondary school level are often seen as completely separate areas of the curriculum. There are, however, useful links that can be made between them. Indeed, some of the earliest

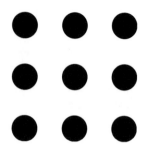

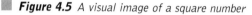

Figure 4.5 *A visual image of a square number*

developments in algebra can be seen to have arisen from geometry. Problems found in ancient Babylonian texts include examples of what is called 'syncopated algebra' (using words in a stylised vocabulary rather than symbols) in which the word for 'side' plays the role that x might in modern symbolic algebra, while 'area of a square' plays the role of x^2. Thus, a statement such as 'I have subtracted the side of the square from the area and the result is 14,30' (14,30 is a base 60 representation of 870) is not just nonsense but can be seen as equivalent to the modern equation: $x^2 - x = 870$ (Joseph, 1991: 108).

The introduction to square numbers is often made through considering the areas of squares with whole number length sides or square

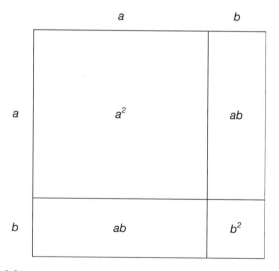

Figure 4.6 *A geometric representation of $(a + b)^2 = a^2 + 2ab + b^2$*

arrays of units (see Figure 4.5). From this, the idea of a square number as one formed by multiplying a whole number by itself is constructed. Further steps of abstraction lead to the ideas that any number can have a corresponding square and that any number can have a square root – and hence to the construction of surds and imaginary numbers as discussed above in relation to negative numbers.

While this process of abstraction is a powerful and creative tool of mathematical thinking, it is also sometimes useful to move in the opposite direction – to construct physical models or visualisations in order to make sense of an abstract entity. For example, drawing a picture (see Figure 4.6) to illustrate the square $(a + b)^2$ and returning to the original physical idea of square numbers as measures of area can help learners to see why and how it can be expressed in expanded form as $a^2 + 2ab + b^2$.

UNDERLYING CENTRAL MATHEMATICAL ISSUES

In this chapter, we have looked at two rather different topic areas from the secondary curriculum and, we hope, indicated some of the ways of thinking about these (and other) topics that will help you and your students make coherent sense of mathematics. It is an interesting and useful activity to look more generally at what is taught in secondary mathematics and see what central issues permeate the content. To conclude this chapter, we offer you a collection of brief overviews of a few such issues, some of which have already emerged in the discussions above of negative numbers and quadrilaterals – our categorisation may not coincide with yours, and it has overlaps, but it serves to give a sense of the range of possibilities for making connections.

Ratio

Ratio is an underlying idea in fractions, percentages, proportionality, trigonometry, rates of change, conversion, social and everyday mathematics, similarity, use of π, and several geometrical ideas. Students have to shift from comparing things by counting them and thinking of the difference, an additive comparison, to comparing things multiplicatively. This is a huge and difficult shift, but one that opens up a wide range of higher level mathematics.

Equivalence

To know that two things which are equivalent can be substituted for each other gives the student power to choose what to do, and to evaluate the choice and decide what sort of choices are best. Equivalence of fractions makes addition and subtraction possible and also encapsulates rules for manipulating algebraic fractions. Equivalence of equations allows students to find the values of unknowns; for example, to know that the statement $2x + 3 = 5$ is equivalent to the statement $2x = 2$ contributes to understanding and being able to create procedures for solving for x. To know that $2x + 3$ is equivalent to 5 also allows 5 to be substituted for $2x + 3$ and vice versa. To know that dividing by a third is equivalent to multiplying by three is useful in a wide range of contexts.

Transformations

The availability of dynamic geometry and graph plotting software makes experiencing transformations of graphs of functions very easy. To see straight lines as translations and rotations of $y = x$ gives a deep sense of the roles of m and c in $y = mx + c$. It also opens up a variety of ways to learn about other aspects of analytical geometry, such as features of quadratic curves, how to find intersections and so on. Exploring the enlargements of shapes relates to similarity and ratio, but transformation also gives ways to explore properties and simple theorems. For example, to see angles relating to parallel lines as translations and reflections of each other makes their equalities very obvious. Students who can describe shapes and geometrical changes in terms of transformations, rather than static relationships, have enhanced powers of generalisation and justification.

Distributivity

An understanding of the structure of distributivity underlies many algebraic manipulations that otherwise would have to be separately learnt. In some countries, students have to learn separate incantations for factorising many different types of expression, whereas a wide experience with using the fundamental law would probably be more useful and easier to use.

Proof

A special feature of mathematics is the place of rigorous proof as a way to convince others. When teaching any topic area there should be opportunities provided for students to justify and provide counter-examples for their own ideas and those of others. Forms of language such as 'if ... then ... because' can permeate mathematics classrooms whatever the topic. Classically, proof in school mathematics appears mainly in geometry, but logical reasoning is just as applicable in discussions about political-mathematical issues as in discussions about number patterns or angles in circles.

Generality

Most of what is taught in school mathematics is a generality of some kind, but students learn about these through examples. The traditional algorithm for long division is a generalisation of a method that works for all pairs of numbers – students learn about it through particular pairs of numbers. The fact that angles of any triangle add up to 180 degrees is a generality – students learn about it through particular triangles and some kind of proof or dynamic demonstration. Means and ranges are generalisations of particular data sets so that something general can be said about a field. Rules for differentiation are generalities and students often have difficulty knowing when to apply each one. Throughout the secondary curriculum, students have to make sense of whether what they are being offered is a special case or a generality and, if so, how far the generality can be applied.

These ideas do not cover everything but are intended to show that some big, general statements can be made about the content of school mathematics, overarching the lists of somewhat fragmented content given in official documents. It may be possible to imagine a lesson in which ratio, equivalence, generality and proof are all featured explicitly, but the lesson is apparently about something else – functions of the form $y = mx$ for example, or the equity of school performance league tables. In Chapters 6 and 7, we will suggest some lessons incorporating a few of these ideas.

THINKING ABOUT PRACTICE

When preparing to teach a topic:

- What historical, cultural and social contexts might help students to appreciate mathematics as a human activity?
- How does the topic relate to others that the students have already studied or will study in the future?
- What opportunities does the topic offer for you to draw attention to generally important characteristics of mathematics and mathematical thinking (e.g., duality, definitions, deductive reasoning)?
- Are there opportunities for making connections between numerical, algebraic and geometrical ways of thinking or for switching between different visual and symbolic representations?

Part II

Learning and teaching mathematics

Teaching mathematics depends not only upon knowledge of the subject but also on knowledge about learning and learners. In this part, we start by thinking about how learning happens, not only by reviewing what theories of learning and intelligence have to say, but also by reflecting on particular experiences of learning mathematics and on the diversity of approaches to learning that teachers will encounter in their classrooms. Continuing our theme that the subject itself makes a difference to the nature of teaching and learning, we consider aspects of mathematical thinking that can make learning mathematics different from learning other subjects.

One of the most immediate challenges for any beginning teacher is the need to plan lessons and to think of activities that will motivate learners and help them to progress in their mathematical understanding. In Chapters 6 and 7, we provide some outline ideas for lessons, addressing a range of mathematical topics. These outlines do not provide a template for lesson planning, nor do they attempt to exemplify a full range of teaching styles, resources or classroom organisation, although they do illustrate a wide variety of approaches. Our aim in presenting the lesson ideas has been to show how it is possible to construct lessons that address critical themes related to learning mathematics.

Finally, how can we know when and what our students have learnt? Having some idea of what understandings students already have is a fundamental requirement for teaching effectively, but can we ever be certain that our judgements about our students are valid and fair? We consider ways in which mathematical learning can be assessed, as well as some of the problems and pitfalls associated with various methods of assessment.

Chapter 5

Understanding learning

KEY QUESTIONS

- What is it like for you to *do* and to *learn* mathematics?
- How do others learn mathematics?
- How can your experiences with mathematics inform your teaching?

In this chapter we focus on practical, classroom, inter-human under-standings about learning, starting mainly from the point of view of the learner. We refer to some of the main theories of learning, but the main purpose is for you to review your own experience of learning math-ematics as a starting point for extending your understanding of what it might be like for your students. Learning theories (described briefly in boxes) may provide some illumination for this process and can give insight into the complexities of teaching, providing new ways to concep-tualise the teaching task.

We probe your experience of doing and learning mathematics to try to show that there is a variety of approach even among relatively successful mathematics students.

THEORIES ABOUT LEARNING MATHEMATICS

A very common reason for choosing to learn mathematics is a desire for certainty. Mathematics gives answers and a sense of closure when you have reached the end of a proof or a long calculation. Many potential teachers report a satisfying feeling of getting it *right*, of being accepted as someone who can demonstrate mental prowess (even if they have lost touch with this feeling during the later stages of their degree studies!). This same feeling may also be a feature of doing mathematics for pleasure, solving puzzles, or using mathematical ideas as a stimulus for creative activities. There is an exciting tension in having an unresolved puzzle or problem in the background of your mind, knowing that eventually it will all fall into place with an elegant satisfaction.

But what if you don't get it right? What if the pieces never fall into place? The two questions above may have led you to give different answers – the word 'do' may imply churning through questions without much effort or engagement, or working on puzzles and questions for enjoyment; the word 'learn' may imply struggle, effort, anxiety and frustration. Many new teachers have experienced difficulty at some stage of their mathematical education, and may, in the end, have not overcome this. Stories of mathematicians achieving insight after long lonely struggles (such as Andrew Wiles proving Fermat's last theorem after years of effort) do not closely relate to their own experiences of trying to finish assignments on time. Such stories do not promulgate an attractive view of being a mathematician – for every Andrew Wiles there are many who never achieve a goal of completion.

So what motivates people who carry on learning and doing mathematics even when they are not getting complete success? Hidden behind your delight at getting right answers, and of knowing you are right, is the long-winded business of building up a complex understanding of structures, language, useful habits, knowledge of useful representations and transformations, ways of communicating about mathematics, and of understanding mathematical text. You have spent many years learning how to work on mathematics. This knowledge is as important as factual and procedural mathematical knowledge, if not more so.

When children start doing mathematics, answers come quickly and praise (or retribution) follows soon after. Whether they are working at school with a teacher, or in the home with parents or other adults, they may come to believe that understanding the question and giving a quick, accurate answer is the stuff of mathematics. Later experience at school challenges this belief. Is there something wrong if I do not understand immediately? Is there something wrong if I cannot remember all the stages of this complicated method? Learning mathematics becomes, all too often, the failure to get the right answer and confusion about how it all hangs together. The experience of not being able to do work which is set by the teacher and has a deadline is very different from the feeling of having an interesting mathematical puzzle unresolved which you have chosen to do and has no deadline.

Those who survive school mathematics taught as 'do this method and get the right answer' are often those who easily pick up and reproduce methods, either by having good recall or by constructing a personal understanding which makes it appear coherent. Those who have a good recall for procedures may be mystified by those who cannot do this. Surely, they may believe, all that is required is to pay attention and copy what the teacher has done, but with different numbers or in a different context.

NOTE

Much mathematics teaching in the past assumed that students learn by imitation, but since every situation is slightly different, even if it is only the numbers that change, a degree of generalisation or appreciation of pattern is required for this to work. Clearly, more sophisticated theories are needed.

Behaviourist theories of learning suggest that people develop habitual responses to stimuli in order to gain the rewards of positive feedback. The data that are needed to see these theories in action are all observable, such as 'the teacher did this and the students did that'. Teaching according to these theories would involve finding out what to do to get the desired result. This is to some extent a useful approach, but fails to explain why adolescents respond so differently and why teaching is not a scientific activity.

Not everyone works in the same way, however. Other successful learners may succeed with a different approach; they may be more motivated by the feeling of learning than the feeling of finishing what others ask them to do – they will treat an unsolved problem as something to which they can return again and again, trying new approaches and hoping for insight. They may continue to think about a problem long after they have handed it in to be marked; they may be unable to tackle any problem until they have developed a personal image of the concepts involved. Teachers may be unaware that this is the case, or may unintentionally

NOTE

It is generally accepted now that all learning is an effort to construct understanding even if this results in imitation (Wood, 1998). *Constructivist* theories see individuals as actively responding to the environment and other people by building structures of meaning that are constantly adapted and developed under the influence of events outside themselves. Some constructivists see mathematical meaning as only existing in individual constructions (e.g. von Glasersfeld, 1995). This explains differences in learning to some extent, and is useful for thinking about what kinds of experience learners need to construct suitable mathematical meanings. But this story does not explain why so many people end up with knowledge that seems similar when communicated to others. *Social constructivism* is a development in which meaning-making is seen as social rather than individual, and develops through language and other forms of interaction with others (Vygotsky, 1986). The role of teachers in organising whole-class discussion, and enabling student–student discussion, is thus central to the learning process.

discourage it by rushing through the curriculum and/or merely failing to give students the opportunity to talk about their further thoughts.

Some teachers may have been drawn to mathematics because they find it useful, giving tools and insights that have granted access to some other subjects. Mathematics, they might say, is important because it gives skills that offer many employment and educational opportunities. Those who have studied engineering, sports science, psychology or computing may have this view and find familiarity in stories of past scientists who have used mathematics to verify their hunches, or to make new discoveries, or to create conjectures about what might be happening, or just to work out the details. They may say that it is important for students to see mathematics in 'relevant' contexts, as an accompaniment to everyday and economic activity. Seeing how mathematics can be used to interpret the world might be enough to provide understanding and motivation for students – and furthermore they can always check their answers against reality. Why isn't this enough for everybody?

As you read these paragraphs you may have been analysing your own kind of mathematics and your own learning experiences. Are you excited

NOTE

Policy-makers often talk as if what is learnt in school classrooms can somehow be picked up and carried out usefully into other situations. In other words, it can be 'transferred'. Yet every science teacher knows that what is learnt in mathematics lessons cannot easily be carried into science lessons! Theories of *situated cognition* claim that learning is always about acting in a particular physical, social, economic and geographical situation. Knowledge is integral to the situation and cannot be detached from this and taken somewhere else (e.g. Lave and Wenger, 1991). These theories explain why people do different mathematics to survive in the supermarket than in artificial shopping contexts in the classroom. They are useful when thinking about the classroom as an arena in which certain actions, interactions, normal behaviours and kinds of knowledge can be developed, but they fail to explain how some people *do* successfully 'transfer' knowledge into different contexts.

by right answers, or by understanding, or by application, or by some other feature of mathematics? Do you enjoy doing mathematics, finishing mathematics, struggling with mathematics, seeing mathematics sort out a real problem? Mathematics is all of these things, and one of the problems facing new teachers is to work with multiple meanings of mathematics, some of which they may find personally unappealing, and to recognise that their students will respond in a variety of ways to different kinds of activity.

Your own learning experience can help you to make sense of different learners, but it can also limit. If teachers only respond positively to those students whose ways of seeing and doing mathematics are like their own, if they only offer activities which ensure success for those whose mathematical approach is like their own, then they fail to reach others. Critical reflection on their own experience, rather than telling them what to do, allows students to identify differences and see contrasts, to wonder about what it is like to see things differently. What would it be like if solving problems is a disappointment, because there is no more thinking to be done, rather than a pleasure? What would it be like to understand only what can be seen in action? What would it be like to have such a strong visual memory of what is on the chalkboard or in the textbook that every procedure ever seen can easily be mechanically reproduced?

NOTE

Socio-cultural theories offer descriptions of classrooms as places in which participants are gradually enculturated into behaving in certain ways which are generally accepted as being, in our case, 'mathematical' (Daniels, 2001). Students gradually come to know the norms of mathematical activity: how to organise their efforts to learn, how to interact with the teacher and each other, how to interpret, communicate and think about mathematics, and so on. What they bring to classrooms is a product of all their previous experiences as learners of mathematics. What happens to them becomes incorporated into their identity as mathematics learners. Teaching is a process of inducting learners into mathematical behaviour through the tasks, goals and interactions of the community. Such theories explain both the differences and similarities that develop among learners, and also point to the importance of seeing the social and academic habits of classrooms as interrelated.

The central problem in all theories of learning is: how do individuals come to know mathematics in ways which are agreed in the mathematical community, given the abstract nature of mathematical ideas and the many kinds of communication and activity with which teachers and learners engage?

WHY DO PEOPLE HAVE DIFFERENT VIEWS OF WHAT IT MEANS TO DO MATHEMATICS?

Contrast these stories. First there is the experience of Sarah Flannery whose father posed mathematical problems for the family to discuss as they went around their domestic life and who, at the age of 16, provided a tentative new approach to the Cayley–Purser algorithm in coding theory (Flannery, 2002). Then there is a child – we shall call her Jade – who is sent to an after-school tutorial 'club' to practise exercises of mathematics, but finds that what she learns there is not valued at school and, eventually, gives up trying to grasp mathematics. Contrast this further with the experience of a child of uneducated parents – we shall call him Jim – who bought some early twentieth-century maths textbooks at a jumble sale and worked through them on his own alongside the exploratory curriculum he was pursuing at school. He did very well at A-level and went on to study mathematics at university, the first in his family to go beyond compulsory education. Not only do these stories create different views of what it means to work on the cognitive aspects of mathematics, but they show that those views are bound up with the emotions of shared working in a loving family, the emotions of moving through a programme of repetitive exercises with systematic reward, and the emotions of ploughing a lonely, studious furrow which, ultimately, removes you from your family experience.

Furthermore, the status society gives to those who succeed at mathematics affects such views. Each of these stories reflects that high status, but in some it is the status of achievement in mathematics that drives the story, in others it is the enjoyment of learning mathematics. And each story becomes more complex when the school experience is added in. For Sarah, school and home appear to have worked in harmony and she progressed to university and beyond. In Jade's case, the school wanted her to use different methods from those she had used to succeed in her after-school class and would not promote her to the 'top table' until she succumbed and set out her long divisions in the way they favoured. In Jim's case, by contrast, the school teaching was flexible enough to allow him to use and make sense of his private knowledge side by side with the problem-solving approaches. Thus he learnt Euclidean geometry alongside transformational geometry; iterative methods alongside algebraic methods; static approaches to calculus alongside those using dynamic graph-plotting methods. The cognitive and emotional embedding of mathematics was affected by the interplay of home and school attitudes.

In the cases described so far, the students saw themselves as 'good' at mathematics, even if that self-perception was not appreciated by everyone. None of them fits an image of students who, *solely* because of the educational norms of their schools, are successful academically as well-balanced, intelligent and competent learners. Why have we described these cases then? First, we wanted to demonstrate how what is going on out of school can influence achievement within school, positively or negatively, even for those who are perceived to do very well. Second, we wanted to raise questions about those who might not achieve very much in school mathematics, or who are merely bobbing along just keeping their heads above water. If capable students can have such a variety of views impinging on their school performance, then surely less successful students must have at least a similar range of emotional and social baggage, and views of mathematics and how it is learnt, which will affect their mathematics learning. Learners' views of what mathematics is will vary according to their histories of success or failure, and also according to how mathematics is perceived by those around them in and out of school. Schools can go some way towards helping influential adults know more about the school's expectations through parents' evenings, reports and the nature of homework tasks, but changing attitudes and understandings takes time. Meanwhile, it will make a difference to students whether their past mathematical experience has been of a sequence of unconnected methods with which they usually get, or usually do not get, right answers, or whether it has been presented as an arena for exploration of abstract structures in which one can make conjectures and test generalisations in an encouraging environment.

DIFFERENT KINDS OF LEARNING

We may be tempted to use Howard Gardner's theoretical categorisation of different kinds of intelligence here (Gardner, 1999). His theory of multiple intelligences tells us that people have seven different kinds of intelligence, which are distributed throughout their interactions with their experiences. Many mathematicians like lists because they suggest completeness and the possibility of a system. Perhaps if we look at people's intelligences we can know how to teach them accurately. Gardner describes linguistic, logical–mathematical, musical, spatial, bodily kinaesthetic, interpersonal and intrapersonal intelligences and points out that these are all triggered by different experiences in different learners. It is a short step from this list to draw up, using appropriate tests, detailed pictures of the preferred learning styles for a class of students and then to try to design lessons that will appeal to the different learners within it.

But hang on! Suppose, in an extreme case, all the students have great musical strengths but little else – what then? Apart from baulking at the challenge of teaching all secondary mathematics through music, we would guess that maybe these students have not had their other intelligences developed adequately by their previous education. Thus we accept that teaching should not merely confirm existing intelligences but could also develop others. As well as this, we need to maintain integrity with the subject as it is generally seen to be, both in school and beyond, and to recognise that some intelligences are more intimately bound up with mathematical achievement than others. If we accept Gardner's list we are also accepting the challenge of describing mathematics as concerning a subset of these, and of learning mathematics in the social context of school classrooms as potentially involving all of these.

The theory of multiple intelligences does not, therefore, provide a teaching recipe for mathematics and its use as a diagnosis–treatment tool might lead us away from offering the full complexity of mathematics to everyone. However, it does alert teachers to the variety of different triggers that could be used in classrooms to engage the interest of all students. It describes a diversity of dispositions.

Treating different intelligences as if they are fixed learning styles is, we have seen, problematic. There are other ways to characterise learning styles that you may come across. Many of them are dichotomies. For example, you might read of surface and deep learners (Marton and Saljo, 1984), of holist and serialist learners (Pask, 1976), of those who learn by rote and those who learn for understanding; of those whose goal is performance and those whose goal is to learn more (Dweck, 2000). These are attempts to distinguish between different kinds of learning, but it is unimaginable that any teacher would ever be able to identify every student in every situation as being one or the other. As with Gardner's list, the value of these characterisations is to inform your planning to take account of all kinds of students and perhaps to help them develop learning styles that do not seem to be their natural preference. It might be appropriate to help holist learners, who prefer to grasp complex situations all at once, to pay attention to the detailed structure of a mathematical argument; it might be appropriate to help serialist learners, who prefer to learn in a step-by-step manner, to develop a complex overview of a mathematical situation.

The theory we find most useful does not come as a neat list; rather, it is a way of thinking about individuals in the interactive settings of classrooms. Each student enters at the start of a lesson with baggage. That baggage includes a variety of adolescent emotions, worries and extra-curricular concerns which contribute to attention, engagement and self-esteem. In addition, a student has a mathematics history that contributes to her view of herself as a learner of mathematics, her relationship with the school and with the teacher. Further, each person has some knowledge that may or may not be brought to bear on the lesson – it depends on what happens, what examples, what words, what diagrams,

79

what visual stimuli are used. These experiences, and the words and discussions and sense making that go with them, are candidates for being incorporated into her memory and connected to her existing knowledge of mathematics. She needs to know which of these it is worth making an effort over for the long term, as well as those she makes an effort over because of the structure and interactions in the lesson. The lesson may have been about expanding brackets, but she may have spent her effort only on worrying about negative signs and not noticed the more general purpose of the lesson. Her memory of the lesson might be triggered by the sight of future questions that look like those she was given to do, but it might equally be triggered by the memory of an off-task incident that caught her attention, or the sound of the teacher's voice as some instruction is intoned. If she sees mathematics as something to be understood, she may have tried to grasp why brackets are dealt with this way and developed her own reasons and incantations to help her relate this to something more familiar. Her ideas may or may not match what the teacher says, but they may have worked far enough to give her right answers in the lesson ... or they may not have worked and she does not know why. Perhaps she has been thinking about the use of brackets as punctuation and does not see why in language the contents can be omitted but in mathematics they have to be included.

Such a view – of individuals acting in a social context which is, for them, part of a chronological sequence of possibly disparate contexts – does not easily lead to recipes for teaching mathematics, but *does* lead to a sense of the diversity of adolescent experience of which Gardner's list is but a small part.

RECOGNISING AND WORKING WITH DIVERSITY

We know what happened to Sarah: she became famous and went on to give inspiring talks to young people alongside pursuing an academic career. The more anonymous Jim was destined for an early mathematics degree and a rather isolated social life. You probably already want to save Jade from the conflicting tangle of rules and methods and judgements which may have left her not knowing what to do for the best.

Fortunately, there is plenty of help available in research literature. School students are very adaptable and, so long as what they are offered is coherent and carried through with commitment, conviction and integrity, they will adapt to new ways to work on mathematics. Those who are inclined to follow rules and accept externally imposed goals will tend to convert what they are asked to do into such rules and goals. Those who are more inclined to make deep connected sense of their experiences will continue to do so, however shallow and unconnected their lesson experiences may be; it is from these students that strong mathematicians can be expected to emerge *whatever their teaching has been like.* How can teachers work with students so that many more become strong mathematicians? How could Jade have been helped to succeed and not give up?

A teacher who gives students pages of exercises for which the goal is to finish is providing something for the reflective learner to work with, but is not challenging rule-followers or those who have previously been taught mathematics as a set of rules beyond their usual behaviour. Students who have only this kind of teaching experience may become very teacher-dependent and overloaded with confusing, meaningless things to remember which give no overall sense of mathematics.

A teacher who offers the same exercises but states a goal of 'learn as much as you can by doing these exercises, and tell me three things you have learnt' is helping the rule-follower to develop less superficial goals, and also offering the reflective learner a structure to support reflection. Dweck (2000) has shown in many research studies that if 'effortful learning', rather than 'finishing', is seen as the purpose of a task, then rule-following students will make more effort and learn more, and those for whom effortful learning was always the goal will also still flourish. Objectives of this type can be expressed to students at the start of each lesson. Think about the contrasting nature of these lesson objectives:

- to convert decimals to percentages;
- to be able to explain to others how to convert decimals to percentages;
- to be able to make up hard examples of converting decimals to percentages;
- to know more about decimals and percentages, including how to convert one to the other.

A learner who prefers to develop deep understanding would do so whatever the lesson objective, but one who was goal-orientated might need the last goal as a prompt to think more and not merely to finish a given exercise. A teacher who uses goals relating to the development of mathematical thought and deep understanding not only benefits all learners but also gives them a view of mathematics which prioritises thinking, effort, struggle and application over procedures, while giving rule-followers new kinds of rules to follow. Instead of rules like 'take things to the other side and multiply' there are rules like 'undo an operation by using its inverse' and 'vary the form of this equation so that the unknown value becomes easier to find'. Studies such as those by Boaler (1997) and Schoenfeld (2002) show that students of such teachers may not learn as much technical content but are far better at applying what they do know. Indeed, in tests they tend to do as well as others on technical aspects and better on problem-solving aspects. The reason they do as well on techniques, even those they have not been taught, seems to be that they approach all questions as problems to be solved rather than things to be remembered and performed. As well as this, their knowledge of mathematics tends to be more holistic, less 'bitty', more about relationships than methods. Psychologists such as Skemp (1976) have shown that relational mathematical knowledge is more easily remembered, used and developed than procedural knowledge, but takes more time to learn.

A further kind of 'rule' of mathematical behaviour could be 'look at several examples and describe what is happening in general in my own words' or 'test what the teacher says by making up my own examples to see what works and what doesn't'. These new kinds of rule are perhaps better described as norms of mathematics classrooms, the regular habits which teachers expect learners to adopt in their classrooms. We have imagined two contrasting classrooms to illustrate the importance of these 'rules of behaviour' or norms.

Pedagogic norms about how mathematics is usually taught

In classroom A it is usual for students to be offered a problem to think about and to offer possible ways forward with it. In classroom B students are given a worked example and an exercise to do which mimics that example. In classroom A students are expected to think about possible approaches and share in offering their ideas and thus develop their problem-solving skills. In classroom B students are expected to imitate what the teacher has done until they get stuck; mathematics is a collection of given techniques.

 82

Communication norms about what kinds of interaction are encouraged

In classroom A discussion, debate and disagreement over answers, methods, accuracy and extreme cases are seen as necessary; for example, students offer examples and counter-examples to the teacher (rather than all such examples coming from teachers and textbooks). Mathematics is seen as a human, discursive activity. In classroom B there is no real discussion; students listen to the teacher, answer 'yes' when he says 'do you understand?' and do not speak to each other while working through exercises. Mathematics, in the second classroom, is a sequence of rules and methods to perform correctly – there is nothing to discuss – the teacher is the source of knowledge.

Social norms about how to interact and how different ways of thinking are valued

In classroom A students typically listen to each other's ideas, comment on each other's ideas, work together on problems and thus have access to a variety of ways of understanding mathematics. They see mathematics as a social activity in which meaning is constructed through collaboration. The teacher organises and orchestrates different kinds of learning activity. In classroom B students put their hands up when they can answer the teacher's closed questions. Right answers receive praise, wrong answers are corrected. The teacher maintains social control and is totally in charge of the direction of the lesson. The construction of mathematical meaning is a private matter.

Curriculum norms about how mathematics is presented

In classroom A mathematics is always networked and connected, rather than fragmented; no new topic is started without asking what students already know and exploring it in everyday language and experience. Thus students can always relate to the topic in some way as it unfolds, and their own prior knowledge has been valued and included in the lesson. In classroom B a new topic might start with a heading written on the board, with a definition or worked example, which has to be copied without any discussion of how this relates to what is already known. The unwritten rules of behaviour in classroom A would be that students take part in the initial discussion and try to make links for themselves between different mathematical ideas. In classroom B the order of delivery is the only order available to students.

Cognitive norms about what it means to learn mathematics

In classroom A mathematics is about gaining understanding, rather than superficial rule following: students expect to give reasons and methods with their answers rather than just giving an answer. Praise is given for interesting and thoughtful contributions, not so much for right answers, which are often incidental to the progress of the lesson. Students are self-motivated and confident with unfamiliar mathematics. In classroom B mathematics is about following rules and getting right answers, so there is emphasis on examination tricks and memory for these. Students are rule-dependent and teacher-dependent.

In classroom A, diversity is important because it leads to fertile and lively discussion and the valuing of many different ways to see and think about mathematics. In classroom B diversity is a nuisance because it means there are no perfect explanations and the teacher spends a lot of time helping students who are stuck.

The different norms of classrooms A and B reflect, and generate, very different views of mathematics and what it means to teach and learn it. We have invented deliberately strong contrasts, and most classrooms operate somewhere between the two, but classroom A gives the freedom to explore for those who prefer to learn that way, and offers behavioural and mathematical rules which encourage exploration for those who prefer to follow rules. Classroom B offers rules for those who like rules, but little for those who need to explore and create their own understandings.

It is not trivial for learners to change from one set of expectations to another. Kevin, a new teacher, felt very frustrated when the class he was trying to get to discuss methods kept saying: 'Just tell us what to do!' Vicky, in similar circumstances with a high-achieving group who were used to following algorithms, described the problem as: 'They don't know me well enough to keep at it long enough to see the rewards.' She found ways to comment on the importance of each thought they expressed and made sure that she referred back to these when she summed up the discussion.

MATHEMATICAL STRUCTURE

Despite the diversity among learners, there are enough similarities about how people learn to help us be certain about some things in the teaching and learning of mathematics. We know individual learners try to make sense of their experiences, even if those experiences are repetitive and mundane. If their sense making is mediated by discussion, language and the encouragement to reflect, then they have more opportunity to see what is going on, perhaps through someone else's description of it or by trying to explain their own point of view. Technical language can be introduced by the teacher as a means of communicating, and through trying to use technical words and hearing others use them students can become more precise in their understanding of the concepts. In discussions, probing questions such as 'Have you considered so-and-so?' can help a class of learners explore their understanding of an idea and even reach a shared understanding. For example, a discussion of the meaning of the word 'multiply' could be very fruitful if the teacher pushes students beyond the obvious 'times tables' towards a range of decimal multiplications they could explore with a calculator.

In mathematics there are some fundamental ways of thinking that have particularly strong applicability both within mathematics and in other contexts. For example, discerning what is the same and what is different about situations is a natural human act and can be used in mathematics to identify categories and relationships. One can do this in a mathematically worthwhile way only if there is special attention given to what varies and what stays the same. Then looking for what varies leads to recognition of relationships, so that a learner might conjecture about special relationships that might 'always' happen.

A sequence of linear equations that encourages learners to focus on a particular aspect: the role of the multiplier:

$$x - 1 = 0$$
$$2x - 1 = 0$$
$$3x - 1 = 0$$
$$\vdots$$
$$kx - 1 = 0$$

Some generalisations are not very useful, although they seem so at the time, such as, 'multiplication makes things bigger' and 'subtract the smaller from the larger'. Students cannot stop themselves making such generalisations, but the public articulation and discussion of them encourages the use of counter-examples or exploration to find out when they are useful and when they are not. Naming mathematical objects with conventional names and talking about their relationships in conventional ways help everyone feel included in the mathematics, and the use of such language can itself call mathematics into being. By this we mean that the ability to say 'if . . . then . . .' makes it possible to discuss causal relationships. The word 'because' allows us to give reasons for relationships. Consequently, the frequent use of 'if . . . then . . .' and 'because' in lessons causes students to reason in the normal course of classroom life.

Even with widely differing backgrounds, students can more easily learn mathematical relationships if they experience them without too much clutter around. For instance, if 'they are always taught about 'area and perimeter' together (two very different kinds of concept, one easily measurable, the other not), many will confuse area and perimeter. They will learn more easily if they can relate new ideas to what they already believe to be the case, either by adding to their knowledge or by comparing new ideas to old. Thus, perimeter extends their previous experiences with linear measure, while area relates more easily to experience with painting than with measuring! Applying algebraic formulae to these without building up a sense of generalisation adds to the confusion. To tackle this, many teachers offer activities in which shapes may change in ways that preserve area but change perimeter, or preserve perimeter but change area.

If they are embedded in a culture of discussion about what changes and what stays the same (such as when comparing graphs with the same gradient), and are used to making hypotheses and deciding when and why they might be true (such as wondering if all squares have an odd number of factors), they will begin to apply those ways of thinking in all their mathematics, not just when the teacher tells them to do so. They can only discern what changes against a background of stability, in an environment which allows them to develop their understanding with others, including the teacher, and, in particular, with language and examples derived from the conventions of mathematics.

Instead of trying to provide thirty individually styled learning environments, it is possible to teach in ways which allow all learners to make sense of mathematics and, through enculturation into habits of mathematical interaction, discussion, argument and thought, check out and develop their mathematics by comparing it to that of others and the expected conventions. The ultimate aim of developing such habits in class is that learners will come to use the same habits when working on their own, thus developing inner dialogue, inner challenge, inner questioning and inner argument and becoming strong, independent mathematical learners. For example, if in class the teacher is frequently comparing the current mathematical topic to other related topics and then shifts to asking 'Can you think of any other mathematics we have done which connects to this?', we can expect students to learn that it is useful to speculate about how mathematics interconnects. Similarly, if the teacher habitually encourages students to make conjectures and to look for counter-examples, then students may do these things voluntarily when studying on their own.

EXAMPLE

Keith asked his students 'What question do you think occurs to me?' and then produced the word 'why?' written on a large piece of card from his briefcase. In Ed's classroom, learners who gaze at the ceiling for inspiration see prompts about ways to think about mathematics stuck up there on little posters. He realised that this was a fun way to introduce them into the classroom ethos and that students would be likely to remember at least their existence ('Do you recall how Mr X had instructions on his ceiling?'), if not their content. In each case the teachers had thought about how to mark out these prompts and questions as special in their lessons.

There are more examples in Chapters 6 and 7 of how teachers might 'model' useful ways to work with mathematics.

LEARNING FROM, AND ABOUT, STUDENTS' MATHEMATICS

When anyone first observes classrooms, either their own or those of other teachers, they tend to interpret students' responses and behaviour in terms of whether they are or are not doing what the teacher expects and asks. Gut feelings might be on the 'side' of the teacher or the 'side' of the students.

Thus, if someone is lolling back in a chair, not looking at the board and poking the desk with a ruler, this might be interpreted to show that she is 'not paying attention', 'off-task', 'lazy', and so on, and thus the problem is seen as hers. The teacher must somehow 'make' her attend by asking her a direct question (thus revealing her lack of attention), by commenting about her failure to listen if she cannot do the ensuing written work, by dealing dismissively or wearily with requests for help, and so on. Somehow this student has to be taught that she must pay attention, listen hard and thus she will know what to do when it comes to working on her own.

On the other hand, her behaviour might be interpreted to be an indication that the work is too easy, that the teacher has failed to catch her attention, that the work is so unrelated to what she understands that there is no point in listening as none of it makes sense to her, or that she is generally negatively treated by the teacher, so sees no point in asking questions. In extreme cases, she may have a sight, hearing or language problem which makes 'paying attention' impossible.

How would you find out what is really the case, rather than rushing to either kind of judgement? Ultimately, the only way we can know anything about someone's mathematical understanding is through mathematics.

EXAMPLE

The lesson was about adding fractions and the teacher decided to start with fractions of the same simple denominator. She drew a circle on the board and divided it into thirds. As many teachers do, she called the circle a 'pizza'. You may like to think about why she did this and how helpful it is for students.[1] She shaded one-third of it and said:

We are going to add a third of a pizza to a third of a pizza.

She then drew another similar diagram (see Figure 5.1) and, pointing to the two shaded regions, asked:

What will we get when we add this third to that third?

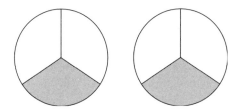

Figure 5.1 *One-third of one pizza plus one-third of another pizza makes two-sixths of two pizzas*

Some students called out 'two-thirds' and some called out 'two-sixths'. She replied:

> Those who said 'two-thirds' are right because there is one-third here and one-third there and that makes two-thirds. It cannot be two-sixths because we only have thirds . . . we do not add the denominators.

One girl at the back, who had thought the answer was two-sixths, called out:

> I do not understand . . . miss, I do not understand.

She then continued in a quieter voice to her neighbour:

> We have six bits and two of them are shaded, so it is two-sixths.

In discussion later the teacher described this girl as disruptive and rude – 'she always says she doesn't understand'.

Before reading on, it may be useful for you to think about the lesson from the girl's point of view. What could she see on the board? What had been said? From this perspective it suddenly makes sense that 'two-sixths' was, for her, a logical answer, whether or not she was usually disruptive or rude. There were six pieces and two had been shaded and in many previous experiences in school this meant the answer was 'two over six'. Talk of 'denominators' may have been unconnected for her as there were no fractions written on the board, only spoken ones. The teacher did not take her request seriously (possibly because she had already developed a negative view of this student) and there was no opportunity to explain why she thought the answer 'two-sixths' was correct, nor did she try to explain to the teacher (possibly she did not expect the teacher to listen to her).

Seen from this perspective, a very ordinary mathematics lesson becomes a negative experience for a student who had two problems: first, that she misinterpreted, in a very logical way, the diagram drawn by the teacher; second, that she had used inappropriate ways to communicate her confusion to the teacher. If she had been able to explain why she thought the answer should be 2/6, it is possible that the teacher would have learned something about teaching mathematics – that however clear you think you are being, you cannot predict how students will interpret what you are doing. For this reason, as this story shows, it is important to keep an open mind about *what* students understand and *how* they understand it.

How, then, can you be sure that you are learning from students' mathematics and not making assumptions based on wrong answers and/or adolescent behaviour? How could this lesson have been organised so that the teacher could learn that her carefully thought-out plans had legitimately confused at least one student? If we could go back to the point at which some called out 'two-thirds' and some called out 'two-sixths' and apply some of our earlier comments about discussion, the lesson could have been very different. If the students are used to giving reasons, and the teacher is ready to respect and listen to all of them, then the explanations given for the two answers could be compared and the students themselves could be saying 'yes, because . . .' or 'no, because . . .'. The teacher might realise that her diagram had led to confusion and could provide another, or a student might offer a new diagram or an example using a different representation, such as placing a third on a number line and adding a third to it. Indeed, if the teacher had planned to use several representations in the lesson, the confusion might have been resolved anyway. In classrooms where this kind of argument is well established, students recognise that it is their own responsibility to say that they are confused and explain how they see things, but there is a world of difference between this kind of discussion and the traditional comment often written on badly done homework: 'You should ask if you don't understand' or, even less helpfully, 'See me.' More can be read about strategies to learn about students' understandings in Black *et al.* (2002).

If the girl in this story had written '1/3 + 1/3 = 2/6' in work to be handed in, could the teacher know that she had thought it through from the diagram rather than mindlessly added the denominators? Probably not, even with an open mind ready to notice such problems. So closed, single-answer questions do not tell us much. If students get one right, the teacher does not know whether this is because they have remembered a method and used it correctly or because they deeply understand the basic concepts, unless they have some access to their thinking. If students get some answers wrong, teachers also cannot always tell why unless they have some access to their thinking. This is why generations of mathematics teachers have insisted 'show your working' and generations of students have tried to organise their thoughts into the format imposed by teachers, textbooks and testing regimes.

But what does 'showing your working' tell us?

Compare the two excerpts in Figure 5.2, taken from written work in which students have been asked to divide 286 by 22. Of course, the second one is correct and the first one is wrong, but who is the better mathematician? What can you say for sure about the mathematical understanding of the two students? The new teacher in whose lesson this occurred made copies of the work to discuss with others, and from that discussion it became clear that what is valued depends on what is seen as mathematical – being correct does not seem to be enough. As the teacher of these two students, what would you do next?

Excerpt 1:

The answer is 26. I have noticed that, with three-digit numbers, if the middle number is the sum of the outside terms the number will divide by 11 and you have to unscramble the middle number to get two copies of the answer.

Excerpt 2:

$$22 \,)\, 286 \,(\, 13$$
$$\underline{22}$$
$$66$$

Figure 5.2 *Two students' attempts at dividing 286 by 22*

SUMMARY

What we know about students' learning

We summarise the main ideas here.

- Learning mathematics involves building up a complex understanding of structures, language, useful habits, knowledge of useful representations and transformations, ways of communicating about mathematics and of understanding mathematical text.

- Students' past mathematical experiences, in and out of school, contribute to their classroom learning in ways that may be helpful or unhelpful. Some students' past experience will be of unconnected methods; others will have experienced it as an arena for exploration.

- Different students will respond to different tasks in different ways, and teaching can take this into account by using a range of linguistic, logical-mathematical, spatial and interpersonal stimuli.

- Classrooms are social contexts and subject to unwritten rules about behaviour; teachers can develop mathematical norms that establish good mathematical working practices.

- Thinking, effort, struggle and application can be prioritised over procedures so that students learn how to learn.

- Relational knowledge is more easily remembered than procedural knowledge, but takes more time to establish.

- Learning can involve discerning structures, identifying what changes and what stays the same, and generalising from examples.

- Teachers can learn from students what they understand and how they understand it.

Above all, it is our view that understanding the complexity of students' lives, and consequently being able to see the mathematics curriculum and lessons through the eyes of learners, is essential for good teaching.

THINKING ABOUT PRACTICE

■ When selecting resources to use in the classroom, what possible ways may there be to understand, and misunderstand, the mathematics presented in the resource and how could you help learners reach the conventional understanding?

■ How may different kinds of classroom organisation help or hinder mathematical learning?

■ How can you incorporate knowledge of how students learn into planning sequences of lessons?

Chapter 6

Themes in mathematics lessons: emotion and power

KEY QUESTIONS

- What sort of lessons can bring mathematics and adolescents together effectively?
- How can teachers create lessons that take a variety of different factors into account?

There are many books that will help you think about the nuts and bolts of lessons, how to get students into the classroom, how to see all corners of the room at once, how to deal with disruption, and so on. In this book we want to focus specifically on ways to think about mathematics so that your lessons stimulate students, engage them in purposeful mathematical activity, help them learn the subject in meaningful, relational, connected ways, and help them become better learners. Thinking about adolescents, and how they relate to the world, might lead to the suggestion that they may be more interested in the subject if it:

- appeals to their emotions;
- helps them feel mentally powerful;
- is useful;
- contributes to the way they make sense of the world.

There are, of course, many other ways to approach mathematics and this categorisation is rather arbitrary – you may like to think up one which makes more sense to you – but it serves as a framework to think about creating a wider range of types of lesson than you may have experienced recently.

This chapter and the next can be seen as a pair in which we present twelve lesson ideas organised according to this framework. In this chapter we exploit the emotional and powerful appeal of mathematics; in the next we use its more practical aspects and reflect on what the suggested lessons show about learning. The earlier lessons are given as outlines; later ones are expressed merely as ideas. Two of the lessons are given in great detail in order to model some detailed aspects of planning in which the teacher imagines what the students' perspective of the lesson might be and what underlying issues are operating at each stage. Each lesson includes several central features of good mathematics teaching, and offers comments and questions to draw your attention to aspects of lesson planning and task design. In the next chapter we shall draw these comments together to look at some of the themes of Chapter 5 and how they are manifested in these lessons.

APPEALING TO EMOTIONS IN MATHEMATICS

Some people respond well to the sense of completion they find in mathematics, or the pleasure of getting an answer and knowing it is right. In the following three lesson outlines we are trying to approach some mathematical topics with less obvious responses in mind. There are aspects of mathematics that can trigger the same kinds of response in learners as music, the arts and nature – an almost emotional, aesthetic response. Many students find elegance and satisfaction in the patterns and symmetries that emerge, or in some of the concepts that require imagination: infinity, fractal geometry, the denseness of rational and irrational numbers and so on. Patterns in number and geometry have also been used by creative people (composers, artists, designers) to give inspiration or technical support for their work. Students can become engaged with the subject by appealing to their visual senses, or by generating opportunity for other kinds of pattern expectation and surprise. There can be surprises when expectations are not realised and the student is thus challenged to look for alternative patterns.

To illustrate these issues we describe three lessons on the topics of: geometric discussion, differentiation of an exponential function and reflective symmetry.

LESSON 1: GEOMETRIC DISCUSSION AND PROOF USING TILING PATTERNS

This lesson was taught by Geri when the scheme of work gave 'geometric shapes, their names and properties' as the topic. She decided to emphasise a shift from aesthetic responses to rigorous use of geometrical language, concepts, properties and arguments and to encourage proof.

Outline lesson description

Students were asked to look at some Islamic tiling patterns and talk about the geometric shapes contained in them. The idea was that this kind of pattern would be familiar as background or decoration, and that it is relatively easy to spot and describe some of the characteristics that make it a 'pattern'. Students talked about repetition, how the tiles join together, how lines on one continue on to another, how colour is used, and so on. Geri managed the discussion and posed challenging questions designed to move students beyond the obvious to use past knowledge, or create a desire for specific language or precise description. This involved recognising shapes and naming them correctly, sorting out some misconceptions about what a regular polygon means (some confused regular with symmetrical), and finding out more about rotational and reflective symmetry. In some cases there were four axes of reflective symmetry, in others two. The orders of rotational symmetry varied, too. Students were then asked to find out if it is possible to make similar kinds of patterns based on the angles 108, 72, 36. Here, Geri was trying to steer them towards thinking about whether tessellation is possible for pentagons and to give reasoned arguments (proofs) about their findings. The lesson also provided a context for using geometric language and for practising drawing skills; she could have used a software package such as Logo if it had been available.

Comments

Art, familiarity and accessibility were being used as 'hooks' to get students interested in mathematical questions. Students started with something familiar whose patterns and symmetries are easy to see. They described these informally, with choice about the features on which they focus. Precise language was developed in whole class discussion. The mathematical questions were designed to move the students beyond description, to give them some incidental 'practice' which is meaningful within the larger goal, to give them something to explore that will lead to conjectures and discussion.

Questions and issues informing planning

Geri looked for a context that would be attractive for adolescents and which contained many shapes and transformations to discuss, rather than just giving them individual shapes whose names had to be learnt. But she went beyond the obvious features. She also asked: 'What situation can I offer which allows them to search, identify, develop a need to describe, give lots of answers?'; 'What is/is not possible if I change some of the parameters?'; 'Will it be useful to ask students to explore such changes?' She decided it *would* be useful for them to explore and she trusted them to do so.

LESSON 2: DIFFERENTIATING e^x

This lesson is about differentiating e^x, using a graphical approach and taking into account the fact that the students have already had experience of differentiating powers of x. Dalia remembered problems she had had when learning about this for the first time, assumed her students might have the same problems and tried to construct a lesson which would meet these difficulties head on.

Outline lesson description

Dalia was fairly sure the students would not expect the derivative of e^x to be itself. The students were familiar with differentiating polynomials, and were aware that they could do it according to a rule that reduces the powers by one and multiplies coefficients by something. They had done some practice examples for homework and were now moderately confident. Before they reached this level of using an algorithmic approach they had explored gradients of graphs empirically using their own graphs, drawn by hand, using graphical calculators and algebraically from first principles. However, the formula they had been using recently had, for most students, displaced this previous experience in importance. In this lesson they found the derivative of e^x by graphical methods. Most of them confidently predicted that the derivative would be something like e^{x-1} because they were misapplying a recently learnt rule which they had detached from its meaning. Using graph-plotting software they tried to get a gradient function, but it kept looking exactly like the graph they had just drawn of e^x. They were puzzled. Eventually, one of the students thought of drawing the graph of e^{x-1} to see what it *should* look like (if you have a graphical calculator, you may like to try this yourself). Again, they were puzzled because, once they had sorted out the domain, this new graph looked just like the old one, but translated one unit to the right along the x-axis. In order to ensure that, when they finally accepted that the function e^x is its own derivative, they also appreciated that this was not just an apparently random mathematical fact but a powerful feature of mathematics, Dalia gave them time for further exploration of derivatives of exponential functions, students choosing their own numbers, positive or negative, for the constants k and m in ke^{mx}.

Comments

Surprise, puzzlement and a desire for resolution were being used as the emotional hooks here, and this surprise was based on the teacher's prediction that students would misapply a previously learnt rule. She created a situation in which surprise was met head on and provided tools with which to explore this. She trusted them to want to sort out differences between their graphs and their expectations in friendly discussion.

Questions and issues informing planning

Dalia started from the question 'What puzzled me about this topic?' and used that to answer another question, 'What might students find puzzling about a topic?' She then planned to start from the source of puzzlement. In her lessons she had tried to create an atmosphere in which being puzzled and surprised are seen as normal. She also thought about the tools they might require for exploration.

LESSON 3: REFLECTIVE SYMMETRY

This lesson is given in more detail than the other two, with an outline lesson plan presented in Table 6.1. The objective of the lesson is to extend the concept of reflective symmetry to include axes not in obvious positions on shapes and, if there is time, non-vertical axes, using students' sense of balance and symmetry, and their own ideas of these, as a starting place to become more formal about

Table 6.1 Lesson 3 – reflective symmetry

Equipment and preparation: mini-whiteboards; matching pairs of coloured transparent shapes, some irregular, including one half and two complete regular pentagons; overhead projector; very thin rod; whiteboard pens; transparent ruler and set square; board ruler and set square; some irregular polygons already drawn on white board and covered with a large sheet of paper

What the teacher does	What the students do	Purpose, assessment, expectations, reminders
Welcome students as they arrive. Give small slips of paper, asking them to draw a shape that has reflective symmetry on their mini-white boards in two minutes.	Come in, settle, recall concept of symmetry, choose a shape to draw to show some reflective symmetry, e.g. decide to draw a simple one or a complicated one; ask neighbour if stuck, or share ideas if cannot choose.	Use names to welcome.
		If no boards, ask them to use sheets of A4 paper.
Say the lesson is about symmetry. Ask them to hold up their drawings. Ask them to draw in a mirror line and hold them up again.	Hold up drawings, draw mirror line if not already done and hold up again. Might have to choose which line to draw if there are several, or might draw more than one.	If they say 'we've done this', say that they will be doing some harder examples.
		Look for interesting shapes; look for those with drawing difficulties; look for wrong lines (e.g. diagonal of a rectangle)
Choose interesting shapes from those displayed and ask whole class to look at them. Ask how they know the shape is symmetrical, and the axis of symmetry	Think about why the shapes are symmetrical. Are they symmetrical? Put reasons into words, maybe try it out with partner first. Articulate reasons for	Get them to use 'axis of symmetry'.
		Try to prompt the idea that the significant points of the shape are

Table 6.1 Lesson 3 – reflective symmetry (continued)

What the teacher does	What the students do	Purpose, assessment, expectations, reminders
(mirror line) is right. Get them to talk to neighbours about this before they contribute to whole class. Write 3, 4 or 5 ideas on the whiteboard for future reference.	symmetry for whole class. Listen to others and think about adding to or arguing with what is said. Does what is said match my diagram or not?	equidistant from the axis. If this doesn't work, offer ruler.
Put the half regular pentagon on the overhead and put the thin rod along the long edge. Ask how to make a full pentagon using reflection. Put full pentagon on as overlay when the instructions are correct. Ask: How do we know the final shape is symmetrical?	Imagine full pentagon – can I remember what one is? Call out instructions, politely, listen to others, applying rules of reflection such as corresponding points have to be the same distance from the line, lines are the same length, angles are the same.	So far this may be revision; shift from recognising symmetry to constructing symmetry. Use technical language as well as everyday. Try to get them to look at significant points. … most likely that only points will be thought about.
Announce we are going to look at the idea of symmetry a different way. Put irregular shape on overhead transparency and ask where to put the axis so we can create a symmetrical shape. Offer rod to someone to put it anywhere on the shape. Wait for ideas. Indicate ideas on board to see if they help.	Think about what it means to be symmetrical; call out instructions to others. Try to sort out 'symmetrical' from 'regular': ask if not sure, or choose where to put rod to find out. Make up own mind.	Puzzle, because there is no obvious place to put axis. Hope for someone to say something about significant points. Ask for agreement or disagreement. If anyone puts the axis not vertical, say we will do that one later.

Teacher	Students	Notes
Offer the matching shape and ask if anyone wants to put it on the overhead transparency where it would be when reflected. Do several of these.		
Demonstrate how to get proper place for significant points using ruler and set square. Ask some pairs or threes to do this on the board, choosing where to put the axis. Go round room discussing with students what is going on: 'What are they doing now, why?'; 'What are you going to do next, why?' etc.	Try some of their own examples on paper or watch others working on whiteboard. Keep thinking about symmetry and reflection. Try to say what they mean; discuss with neighbour if necessary.	Those who have got the idea strongly can do it on coordinate grids with the y-axis as axis of symmetry and see where the new coordinates are (predict). Get assistants to do the drawing for those who had problems at the start of lesson.
Ask them what are the most important things to remember about constructing shapes reflected in an axis of symmetry. Get everyone to check whether answers apply to every example we/they have done. Choose best answer and write on board.	Decide what is important. Write chosen answer in books. Compare what others say and change what I say if theirs is more general, or said better.	Choose an answer with them if possible; key issues: the distance of significant points from the mirror line, measured at right-angles to the line.
Depending on timing, try a non-vertical axis on overhead transparency. Homework: make up examples which they think are hard.	Note homework, check I understand the words I need.	

what it means. Note that the teacher has thought carefully about what the students do, trying to see the lesson from their perspective. She has also thought about how to work productively with classroom assistants.

Comments

Since their early years in primary school, students will have designed, coloured and decorated symmetrical patterns, which are then displayed on the walls of the classroom. Most will have a well-developed sense of reflective symmetry where the mirror line (axis of symmetry) is vertical. In this lesson the teacher is trying to use the students' past experiences to extend their conceptual understanding of symmetry. She is aware that this will involve some challenges to ideas to which they have become attached through many visual and artistic experiences. Her awareness comes from experience, or by talking to colleagues, or by reading the National Curriculum, or by reading reports from the Qualifications and Curriculum Authority about national tests, or by recently asking students to draw her examples of what they understand by certain key words and concepts. Of these five possible contributions, only one, experience, is unavailable to new teachers.

This lesson may have several features that seem unusual to you. There is no work from textbooks; the varied examples come from the students themselves and thus they are personally engaged with the work. The teacher does not provide a definition; rather, the students create informal definitions. Those who have grasped the idea are given an algebraic perspective to work with, focusing on expressing the general relationships, rather than being asked to think about non-vertical axes (the teacher clearly wants to work on these with the whole class). Provision of extra work for those who need to do no more practice at a simple level focuses on generalisation and linking topics across mathematics, rather than on new ideas.

Questions and issues informing planning

- What do students already know?
- What has students' previous experience been and how deeply are they attached to it?
- How might students' previous experience and ways of 'seeing' have limited a broader view of the topic?

- Can students become involved in the process of change by contributing their own examples for exploration?
- How and when can I get students to make statements about what they are seeing?

FEELING POWERFUL THROUGH LEARNING ABOUT STRUCTURE

Being able to say for themselves something general about a class of mathematical objects can help learners feel powerful, and if that has come about as a result of effort, the feeling of success can be exciting. Research into what successful mathematicians do when they think about mathematics reveals, among other things, that they pay attention to structures rather than individual examples. What can be done to help students focus on structure so that they can reason for themselves and make general statements? Teachers can assume that nearly all students have basic pattern-spotting abilities and then try to guide the way they make sense of patterns so that they become familiar with the accepted mathematical structures.

But how does engagement with structure relate to the logic and certainty that some people appreciate in the subject? Working with structure rather than separate topics or separate examples gives students the opportunity to make general statements for themselves, rather than be given them by teachers in what might seem to be a haphazard, arbitrary, disconnected fashion. In the first lesson below, students can reason, predict and verify results about reflections on a coordinate grid. They can try to find counter-examples to break their own rules. They can be encouraged to sharpen their arguments by considering all possibilities. In the second lesson, engagement with structure enables them to understand the purpose of the measures and their power; they become better able to choose appropriate measures in future and thus create meaningful arguments about given data. In the third lesson, students might learn to use the inverse relationship between division and multiplication as a tool in mathematical arguments and manipulations. They can use it to check answers and may progress to using it to transform equations.

In the three lessons that follow you may also see that a certain kind of mathematical beauty may be revealed to students. For many mathematicians there is a link between beauty and structure – we could not find a classification of the multiple faces of mathematics that would not have included overlapping categories for many people. As we have said before, what is important here is to get a sense of plurality and variety.

LESSON 4: EXPRESSING GENERAL REFLECTIONS ALGEBRAICALLY

This lesson is about expressing some reflections algebraically and thus seeing how spatial and symbolic patterns relate. It also includes some very useful aspects of mathematical thinking applied to a core curriculum topic.

Outline lesson description

Students have been looking at the coordinates of points on shapes reflected in the y-axis. Some students will use pattern-spotting abilities to see that a point such as $(2, 3)$ becomes $(^-2, 3)$ and so on. They are asked to give a general description in words: 'the x-coordinate becomes negative, the y-coordinate stays the same'. This easily lends itself to being expressed in algebra; even if students are not entirely sure what letters signify, they will not have much difficulty continuing their pattern to (a, b) by saying it would become $(^-a, b)$. This can then be used to predict what will happen for new shapes not yet drawn. Imagine the feeling of being able to predict what will happen from a general argument, compared to drawing shapes and finding coordinates from them! However, many students will find it harder to see what happens if the shape has negative coordinates, and to still express the result as $(^-a, b)$.

Comments

You could compare this lesson to lesson 3, which was also about reflective symmetry. In this one the teacher has thought about what generalities can arise from considering reflective symmetry and constructed tasks that allow students to use their generalisations, combined with visual imagery, to make predictions that they can check for themselves. Thus they are in charge of their own 'marking' and can self-correct as a contribution to their learning. Generalisations arise from the students' emerging sense of structure. There are four representations used here which they can use to develop understanding: numbers, symbols, coordinates and shapes.

Questions and issues which inform planning

- What are the generalities in this topic?
- Stating general mathematical structures algebraically is more meaningful than learning about algebra as a separate topic.
- Having several ways to express mathematical structure helps learners to see mathematics as connected and meaningful.
- Self-assessment helps students become more interested in their work.
- Can I trust my students to get excited about grasping a structure and being able to express it in several ways?

LESSON 5: MODE, MEDIAN AND MEAN

Toby had been asked to teach the three 'averages': mode, median and mean. He knew from his observations of other teachers that these can be confused and that learners may not understand why there is a need for different measures of 'middle'. He decided that his class would be able to handle a theoretical approach and see them as mathematical structures to explore, comparing how they describe data.

Outline lesson description

Each student had to make up a list of data which would have 32 as the modal value, the lists being as long or as short as they liked. Toby suggested some extreme cases, such as 32 being the only value to appear, or 32 appearing twice and a wide range of other values only appearing once. The data sets were displayed on mini-whiteboards and there was discussion in pairs about what they had in common. The fact that having the same mode does not imply that they have the same mean, median or range was also discussed, and students were encouraged to work out what the medians and means would be in each case. They repeated the exercise for other values. They were then asked to create sets which all had 15.5 as median and again contrast their means and modes, Toby always making sure that contrasting examples were included which showed up the important features. He was fairly sure that all the students ended up knowing why there are different measures of 'middle', even if they could not recall which was which. An extension of this task would be to have fixed values for two statistical measures and to see if and how

Table 6.2 Lesson 6 – multiplication and division

What the teacher does	What the students do	Purpose, assessment, expectations, reminders
Ask class to think of three difficult multiplication facts each as they come into class, and write them down. Circulate, helping them settle and seeing what they do. Find students who choose from 6, 7, 8 and 9 times tables.	Settle, recall or work out three multiplication facts; choose from several possibilities; decide what is meant by 'difficult'; write them down.	Get started; get some raw material for the lesson from them so they are involved; note the range of what they say is 'difficult'.
Choose someone to give an example from 7 or 8 times table on the board, e.g. $7 \times 8 = 56$ Write $56 \div 7 = 8$ $56 \div 8 = 7$ say nothing Choose another and do same thing. Pause. 'Can you see what I am doing?' 'Write the same sort of thing under or next to your examples.'	Watch; think about what is going on. Notice patterns in the way the numbers appear. Notice patterns in the next one; are they the same? Decide what 'same sort of things' means. Write division statements next to multiplication facts. Check them? Discuss with partner.	There may be layout problems. It is important that the three statements are near each other. Some might want to put thought bubbles around the sets of three statements. People who finish can make up harder statements and check answers on a calculator or other method.
Circulate; prompt discussion with 'Will this be true for all multiplications?'		
Choose a harder example to be written on board.	Listen; watch; think of other examples; recognise three versions of statements. Look for multiplication and division in	Circulate, listening to descriptions, expecting to get some which are mechanical (moving numbers and

Ask if anyone can give an example from e.g. science, where you have to divide or multiply two values. Generate three statements.	examples given by others and teacher. Try to match letters with patterns recognised so far.	changing signs) and some which are conceptual (e.g. division undoes multiplication).
Give distance, velocity, time as example . . . imagine car or bike journey . . . use words, offer letters as quicker way.	Describe the way we get the three statements.	
How would you explain to someone who hasn't been in this lesson what we have worked on so far?		
Get someone to say that division undoes multiplication, multiplication undoes division. Use phrase 'inverse of'.	Find a way to say how multiplication and division relate; try to understand what others say. Continue to think of own way to tell others. Reorganise thinking to start with division.	May have to do easy numerical ones first if I start with division.
Write $a \times b =$ and ask for two other versions.		Is it worth going for something they haven't yet met?
Then try writing some with division first, e.g. $12/3 = 4$; what are the other two statements?		
Possibly, offer Boyle's law. Also offer example: what can I buy with £24? 6 things costing £4, etc., to see if they can give different ways of saying the same thing.	Refine written version. Match new examples with what I understand so far. See that this can be graphed!	Try to get answers from all students; if OK, could go for drawing graphs of $xy = k$ on overhead calculator screen (or interactive whiteboard) as interesting bit of fun at end.
Make sure everyone has a good written version of the three statements.		

this constrains the possibilities for other statistics. For instance, is it possible to have datasets that have the same mean, the same median, but different ranges? What might they look like?

Comments

Toby created this lesson as a contrast to the more usual approach to mean, median and mode, which focuses on numbers from an existing data set and thus appeals to the need to make sense of the world. He assumed that working directly on the mathematical ideas that cause confusion would be a good way to become less confused, and that applying them to actual data could be done later.

Questions and issues informing planning

In creating this lesson Toby had asked a very powerful mathematical question: 'In this topic, what can be varied and what must stay the same?' He knew that asking students to make up their own examples would encourage them to explore the range of possibilities. He also planned special examples that would help them extend the range of possibilities. Playing with these ideas himself enabled him to have some idea of the theoretical and structural understandings that students might develop.

LESSON 6: MULTIPLICATION AND DIVISION

This lesson is about the relationship between multiplication and division, expressing it in three ways, and as a generality. It includes helping students recognise and use this relationship wherever it occurs. As with Lesson 3, we present this lesson in rather more detail with an outline lesson plan in Table 6.2 (pp. 106–7).

Comments

In this lesson the teacher intends to use students' knowledge of some numerical relationships as a starting point for working explicitly on the structure of rational expressions. The central idea is that students will get used to thinking of multiplication and division not just as ways to get answers, but as operations that are inverses of each other, related through the three ways of representing essentially the same structure.

This teacher has thought about how to engage students in thinking about a key mathematical structure, generalising it for themselves in an environment that allows them to explore and refine their ideas. Multiplication and division are no longer seen just as techniques to be learnt, but as relationships to be understood.

The teacher expects students to call out suggestions sometimes. You may be concerned that having got them excited they may not be able to control their excitement, so you may prefer students to wait quietly with their hands up, or to talk to a neighbour first and then agree on a contribution which they indicate with 'hands up'. This teacher also assumes that students will have calculators with them and that there will be a way to draw electronic graphs available, though this is not the norm in all schools.

Questions and issues informing planning

- What is the underlying structure in this topic?
- How can I use students' contributions to get started?
- Asking for 'hard' examples encourages creativity and can generate examples that go beyond the obvious.
- There are three forms of the generalisation of this relationship; is it better to offer all three at once or separately?
- What practical examples, or examples from other subjects, can I use?
- What is the best way to get whole class discussion going so that excitement is generated and maintained, everyone can contribute, but it won't become unmanageable?

SUMMARY

In this chapter we have looked in detail at some lessons which use the potential of mathematics to appeal to adolescent emotional and aesthetic awareness, and which also use and develop engagement with structures and generalisations. The underlying idea is that these features of good teaching need not be separate but can be fully integrated. This is in contrast to lessons that offer mathematics as tasks to be imitated and use future test results as a motivational carrot. There will be further reflective comments about these lessons at the end of the next chapter.

THINKING ABOUT PRACTICE

■ When observing other teachers: how do teachers structure their teaching to help students engage with mathematics?

■ In what ways have you seen teachers incorporate students' ideas into the structure of lessons?

■ What problems of motivation and engagement have you seen in classrooms which are not addressed by the themes of this chapter?

Chapter 7

More themes in mathematics lessons: usefulness, sense and learning

---

KEY QUESTIONS

- The ideas in the last chapter were very learner-focused, but what about the practical aspects of mathematics and the learning of techniques?
- How does knowledge about mathematical learning contribute to lesson planning?

This chapter continues from the previous one, offering more lesson ideas. We now build on the practical aspects of mathematics: its usefulness and its capacity for making sense of the world. At the end of the chapter we reflect on all twelve lessons presented in this chapter and Chapter 6, to show how the lessons have been based on the theories in Chapter 5, as well as on practical knowledge of students and of teaching. Finally, we reflect on the place of practice and routine in mathematics learning, since this is a common approach in many lessons, and, by contrast, consider the role of creativity in what is often seen as a rather uncreative subject.

USING 'USEFULNESS'

It is sometimes supposed that the lack of relevance of school mathematics is problematic. But there is a trap here! An honest answer to the question 'what use are quadratic equations when I leave school?' is probably 'none specifically' for most students, yet they will be important for some.

However, the same can also be said for much of the content taught in other secondary school subjects: art, poetry, music, specific bits of history – not many of these are 'useful'. Why should mathematics be any more immediately useful than any other subject? Probably the expectation that it should all be useful, and easily transferable from the classroom to other places, comes from the fact that arithmetic, understanding money and measures, and deciphering graphs and data *are* useful skills to have in many contexts. In this sense, part of the function of mathematics teachers is to help students become numerically functional in outside life.

One difficulty in working with adolescents is that many of the obvious questions arising from the environment and the behaviour of objects and machines that can be answered mathematically require quite a high level of applied mathematics to resolve. Simple questions, such as why it is shorter to walk across a rectangular lawn from corner to corner than round the edges, tend to be seen as obvious or can be answered by practical means, such as measuring. Finding applications that are mathematically accessible and for which students will see the point of using mathematics is not straightforward.

New teachers often feel that they need to make everything 'relevant' for their students, but it is hard to decide what is relevant for adolescents and how to relate this to mathematics. Obvious candidates for 'relevance' are the mathematics of pocket money, football, the music industry, warfare or ecological and humanitarian concerns such as fair trade, relief work, forestry, and so on.[1] Some teachers are successful at getting their students to accept that mortgages, hire purchase and work-related mathematics might some day be relevant for them and hence that it is worth taking time to learn about them in school, but most teachers find that these far-off concerns fail to engage the majority of teenagers. For most secondary school mathematics the relevance is, at its lowest level, that it is required for passing exams and, at its highest level, that it is part of education to learn about the wide range of things which human beings have done and can do. However, students can at least have a glimpse of how mathematics is used in current technological advances. It can also be argued that students are entitled to taste the full range of human activities and that opportunities for achieving this entitlement are thus relevant. Doing mathematics successfully, either by enjoying puzzles, or by becoming a skilled mental calculator, or by using it when needed, or by studying more mathematics, are such possible activities.

Having said all that, however, there *are* ways in which mathematics can be shown to be useful as a tool for informing, explaining and predicting. The next three outline lessons treat the subject in this way.

LESSON 7: PERCENTAGES

Anna had to teach percentages to students who would have met them before, but probably would recall little, and lacked motivation and confidence in mathematics. She exploited their interest in money so that they could see a use for the topic.

Outline lesson description

Anna asked the students to imagine a realistic sum of money they could save and to find out what rates of interest they could get from nearby banks or building societies. In the lesson she showed them how to calculate the first lot of interest at a rate of 4.5 per cent. She decided not to explain the calculation directly but instead to get them to compare two methods. First, she worked out 4.5 per cent on the calculator screen projected on to the whiteboard and added it to the original amount; second, she calculated 104.5 per cent directly. While working these out she recognised there are several possible sub-methods and allowed students to describe them. For some students it made more sense to find 1 per cent, then multiply by 4 or 104, then add a half of 1 per cent. For others, a more compacted method was acceptable. Even though the operations are essentially the same, different students thought about them in different ways. They then discussed which was most efficient and, while some opted for using 104.5 per cent directly as needing fewer calculations, others chose methods which kept detailed track of what was happening. Having found out what they would gain with different interest rates after one imaginary time period, they repeated the method for subsequent time periods and compared how much extra they would get for different starting values and different rates of interest. Reducing the number of variables by fixing the starting value would have given a clearer picture of which investment was better, but Anna wanted them to realise this for themselves and to suggest it to get a 'fairer' comparison. This happened eventually when students were comparing their answers in pairs. They also had further discussion about which methods of calculation were faster, and some admitted that using 104.5 per cent would have been faster than using their own methods.

Comments

In this lesson the motivation is money and the amount chosen was one that had realistic personal meaning for students. Anna offered two methods, not just one, to do the calculations, and allowed for further methods to be seen as more accessible by students. The lesson could have included the use of spreadsheets. The idea of fixing a variable to make comparisons emerged towards the end. It was motivating that the lesson was about something that could be clearly named, so that at the end students could claim to know something they might not have known before.

Questions and issues informing planning

Anna had asked herself if there was something in students' immediate lives and experience that could show how percentages were useful. Thus she avoided making artificial claims of usefulness. She allowed several ways to do the calculations, but included discussion about efficiency to inform their choices. Working out the answers was not an end in itself; there was something the answers could be used for, i.e. they could be compared to find the best investment.

LESSON 8: ANGLES AND STRUCTURES

This lesson is about using geometrical properties to explain some practical design decisions, leading to examination of the properties of triangles and rectangles with given side lengths.

Outline lesson description

In this lesson suggestion geometry is being used as a tool to explain the construction of some familiar objects. The question is: 'Why is it better to build a tent with a triangular frame than one with a rectangular frame?' Students have some strips of various lengths that can be fastened with split pins to form flexible joints.[2] They experiment with various frames and find that the rectangular construction is flexible and can collapse sideways, whereas the triangle, so long as it is supported vertically (perhaps by another triangle), will not collapse. Dynamic geometry software can be used to model the situation and demonstrate the problem of the sideways movement. Each group of students is asked to give an explanation, and these will vary from the irrelevant, through the very vague, to comments about 'fixing' angles. The teacher then applies a geometric focus to the discussion by recasting what is said in order to pose questions about the number of different angles it is possible to have, given fixed lengths of sides for triangles and quadrilaterals. Students can experiment with drawings to relate the properties of triangles and quadrilaterals (in this case parallelograms) to the rigidity of tents.

Comments

One way to generate such lesson ideas is to develop a habit of looking for uses of mathematics around you and keep notes about such contexts. Another is to ask students to do the same kind of observation for homework and then to select, as a whole class, contexts in which, for example, triangles might be a crucial design constraint rather than an aesthetic decision. In this lesson the teacher goes beyond description and takes the opportunity to relate rigidity to the question of what shapes are possible with given lengths – that is, a purely geometric question.

Questions and issues informing planning

- If I want students to think about the properties of shapes, it would be a good idea to get them to see how a shape can be changed while certain features remain fixed.
- Use dynamic geometry software to demonstrate such changes.
- How can these examples and results be seen to be useful?
- What would be made possible, or impossible, if a shape changed in a certain way?
- Students can do experiments and conjecture about what they find.

LESSON 9: PROBABILITY

This lesson is about experiencing the predictive power of mathematics by linking experimental and theoretical probabilities.[3]

Outline lesson description

The teacher uses a die that has numbers 17 to 22 on it, rather than the familiar ones, to avoid the common belief that it is harder to get 6 than other numbers. There is discussion about what students expect to happen if the die is fair, what fairness would mean, and so on. She asks them to choose one of the numbers and predict how many times it will appear in 60 throws. By emphasising the word 'fair' and prolonging the discussion, she gets them to agree that each number 'ought' to appear ten times unless the die is 'unfair'. The prediction is written on the board and the test is done. Results are compared and (with a bit of luck!) it should be seen that the mathematical prediction is 'pretty good'. Later on, stickers with numbers 1 to 6 can be put over the numbers and the 'myth' can be confronted head-on.

Comments

A typical lesson introducing probability involves throwing a die to see how many times 6 appears out of a large number of throws and deducing that the probability of getting 6 is a sixth. Thus it looks as if the experiment is predicting the mathematics. This lesson is the other way round and hence makes more mathematical sense. The teacher's use of the everyday notion of 'a pretty good estimate' avoids a debate about which was 'wrong' – the maths or the die – and hence goes some way towards establishing that approximate prediction is also possible.

Questions and issues informing planning

- In what sorts of situation can we use mathematics to predict – and how good do we expect the prediction to be?
- What might students already think? Are their preconceptions going to confuse them, can we meet them head-on or is it better to avoid them?
- How can we deal with the contrast between the theoretical and the experimental mathematics? Which could we do first and how will the results compare?
- How can students be helped to see that approximation is as mathematical as accuracy?

MAKING SENSE WITH MATHEMATICS

In the last section we hinted that adolescents might be motivated by the mathematics of issues outside their own immediate concerns and outside what is immediately available to them. Adolescent students often desire the world to be different, but they feel unable to do anything about it and unable to understand why it is the way it is, and they feel powerless. To some extent this feeling of powerlessness has been addressed by showing ways in which students can be more involved in the direction of lessons, in reasoning things out for themselves and in being offered mental tools that give a sense of intellectual power rather than merely doing what they are told. There is much self-esteem to be gained by being able to say: 'I know I am right because . . .' rather than being dependent on a teacher or on answers in the back of the book.

But while much of adolescence is concerned with becoming a confident adult and pursuing personal development, there is also the desire for the world in general to be better, and this section offers three examples of lessons that draw on the role of mathematics in this area.

LESSON 10: INTERPRETING DATA

This lesson idea is given in rather less detail because its specific content will depend on current issues of concern. The key idea is that teacher and students should use mathematical awareness to analyse, understand and criticise information given in the news media. Students work in groups to develop arguments which they then present to each other.

Outline lesson idea

Students are asked to compare the reporting of an economic issue in the national and local press, on the Internet, in TV coverage and in different kinds of newspapers and magazines. Some aspects that may show differences are:

- How are percentages quoted? Percentages of the whole UK population can mask stark contrasts between groups, such as a national unemployment figure of 10 per cent hiding a local one of 60 per cent.
- Over what time span are increases compared? Is an increase from one year to another part of a trend or a local blip?
- Are rates of change or actual changes being discussed? For example, are readers made aware that a falling rate of inflation still means that prices are going up?

117

- Are similar populations being compared? For example, in election results are actual numbers more useful than percentages, given the very different sizes of constituencies?
- Are graphs shown in ways that exaggerate certain features and hide others?

Students are asked to take one side of a debate and justify their views using quantitative data, different groups using different kinds of data, or different aspects according to the kinds of questions posed above. A particularly good kind of issue for this analysis is one which affects one group of people more than another – for example, the closure of a large factory, or difficulties in a particular industry, or a change in pension laws. Other useful sources of statistics are available on the website reporting Prime Minister's Question Time or on the websites of charities and single-issue pressure groups.

Comments

This analysis might be done alongside similar work in English in which different kinds of persuasive writing are used to emphasise different points, but focusing in the mathematics lesson on the different kinds of statistics quoted. The teacher is harnessing the students' interest in local, national and current issues to develop arguments that involve the use of measures and representations of data, logic, example and counter-example, and so on.

Questions and issues informing planning

- What current issues will motivate my students?
- What questions can I devise to go more deeply into the issue by comparing quantities or mathematical representations?
- What uses of graphs, percentages and rates of change are relevant?
- Will debating real issues enable students to learn how to use these aspects of mathematics better than other methods?
- What other kinds of task will students need to further develop the use of the same mathematical techniques?

LESSON 11: STREET LIGHTING AND WATER TAPS

In this lesson, Jim adapted a well-known activity so that it applied meaningfully to a global issue. He knew that many of his students were interested in the availability of water in developing countries. The lesson included attention to societal values.

Outline lesson idea

There is a frequently used activity in secondary mathematics that involves the placing of street lamps at the corners of a grid of city streets. The idea is to predict the minimum number of lights and their positions to light the whole grid. Another version is to find out how many beat police are needed to ensure the whole grid is under surveillance. The implication in each of these is that the streets need light and surveillance, otherwise dreadful things might happen, and that minimising the costs of provision is a good thing. The economics of cost efficiency and social control are accepted as given. In Jim's lesson these assumptions were challenged in what appears to be the same mathematical problem. Jim wanted his students to see mathematics as a tool with which political assumptions could be challenged. He offered a grid of squatter shacks outside a city in the developing world and posed the problem of where to place water taps. The class had to discuss if the object was to minimise the distance, the number of taps or the length of piping. There was discussion about whether it is fairer to base this on the distance that people *can* walk to a tap, or the smallest distance they should have to walk. Different groups of students made different assumptions, so several models emerged. Most were far messier than the neat equations the police and lighting problems would produce, although there were a few students who were unhappy about messy answers. After the lesson Jim thought that it could have been explored in a more structured fashion by controlling the number of water taps and asking: 'What is the length of the longest distance to a tap if there are $1, 2, 3 \ldots n$ taps for a given grid?' This approach might have appealed more to those for whom the certainties of mathematics are attractive, but still sets it firmly in the context of the role mathematics plays in formatting societies. However, it may have reduced the commitment students had to finding 'their' answers.

Comments

Many published resources present versions of this activity in the form of a diagram and some structured questioning. Clearly, in this version, much whole class discussion is needed in order to decide what assumptions can be made. This makes the solution less simple than a purely mathematical minimal solution.

Questions and issues informing planning

Jim had to decide if it was worthwhile to give mathematics lesson time to the discussions of fairness that would emerge from this lesson idea. He asked himself if any mathematics from the official syllabus was involved, and decided that this did not matter as much as getting students to see mathematics as having a powerful political role. He had to decide how to manage the discussion, which was bound to get passionate, and decided he could manage it as a whole class discussion; he could have used small groups or pairs instead. He rejected structuring the problem for the students, as he wanted them to make their own assumptions and then to see how these would affect the mathematics.

LESSON 12: SPEED AND DISTANCE

This lesson presents another kind of idea for embedding mathematics in meaningful contexts, so that students learn more about the context as well as about the mathematics involved.

Outline lesson idea

It is illegal to park within a certain distance of a zebra crossing because cars and people have to be able to see each other clearly in order to allow each time to stop safely. Students can model stopping distances of a car and decide if these parking restrictions are reasonable (too long or too short). There are several variables that can be controlled: starting speed, rate of deceleration, how close the car is to the crossing when a person steps on to it. The basic relationship between speed, distance and acceleration can be understood in a variety of diagrammatic or graphical ways, as well as by using formulae.

Comments

This lesson demonstrates the uses of mathematics, but also imbues formulae and graphs with meaning, including the notion of rates of change as gradient. It would provide a concrete context for working with these concepts, the idea being that the students may be able to develop an abstract understanding for use in other contexts.

Questions and issues informing planning

- Can this topic be presented in a form that can usefully be visualised or imagined?
- How could students develop an abstract understanding of mathematical ideas that have been presented in a realistic form?
- This exploration could take some time; how can motivation be maintained over several lessons?

SOME THEMES IN THINKING ABOUT MATHEMATICS TEACHING

The lessons in this chapter and the previous one all contain many features of good mathematics planning and teaching. To concentrate on features concerned with the learning of mathematics, we shall restate some of the important aspects of learning given at the end of Chapter 5 and relate these to the lesson ideas above.

Learning mathematics involves building up a complex understanding of structures, language, applicable habits, knowledge of useful representations and transformations, ways of communicating about mathematics and of understanding mathematical text.

Since we have only illustrated single lessons, we have not shown how understanding can accumulate over a sequence of lessons. However, the two lessons on reflective symmetry could flow together meaningfully, with work arising from the first lesson being continued and formalised in the second. Similarly, notice how the lesson about differentiation built on the teacher's expectation that recent previous work would have created a false assumption. Within most of these lessons teachers have not shied away from the complexities of mathematics. Rather, they have tried to give students access by using a range of representations and helping students pick their way through to what is important and central. Note how these teachers are *not* trying to over-simplify mathematics but instead are asking: 'How can students develop an abstract understanding of mathematical ideas which have been presented in a realistic form?'; 'What other kinds of task will they need using the same mathematical techniques?'; 'What questions can I devise which will go more deeply into the issue by comparing quantities or mathematical representations?'

Students' past mathematical experiences, in and out of school, contribute to their classroom learning in ways that may be helpful or unhelpful. Some students' past experience will be of unconnected methods; others will have experienced it as an arena for exploration.

The lessons, even those that are about introducing new topics, do not assume ignorance. Every topic in mathematics can be seen to arise from some previous topic, and hence all students will already have some under-standing that will be a relevant basis for new ideas. The teachers ask questions like: 'What do students already know?'; 'How can I use their contributions to get started?'; 'What has their previous experience been and how deeply are they attached to it?' For example, the teacher of the lesson on probability (Lesson 9) assumes that students have experienced only exact answers before, so she asks: 'How can students be helped to see that approximation is as mathematical as accuracy?' Similarly, if students' previous experience has been only about trying to get correct answers, the teacher could introduce the principle that answers are only a starting point for some wider generalisations, or some new patterns and questions.

Different students will respond to different tasks in different ways, and teaching can take this into account by using a range of linguistic, logical-mathematical, spatial and interpersonal stimuli.

The lessons we have presented do not expect everyone to engage in the same way; indeed, they include many points at which students are expected to respond in a variety of ways. Thus, it is sensible to plan to offer mathematical ideas in more than one way and to plan to take students' varied responses into account. So the teachers ask questions like: 'Can this topic be presented in a form which can usefully be visualised or imagined?'; 'Do we need equipment and/or special paper to help model the situation?'; 'How might students' previous experience and ways of "seeing" influence their view of the topic?'

Classrooms are social contexts and subject to unwritten rules about behaviour; teachers can develop mathematical norms that establish good mathematical working practices.

Few of these lessons involve students sitting in rows and listening to the teacher, then working on their own. Most of them include some form of discussion, some enquiry and the expectation that students will 'have a go'. If students are not used to working in these ways, teachers have to plan the detail of using different kinds of class dynamics. We cannot just expect students to adapt to new behavioural expectations. The sorts of questions that arise are: 'Is this topic best dealt with through whole class discussion, pair work or groups?'; 'What is the best way to get whole class discussion going so that excitement is generated and maintained, everyone can contribute, but it won't become unmanageable?' Anticipation is important: 'This exploration could take some time; how can motivation be maintained over several lessons?'

The gradual creation of a classroom atmosphere in which students will feel comfortable with open-ended enquiry approaches takes time. Teachers may ask: 'Is there an atmosphere in my classroom in which being puzzled and surprised are seen as normal?'; 'Can I trust my students to get excited about grasping a structure and being able to translate it several ways?'; 'Can they become involved in the process of change by contributing their own examples for exploration?'; 'How and when can I get them to make statements about what they are seeing?'

Thinking, effort, struggle and application can be prioritised over procedures so that students learn how to learn.

Most of the lessons expect students to do some hard thinking and perhaps to have some questions left unanswered. None of them involves straightforward practice examples, although nearly all entail the necessity for procedures to be repeated several times in the context of a more complex, more conceptual task. We have more to say about 'practice' below.

Teachers have designed tasks by interrogating the mathematics: 'What puzzled me about this topic?'; 'What might students find puzzling about a topic?'; 'Can we start with the source of puzzlement?'; 'What situation can I offer which allows them to search, identify, develop a need to describe, give lots of answers?' They help students work harder by asking for 'hard' examples to encourage creativity.

There is recognition that some students may be unable to start exploring without help, due to a lack of confidence or not having sufficient choice of strategies at their disposal. There is a constant tension between giving help and avoiding over-simplification of the task. 'What about students who will not be able to get started?'; 'What hints can I give without taking away the need to do their own thinking?'; 'Could I provide structured questions for students to work through, or let them devise their own methods of solution and then compare them to see which were better?'

Relational knowledge is more easily remembered than procedural knowledge, but takes more time to establish.

These lessons show a belief that all students need to do experiments and conjecture about what they find, that they need to relate new ideas to what they already know. In the lessons about structure, students are empowered by explicitly working with relationships, rather than just learning manipulative procedures. Time is a constant problem because teachers feel pressure to 'cover' the curriculum but know that learning takes time. They may be tempted to curtail students' explorations or to rush on before deep, connected, familiar understanding has been established. In contextual tasks they may ask: 'Is any syllabus mathematics involved and does it matter if there isn't?' In the lesson about multiplication and division (Lesson 6), it would have taken moments to just say 'multiplication is the inverse of division' and give a few examples and an exercise, but the meaning and generality of such a statement might then only have been appreciated at a superficial level.

Learning can involve discerning structures, identifying what changes and what stays the same, and generalising from examples.

Many teachers have a belief that all students can spot patterns and hence see underlying structures at work in mathematics. The process of identifying what changes and what stays the same can be seen in some of the examples offered and the questions posed in order to 'lead' students to seeing a method or to expressing a structure in algebra. Much conceptual learning is about comparing different examples or different representations. In these lessons teachers ask: 'How can we deal with the contrast between theoretical and experimental mathematics?'; 'How will the results compare?'; 'What would be made possible, or impossible, if a shape changed in a certain way?'; 'There are several forms of the generalisation of this relationship; is it better to offer all three at once or separately?' and 'If I want students to think about the properties of shapes, it would be a good idea to get them to see how a shape can be changed but certain features remain fixed.'

The teachers also think about whether students will see what they hope they will see, or whether students will be distracted by features which are not central to the unfolding mathematical story.

Teachers can learn from students what they understand and how they understand it.

The lessons include opportunities for teachers to monitor students' understanding through activities that are fully integrated with the teaching. There are also self-assessment features in some lessons because self-assessment helps students become more interested in their work. (Issues of assessment are discussed further in Chapter 8.) When planning, these teachers think about what students bring into the classroom in terms of knowledge, experience and possibilities, and ask questions like: 'What current issues will motivate my students and can I give lesson time to the discussion?'; 'What might students already think?'; 'Is there something in their immediate lives and experience which could be used to show how mathematics is useful?'; 'What examples might I introduce to ensure they extend their range of possibilities?'; 'What theoretical, structural understandings can they develop?'; and, where there is the potential for confusion, 'Is this going to confuse them? Can we meet it head-on or is it better to avoid it?'

Finding answers to these questions takes time, but we have tried to present you with a range of thoughts to inform your planning. These can, at the very least, give you some precise questions to pose to more experienced colleagues.

You may have noticed that the lessons we offer have two particular features: an absence of practice exercises and a dependence on the creativity of students. Instead of asking them to do lots of the same thing, the teachers offer students a wide variety of different things.

WHAT ABOUT PRACTICE?

Reference was made in one of the lessons to students having practised differentiation of polynomials for homework and thus being submerged in the technical details rather than thinking about the meaning of what they were doing. This recognises that differentiation, when first met, is a topic in itself, but that the ultimate aim may be to be able to differentiate fluently when it is needed as a tool and when this contributes to other mathematical ideas (e.g. the Taylor expansion) and to use differentiation to explore and define more complicated functions. Fluency without thought is useful as it frees the learner to think about more complex matters of meaning. However, lack of accompanying understanding is likely to lead to problems in applying the technique or in adapting it for unfamiliar examples. Of course, fluency does not have to be the result of meaningless repetition, but can be a product of practice involving understanding and the creation of personal shortcuts.

Algebraic manipulations may be a focus of hard work for some time in school, but the ultimate aim is likely to be to do them fluently when appropriate. (It helps to ask professional mathematicians about their most frequent mistakes and hear that dropping negative signs happens for everyone except those who now let software do their manipulations.) However, fluency on its own can lead to being stuck when the situation is unfamiliar or applying personal versions of rules inappropriately. For example, students tell themselves to 'take out the common factor' when factorising and simplifying algebraic expressions. Because the common factors in algebraic fractions can be cancelled, and hence omitted, students often inappropriately omit the common factors in other procedures as well. Their personal rule connects 'take out the common factor' with 'I can now leave it out altogether'. They are applying a rule automatically, not thinking about the meaning of what they do.

It is also tempting to rely on rules and procedures where an understanding of the distributive law would be much more powerful. For example, a deep familiarity with the structure $a(b + c) = ab + ac$ is all that is needed to decide on the order in which to evaluate an expression, where reliance on BODMAS[4] without understanding can lead to problems. For example, $-3 + 5 - 7$ can be calculated as $-8 - 7$ by a student who meaninglessly applies the 'addition before subtraction' aspect of BODMAS. Some people use BEDMAS which contains the instruction to deal with brackets before exponents; think about how this might be wrongly applied!

In the lesson about rates of interest (Lesson 7) there was plenty of experience included in calculating the appropriate percentages. Fluency would clearly be useful here and several performances of whatever method was being used would have led students to become quicker. Often it is the case that people become fluent at something because it is a necessary part of a larger task. The flipside of this comment is that such practice does not mean that students will know what to do when they have to calculate a percentage in some other context, especially if they used a method that only worked for particular numbers. Just as practising mathematical procedures in school does not mean that people can apply them at work, so procedures used in one context do not pop up conveniently in another.

As well as knowing that students can perform procedures, teachers would like to know what is going on inside students' heads as they do so, not because they ought to justify every step (that would slow them down – just as thinking about how you pedal makes you fall off a bicycle!), but because it gives an insight into whether their ways of thinking are universally useful or just happen to work in special cases. For example, the student who starts factorising quadratics by saying 'put x at the start of each bracket' is going to find this muttering unhelpful when the x^2 term has a coefficient other than 1. Asking students to tell you how they did something may not be very revealing: sometimes they may see pictures, sometimes they may have inner verbal instructions. Some ways of thinking about mathematics may not be expressible in words or symbols.

So some, but not all, of the mathematics in school is found in the techniques that enable students to become skilled enough to move on to the next stage. Mathematics is also in the underlying reasoning and structures of mathematics. It is important to know how to divide, but also to understand rational numbers; it is important to know how to 'multiply out' but also to understand distributivity.

Interestingly, mathematicians rarely do practice examples, even when they have just met a new technique. If they do repetitive examples at all, it is usually to look for patterns and habits which emerge in the answers,

127

or in the relationships between questions and answers – you may have found spreadsheets or computer algebra systems to be useful tools for doing this during your university studies.

Consider the difference between needing to know that 'four twelves are forty-eight' and being asked to list all the factors of 48. In the first case, meaning is only important if you cannot say the answer immediately – you have to slow down and start adding and reconstructing the answer by using your knowledge of multiplication. But if you can say the answer straightaway, you do not need to think about how well you understand it. In the second case, listing the factors, you *do* have to engage your understanding of factors and multiplication, however well you know the arena, although it is still true that the less you know automatically, the more you have to think about meaning. A student would be disadvantaged not to have instant automatic answers here. The related question 'What are 4 lots of 1.2?' is a useful one to think about: should the answer be automatic or should we have to think about it?

Conversely, suppose that all you had were the automatic answers, remembered almost as a rhyme, but no understanding of multiplication. You could do little in the second task without reciting all your multiplication table rhymes and listing wherever 48 occurred as an answer – but in doing this you would probably miss 2×24 and 3×16 because they are not in the tables most people have learnt. Clearly, there is a balance to be struck between fluency and understanding – lack of either might slow you down.

Multiplication tables are the most well-known example used in discussions about what students might need to know automatically. What else is automatic for you and how did it become automatic? Perhaps you have little memory aids you use, or a particular way of visualising what to do or say. Thinking about the example of '48' just examined, how would you balance teaching students to understand what they are doing and the need for some things to be automatic? How would you help them to achieve automaticity?

Consider another common example of helping students to develop fluency with a procedure. Students are sometimes taught to draw a 'smiley face' to remind themselves how to multiply two binomial brackets together (see Figure 7.1). What does this offer learners who need to multiply more brackets or brackets with more than two terms? How does it help with the reverse procedure where there may be more than one possible decomposition? How does it help learners to feel that what

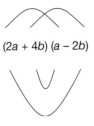

$(2a + 4b) (a - 2b)$

Figure 7.1 *'Smiley faces' for multiplying brackets*

they are doing is worthwhile, when symbolic manipulating software can do it for them?

CREATIVITY IN LEARNING MATHEMATICS

Many mathematics lessons throughout the world take the form of students watching the teacher do a few examples of a technique on the board and then doing a sequence of similar examples themselves, often in silence. This type of lesson is used less in the UK now, due to the gradual realisation over the last four decades that students need to discuss their mathematics in order to make sense of it, that imitation is not the only or best way to learn, and that doing techniques successfully is only a part of learning mathematics. These realisations were eventually included as guidance to all teachers through the National Curriculum from 1988 onwards and, more recently, the National Framework for Mathematics. While successful and accurate reproduction of techniques is a crucial part of mathematics, the development of machines to do this for us makes it more important to understand the concepts and ideas behind the algorithms. It turns out that understanding the concepts enables us to make up our own techniques. This idea now permeates primary school mathematics lessons, in which students are regularly asked to calculate answers and then report how they did so. A variety of mental methods are accepted, many of them based on familiarity with numbers and their combinations rather than following rules given by the teacher. In the hands of skilled teachers this is an elementary example of how working with structure can mentally empower students – they are not dependent on teachers to tell them how to do things in their heads.

In some of the lessons outlined in these two chapters, students make up their own examples to work on. The teacher may ask them to make up hard examples to see how they interpret 'hard'. Suppose you had been asked to make up a 'hard' multiplication question, what would you do to make it harder? Typically, most students choose bigger numbers; some may use different kinds of number – negatives, decimals and fractions; some will use more numbers – multiplying three or four numbers instead of two and thus making an inverse very complicated to sort out. Making up examples is not just a good way to practise mathematics; it is an integral part of exploring mathematical concepts. As well as harnessing students' creative urges, it is more motivating for them to work on their own questions than those of others. Most importantly, the creation of examples also requires engagement with structure. You cannot make up a quadratic expression that has $(x + 1)$ as a factor without developing a better understanding of the role of such a factor. You cannot make up an example of an irregular but symmetrical hexagon without developing your understanding of the technical words and the properties of the shapes.

There are other ways in which students work on mathematics in the lessons above besides following given methods and making up their own methods and examples. Many of those ways *are* mathematics, in that they employ mathematical thought directly on the objects of mathematics. A central feature of mathematics is that it involves symbolic representations of generalities of abstract ideas. Symbolism brings abstract ideas into the world of things that can be seen, manipulated and talked about. The constant π, for example, is an abstract idea, the ratio of the circumference to the diameter of all circles, expressed as a symbol. There is a numerical value, which cannot be known exactly, but mathematics shows that it exists. The use of π to calculate measures of circles is mathematics, but so are the processes of generating examples, hypothesising a constant ratio, symbolising it and refining our understanding of its power – processes that have taken place over centuries. There have even been major historical arguments among mathematicians about its value – these arguments are also mathematics. Thus, to give students a flavour of mathematics as a human activity, lessons need to give the opportunity to question, to hypothesise, to generalise, to try and to err – in other words, to create theories.

Perhaps your own mathematical studies did not give you many opportunities to create your own ideas and avenues for exploration, and your interest grew from a self-motivated desire to understand and achieve. What about those students who are not naturally motivated towards the subject? By offering opportunities to adolescents to bring their own thinking to bear on mathematics and to incorporate their own ideas into lessons, you could help them become interested and even intrigued in the subject – beyond usefulness – by recognising their creativity.

SUMMARY

In these chapters we have given you lesson ideas, attempting to show how the views about the nature of mathematics we have developed in earlier chapters can inform the development of interesting lessons. Within these lessons were some major themes about what it means to learn mathematics and, hence, how it might be taught. In particular, we wish to suggest that an emphasis on creativity and participation, rather than demonstration and practice, will make lessons not only enjoyable but also meaningful and effective.

THINKING ABOUT PRACTICE

- It is quite usual for teachers early in their careers to lack the time to work on mathematics for themselves and hence lose a sense of creativity; how can you make time to work creatively on mathematics, either on your own or with others?
- What are the benefits and losses of using curricula that focus on vocational mathematics?
- What strategies have you seen teachers use to help students achieve fluency, that is, speed and accuracy, in mathematics?

Chapter 8

Why assess and what to assess

KEY QUESTIONS

- What different kinds of assessment are there and what are their purposes?
- How can assessment affect teaching and learning?
- What sorts of things is it useful to know about students' mathematical knowledge?

The word 'assessment' can be used to refer to a wide range of activities in schools, ranging from the most informal judgement by a teacher that a student has understood what has been said to them to timed written examinations, set and marked by external bodies such as examination boards or the QCA (Qualifications and Curriculum Authority). It is also widely acknowledged that different forms of assessment can have very different purposes and that some forms of assessment can serve several purposes at the same time. In this chapter we will focus mainly on the purposes of assessment that relate most centrally to the main themes of this book: improving the learning and the teaching of mathematics (often referred to as 'formative' assessment).[1] In order to be an effective teacher, you need some knowledge of what students already know and how they know it. Learners are also likely to be more effective if they have a realistic view of what they have achieved and of what they have to do in order to progress in their learning. We will look at a number of examples of approaches to assessing mathematical knowledge and consider some of the issues and problems that may arise.

The results of assessment are also used for multiple purposes related to the organisation, management and monitoring of education at departmental, school, local, national and even international levels. We will consider the effects of these kinds of assessment on the work of mathematics teachers, on the experiences of students and on the nature of the mathematics curriculum as it is actually implemented in classrooms.

As a starting point, it is useful to reflect on what it might mean for a teacher to know what his or her students know. We will use the topic of solving equations as an illustration. Checking the solutions to an exercise or a test can inform you whether a student can get the correct solution to the particular equations in the exercise or test – but is this enough information?

When solving equations, some students see the task as being about manipulation of symbols according to certain rules (such as 'change the side, change the sign'), which may have only ritualistic meaning for them. Others may see it as a 'balance' in which one side always has to balance with another, each side of the equals sign. Thus they have to do the same things to each side to maintain the balance and they keep doing things until they end up with the unknown on its own on one side. Others may see it as a process of 'undoing' what has been done to the unknown value to 'hide' it. Others may have a graphical interpretation.

Yet all these students could get the right answer to a given equation. Knowing that they can produce correct solutions is therefore a rather dead-end piece of knowledge for the teacher. It would be more helpful to find out the limitations of the way they currently see the task. Knowing how they see the process and what they say to themselves while doing it, provides you with a starting place for teaching them to solve more complicated equations. If most of them are operating with the rule 'change the side, change the sign', how are you going to help them solve simultaneous equations? If most of them use a 'balance' metaphor, how are you going to help them solve equations involving trigonometric functions? If most of them use an 'undoing' metaphor, how are you going to help them solve quadratic equations? To teach most effectively, therefore, you need to find out not only *what* the students know about and can do, but also *in what form* they know it, how they see it, what they say to themselves when working with it and what methods they have chosen to use.

ASSESSMENT FOR INFORMING LEARNING

As should be clear throughout this book, we consider learning to be an active process, not just a passive reception of information from the teacher. Where learners are aware of their own learning – of what they do and do not know and understand, of their own most effective ways of learning and of their current personal learning objectives – they are more able to take responsibility for their learning and to direct their efforts where they will be most useful. Knowing that you have really learnt something can be both a source of satisfaction and a strong motivation towards further learning. It is far more valuable for students themselves to participate in the assessment process than for teachers to be the sole monitors of progress.

There are many simple adaptations to your classroom practice that will give students opportunities to become aware of and to reflect on their learning. A recent study has shown how the use of a wide range of such strategies can lead to a significant improvement in test grades by, on average, half a GCSE grade (Black *et al.*, 2002). Many of the techniques used by the teacher-researchers in this study provided rough-and-ready information that influenced the direction of a lesson or a sequence of lessons, yet were relatively simple to put in place. This kind of information does not have to be recorded anywhere as it is ephemeral and specific to the course of the current lesson. Students who feel they are always being 'judged' will not want to show that they do not understand, but those who feel that the classroom is a place to converse about understanding will gradually learn to give information which helps the progress of the lesson and will benefit from the insight this can provide them into their own understanding of mathematics.

How can you establish such conversation? Here are some ideas to think about.

1   Students award themselves 'traffic lights' of red, amber or green to indicate how much of the lesson they think they have grasped so far. These self-assessments are communicated to the teacher, perhaps by holding up a coloured card, or by the teacher going quickly round the class looking at books. Another version of this is for students to hold one, three or five fingers above their heads, five indicating full confidence, one indicating total confusion, and so on. At first students might play around with this system, but eventually they realise that it involves them

in creating a good lesson because the teacher responds. But how does the teacher respond? If most students show the red card, what are your options?

- You could explain the work a different way, using different materials, symbols or words, but this would have required prior preparation and you may not have thought about this in advance.
- You could ask some of them to describe what they thought had happened so far because that reveals to you how they understood the work and the process of explaining might itself clear up any confusions.
- You could explain again in the same way, exhorting them to listen better.
- You could ask them to discuss it with their neighbours and then ask you questions for clarification.
- You could use slightly different examples.

Perhaps you can think of other kinds of response.

2   Students make up their own test questions about a topic; both the questions and the responses show what and how they understand. This is likely to be revealing for both the student and the teacher, identifying the different things that have been studied and the critical features of these. It can also be an effective and interesting form of revision for a test, whether the questions in the test are set by the teacher or taken from those constructed by the students themselves.

Similarly, students can be asked to make up hard questions and easy questions as a regular homework activity. This has the disadvantage that you cannot mark homework by just rushing through, ticking and crossing answers, but the value of this kind of marking is dubious anyway (Black *et al.*, 2002). The big advantage is that you can see who understands enough to construct meaningful, answerable questions and who is floundering. Constructing answerable questions can be particularly valuable in establishing the importance and relevance of inverse processes. For example, students can come to realise that the easiest way of making up a quadratic function that is soluble by factorisation is to start by choosing the roots, forming the factors and multiplying them together.

135

Sometimes teachers make use of student questions in their teaching. This not only ensures that your teaching takes students' understanding into account, but it also helps students to feel valued as full participants in the conversation. Some teachers even ask students to mark the tests, prompting further development of their understanding as they have to consider how to value different questions and different kinds of answers.

3   Did you ever have teachers who would call out 'Tell me what I just said'? This technique can be used sarcastically to draw attention to someone who is not listening (not a practice we would advocate), but it can also be used very positively as a regular check on the effectiveness of communication and to find out what students make of the lesson. Moreover, it allows students to decide what it is they know and how to express it. The act of struggling to find the words for an explanation can not only clarify what is known, but can also make a student more aware of gaps in their own understanding. Teachers who regularly ask students to explain the lesson material in their own words learn a lot about what is being understood and how misunderstandings, or partial understandings, can develop.

4   Students make up an example to illustrate or demonstrate what they have been learning and thus show the extent of their understanding. For example, suppose you have been teaching about adding directed numbers by getting some students to walk along a number line on the floor. You could then ask them in pairs to make up their own additions, write them on the board and demonstrate them on the line. This would be even more useful when looking at subtractions of directed numbers, which are a lot trickier; the two of them could stand on the numbers to be subtracted, the difference showing up as a distance between them. This way, you provide a strong visual image of the subtraction, and they have a physical and emotional involvement in demonstrating how their own subtraction works out in practice. Note that the use of pairs of students enables them to discuss their ideas before they go public, thus building confidence, helping more of the class to be involved and giving the teacher more feedback. In making up examples, students have to actively transform their current understanding, to reorganise it, to decide what is relevant, what is constant and what is variable, in order to present it in a different form.

5 Teachers mark work only with comments about what has been achieved and what can be done to get better, not with grades. It has been found that if students are given grades and marks, that is all they will look at, but if no marks are given, only comments, then they will read the comments. This, of course, means that work takes much longer to mark than the traditional way, but the benefits are worthwhile. One way to keep this manageable and the comments useful, is to ensure that the work contains one question that encapsulates the aims of the teacher in some way. Then the marking focuses on that question and the comments can refer to the difficulties or methods that were the reason why that question was chosen.

EXAMPLE

Pauline taught a lesson about finding unknown lengths of sides of right-angled triangles, knowing the angles. She knew that showing students what to do and giving them an exercise would not in itself achieve much, so, as they were working, she made time to check that each one could find the length of the 'opposite' side, given the hypotenuse, and encouraged them to self-check their work by recalculating the sine.

When marking the homework that followed the lesson, she checked that they each had a transformation of the equation that enabled the hypotenuse to be found, given the 'opposite' side. She predicted that some would be confused by dividing by a function and might not be able to translate that into calculator instructions, so she focused carefully on one such question and created a record of how students had tackled it. She found that only a few had managed it successfully and several had omitted to use the sine of the angle so they had become puzzled when doing a self-check. One student had written: 'This is a mystery' after her answer. Pauline also wanted to check that they were rounding appropriately in this context, although she had not reminded them about this. She wanted them to learn that they had to be aware of rounding all the time, even when not reminded. On each student's book, she wrote about aspects of the mathematics they could think about further, including challenges for those who had everything right (such as 'What could it mean for an angle to be over 90 degrees in this situation?').

In the next lesson she gave 15 minutes at the start for people to work on what she had asked them to think about and gave help to those she knew would need it, before moving on to discuss the problems with dividing by a function. The lesson took into account what she had learnt from their work. At the end she inserted a quick game about rounding decimals, including tricky ones containing zeros or strings of nines. Finally, she asked them if they knew why she had done this, and those who had received written comments from her about rounding were quick to call out the reason.

Note that all of the methods of assessment we have suggested and illustrated are participatory and interactive to some extent, and many of them involve explicit or implicit self-assessment. None of them pretend to give complete and accurate pictures, but all of them provide opportunities for a teacher to gauge whether her teaching has been effective, and many of them give students the chance to reflect on what they have learnt, to become more aware of their learning and to express their own confidence or confusion. Helping students to know and use techniques for checking their own answers as Pauline did can develop their independence as well as their appreciation of the power of inverse relationships.

It is worth noting that there is a danger that some kinds of self-evaluation may not really trigger reflection. Repeated filling in of lists of 'I can do . . .' statements can become as much an algorithmic task as arithmetical exercises can be. Self-evaluations can be written with only superficial consideration to their meaning; for example, students may write: 'I did well on this topic, it was about Z and I managed to do all the examples.'

In preparation for more formal types of assessment, including the kind of 'high-stakes' tests we discuss later in this chapter, students can still be involved in the process by having access to the criteria used by teachers and deciding for themselves whether they can achieve these or not. These criteria can sometimes be difficult to interpret. For example, the criteria for assessing GCSE coursework include statements such as 'Candidates develop and follow alternative approaches. They reflect on their own lines of enquiry when exploring mathematical tasks; in doing so they introduce and use a range of mathematical techniques' (Edexcel, 2001: 135). Many teachers need help to interpret this in the context of specific tasks! Students are likely to need to be actively engaged in making sense of the criteria and of the standards required. Your feedback on their work could make it clear which criteria have and have not been met and what they would need to do to meet specific criteria that you believe to be within their grasp. You might also involve them in evaluating work themselves, perhaps working as a class to decide what grade to allocate to a piece of work produced by a student from a previous year. Where students are aware of the criteria by which their work is to be assessed and are involved in the assessment process through peer- and self-assessment, there is some evidence to suggest that they become 'acculturated' and produce work that meets the criteria better (Tanner and Jones, 1994).

ASSESSMENT FOR INFORMING TEACHING

At a most informal, fundamental level teachers assess students as part of getting to know them and as part of a natural two-way process of communication. They make judgements about students by observing types of response, behaviour, mistakes, communication skills and many other ordinary classroom actions and events and, as in any other sort of interaction between human beings, they adapt their own behaviour (words, actions, teaching approaches) on the basis of these judgements. The quality of the judgements and of the consequent teaching depends on what is used as evidence and how it is used. If all you rely on are the nods and smiles of a few students in the front row, then you may end up teaching appropriately for only a few students in the class – assuming their smiles mean something substantial and are not mere politeness.

You may say: 'How can I possibly know what every student knows?' This is a very important question, because to overload yourself with detailed information about every individual's personal state of knowledge and internal mutterings would make lesson planning an impossibly long task. It also supposes that the information you have is, in some way, accurate and meaningful, and that lessons can be scientifically constructed to treat individual cases. This is nonsense. On the other hand, to assume everyone remembers what you taught them last lesson – and remembers it in the way you do – can lead to an inappropriate charge through *your* version of mathematics, leaving many students lost and confused. Somewhere between these two extremes lie collections of rather messy, haphazard information, which give you a suggestion of the range of understandings and competencies in the classroom. These form the basis for lessons that allow a range of ways of knowing to be brought to bear on a central issue, topic or theme.

Starting a new topic

Imagine you are about to teach symmetry to students in early secondary school. They will have some ideas about symmetry of shapes from work done in primary school, from art lessons and from everyday life. How might you start? A good starting point is to identify what ideas the students are likely to bring with them to your first lesson on symmetry. Experienced teachers know a lot about the kinds of limited understandings students might bring with them. For example, they know that most students at this age will recognise symmetry if the axis is vertical or horizontal, but may not if the axis is in any other direction. For newer teachers with less practical experience of students' difficulties, there are useful and accessible sources of research evidence that can provide the necessary insight. For the topic of symmetry and several other important topics, the book *Children's Understanding of Mathematics 11–16* (Hart, 1981) is a good starting point. Other accessible sources include Nickson (2000), the reports of the APU (Assessment of Performance Unit) surveys, reports on Key Stage tests (published by the QCA) and GCSE examiners' reports, all of which identify what students can generally do well, as well as common errors.

Having identified what students are *likely* to know or to have problems with, how do you then match this up with the actual students in your class? If you start by asking 'Have you heard of symmetry?' you may get nods and smiles, but not learn much. If you start by drawing a diagram and asking them to say if it is symmetrical or not, what kind of diagram would you draw? Very often, for teachers as well as students, the first example that comes to mind is unhelpful because it is too special or too simple. If you draw one with a vertical axis of symmetry and the students recognise it, that only tells you that they recognise balance – an everyday notion of symmetry rather than a mathematical notion. So you could look at your first example and think 'What can I vary about this to make it a little more obscure, so I can find out what they know in more complicated cases?' Then, when you have found out whether students recognise symmetry with nasty axes, you may still not have found out the full range of knowledge in the classroom. Perhaps you would get more information by asking *them* to draw examples of shapes that are symmetrical but have axes of symmetry that are really hard to find.

The techniques we have just described are examples of formative assessment, because they give you information about what learners know and how they know it so that you can adjust your teaching to suit their current knowledge. One of the challenges is to collect such information in a reasonably systematic and professional manner as part of your normal teaching and to be able to distinguish between formative assessment, which is temporarily useful for you, and summative assessment, in which you are aiming to make a statement about the state of students' knowledge at some point in time, perhaps communicating this to colleagues or to parents. Students' mistakes and your misunderstandings of their work are part of normal classroom life, but it would be very unfair if these were treated as definitive measures.

Be(a)ware of your expectations of individuals

Judgements made as a result of feedback from the kinds of activities just described help teachers decide how to respond, what sort of challenges to offer and how to adapt their teaching. But they also influence future expectations of students and, without sufficient care, teachers' responses to students can become habitual. An unspoken set of assumptions can build up, based on homespun judgements such as 'Jack is lazy', 'Sara doesn't try', 'Parminder needs reassurance', 'Josiah is bright', 'Tracey is one of my strong ones', and so on. Often these summaries are based on something that happened early on in our teaching with that student when we needed to make instant judgements in order to decide how to react. The problem is that these instant judgements, unchecked, can continue as if they are true. As Blease said: 'In the heat of the moment [teachers] may be more ready to accept their own first impressions . . . myth becomes reality' (1983: 124).

Such first impressions can, of course, be positive or negative.

EXAMPLE

Lorna was observed by a learning support assistant to have several ways of getting other students to do her work and to be frequently involved in arguments, chatting, fiddling with pencils and other off-task activities. However, her teacher found Lorna lively and charming and had high hopes for her as a learner.

141

One person had formed a negative opinion, one a positive. What mattered in this case was not who was right, but that the teacher and the learning support assistant were able to discuss their opinions with each other and hence understand that they needed to avoid premature judgement and to find out more about her mathematics.

In a research study (Watson, 1997), a small number of learners were observed in their normal classrooms and the observational data was compared with the teacher's growing impressions of them.

EXAMPLE

Geraldine frequently asked the teacher for help, giving an impression of weakness and a need for reassurance, but the teacher did not hear that when she talked to her neighbour her speech was dominated by correct mathematical statements.

The teacher, who valued oral contributions, thought Julie was brighter and stronger than Clare at mathematics. Yet Clare talked more about maths than Julie did in whole class sessions; somehow the teacher had noticed Julie's contributions more than Clare's.

The teacher had formed the view that Alan was articulate, yet the researcher noticed that he hardly ever spoke about maths and nearly half the times he did so, he was merely reading what was already on the board. Alan also failed to produce much written work, so a teacher who valued written work might have had a lower opinion of Alan than this teacher did.

We have said nothing about the actual mathematical achievement of these students because the impressions of both the teacher and the researcher were based on surface features of the students' behaviour, not on mathematical knowledge, and yet these kinds of impressions do influence what happens in classrooms.

In order to cope in the classroom we summarise what we expect of students and they usually conform; a two-way process which creates certain types of learners and learning, and is easy to establish and hard to escape. Students conform not because this is really the way they are, but because it is sometimes easier to fit into the teacher's expectations than rebel, or because they accept the teacher's judgement about what kind of mathematician they can be, or because the teacher and student between them subconsciously set up a pattern of interaction that becomes a habit. Houssart (2001) writes of her disturbing observations of some students who set up an alternative discourse in the classroom, one of disagreeing with the teacher, doing the work quickly, mentally and with discussion, and refusing to slow down to work at the teacher's pace, or to write down their work, or to put up their hands to speak. A vivid picture is drawn of potentially strong students being alienated to the point of rebellion as the teacher judges them negatively and treats them accordingly, not really paying attention to the mathematics they are understanding and questioning.

In making judgements about individuals, teachers have to remember that they:

- see only part of the whole story – inevitably missing some of the detail and not having time to explore every student's mathematics fully or to use all the available information;
- may be over-influenced by some kinds of responses and behaviour and may find it harder to notice other patterns in response and behaviour;
- may be over-influenced by students' strong or weak social or communication skills.

You need to be aware that your early impressions of students may unfairly influence later judgements. It may be wise on occasion to adopt a stance of deliberately questioning your own judgements in order to test their validity.

Identifying mathematical knowledge and understanding

How, then, are you to develop knowledge about the mathematical capabilities of your students? The student has three main ways of communicating mathematically with the teacher: orally, in writing or through some kind of physical behaviour. All of these have to be noticed and interpreted by the teacher. Even if the student communicates what appears to be correct mathematics, using conventional symbolism, you cannot know whether the meanings the student is trying to convey by the symbols are the same as your own, or whether they are going to give conventionally correct answers in other situations. For example, many students who say correctly that 0.05 is smaller than 0.5 base their answers on the idea that 0.05 is 'half of a half' and, therefore, a quarter. It is tempting, however, to take the correct answer to be evidence of knowing about decimals and place value.

Suppose, then, that we try to assess understanding instead of performance or behaviour. We will take multiplication as an example.

There are many levels of understanding one might associate with multiplication. It can mean 'lots of'; the terms 'of' or 'how much' can be seen as instructions to multiply; multiplication makes things bigger; multiplication does not always make things bigger; multiplication is scaling; multiplication is about multiplication tables; multiplication can be seen as an operation on two mathematical entities, and so on. All these understandings have legitimate places in the growth of mathematical knowledge and the teacher cannot know precisely what and how the student understands at any stage.

Correct performance when multiplying two numbers together does not give the teacher evidence of which of these forms of understanding a student may or may not have – and nor does incorrect performance in itself. Again, a teacher can lead students towards revealing some of the detail of their understanding through carefully chosen questions. Avoiding easy numbers, ones which encourage the use of doubling, repeated addition and 'making things bigger', can be useful in designing tasks which aim to assess multiplication, as can the use of contexts which require scaling. A popular calculator activity which goes some way towards this is to get students to 'make 20' by giving them starting numbers and asking them to find other numbers by which to multiply them to get 20 as the answer. The teacher can choose starting numbers to see how far their understanding can take them, for instance selecting, eventually, very small (or very large) negative numbers.

Choosing an appropriate question or task is the key to probing students' understanding. Diagnostic questions can be designed to distinguish those students who have particular kinds of understandings. You need to try to avoid questions (like the decimals example described above) that students can get right by using incorrect mathematical reasoning.

A large-scale APU survey (Mason and Ruddock, 1986) found that two apparently similar questions about ordering decimals were answered with very different degrees of success by 11-year-olds across the country. Question 9 asked students to put the decimals 0.3, 0.1, 0.7 and 0.6 in order of size, smallest first. This was answered correctly by 75 per cent of the sample, while 18 per cent gave the numbers in reverse order. Question 10 asked them to put 0.07, 0.23 and 0.1 in order of size, smallest first. This time only 23 per cent gave the correct answer; hardly any responded with the numbers in the reverse order, but 31 per cent answered 0.1, 0.07, 0.23, and 20 per cent answered 0.23, 0.07, 0.1. The researchers concluded from these and responses to similar questions that there are two kinds of common error being made here, which they called 'Decimal Point Ignored' (DPI) and 'Largest is Smallest' (LS). In the case of question 9, those students who made the DPI error, ignoring the decimal point, still gave the correct answer; this question was not successful in distinguishing between those who had a secure understanding of decimal place value and those who were treating the decimals as if they were whole numbers. It was thus not a very useful assessment task.

You also need to use some questions that cannot be answered easily by using informal 'child methods' but need more formal mathematical methods. When dealing with proportion, for example, many students prefer to use methods that involve a mixture of doubling, halving and addition rather than recognising and using multiplicative relationships. The first question in Figure 8.1 can be answered correctly by reasoning along the lines 'The new base is increased by 4 cm, which is half of the old base, so take half of the height and add that on. The new height is 3 cm plus 1.5 cm, which is 4.5 cm.' If you change the length of the new base to 11 cm instead of 12 cm, the question is much more difficult to answer in this informal way as the increase in the base involves using a fraction of 8 cm that is not a half. Looking at students' responses to this revised question will allow you to distinguish those who can already reason multiplicatively about proportion from those who rely entirely on additive strategies.

The Concepts in Secondary Mathematics and Science project (CSMS), (reported in Hart, 1981), developed many such diagnostic questions in a number of different areas of mathematics, which can be very useful when planning lessons or devising tests.

Assessing students' ability to apply their mathematical knowledge and understanding to problems set in 'real world' contexts raises some further

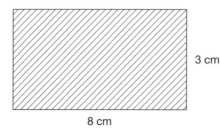

3 cm

8 cm

Enlarge this rectangle so that
the base is 12 cm.

or

Enlarge so that the base is 11cm.

Figure 8.1 *Two contrasting proportion questions*

difficulties in interpreting students' answers. The complexity of using and applying mathematics was discussed in Chapter 3. As soon as students are expected to do more than simply translating a 'word problem' into mathematical terms, they face the problem of knowing how much of the context to take into account, and their teachers face the problem of knowing how much use the students have made of their contextual knowledge. A test question on probability asked students to use some data on the numbers of different kinds of vehicles passing a school to state how likely it was (certain, very likely, unlikely, etc.) that a lorry would pass the school during the next minute. In a research study in which students where interviewed about their answers, some students were found to have given correct answers based on non-mathematical, 'everyday' knowledge rather than using the data provided. One boy, who had given the correct answer 'unlikely', explained why: 'Outside of school, more parents would come to like collect a child in a car than they would in a lorry' (Cooper and Dunne, 2000: 102). It is also possible for the context to lead students to give answers that would make complete sense in the everyday world, but which are considered incorrect in a mathematics lesson or test. Cooper and Dunne's research showed that students from working-class families were more likely than those from middle-class families to find it difficult to judge exactly how much of their knowledge of the everyday context was relevant to the questions, even when they had an adequate grasp of the necessary mathematical concepts and skills.

Modes of assessment – effective means of communication

If you ask teachers what forms of assessment they use, you are likely to find that a high proportion of the responses involve making judgements about the written records of work done by their students. These include: in-class monitoring of answers to exercises; marking books with written classwork and homework; tests set at the end of a unit of work; reports of statistical projects or investigative work; examinations; coursework. As we have discussed above, we need to be careful about the types of questions we ask and the ways we interpret students' answers, but using students' written work has some major advantages:

- Suppose you know that question 5 in the exercise the students are working on requires a change of strategy. You can keep an eye out for students' answers to this question at the same time as responding to requests for help with other questions. This will let you know whether you need to intervene to draw everyone's attention to the change or whether most members of the class have managed to spot what is needed independently.

- As you mark a class set of homework or test papers, you will sometimes find that a high proportion of the class has got a particular question wrong. This can be a useful starting point for a subsequent lesson, identifying the underlying reasons for the errors and helping the students to sort out what was required. Equally, a diagnostic homework or test set before teaching can show you which parts of a topic are already well established and will need little extra attention, allowing the class to progress at an appropriate rate.

- When you have been working with a class doing a substantial investigation or statistical project, it is often difficult to keep track of the individual contributions or to be sure that each member of a group has fully understood the outcomes their group seems to have achieved. An individual written report provides you with a way of seeing each student's attainment.

From the teacher's point of view, using students' written records has the advantages that it allows you to get a relatively quick overview of the general level of understanding and the kinds of errors that are being made within a class and it also allows you to distinguish the individual student's work from that of a larger group. In contrast to oral interactions and observation of students' actions in the class, students' writing provides a record that you can take away to read, thus giving you time not only to reflect on its meaning, but also to consider how to respond. Do you write a comment on a correctly worked example? Do you plan to speak to an individual during the next lesson? Do you start the next lesson with a discussion about a common error? Do you praise good work publicly or privately?

In addition to written answers to traditional mathematical exercises and problems, writing about a mathematical topic can give students a chance to reflect on their own understanding. A group of teachers who tried using regular 'writing prompts' with their classes found that this kind of written response gave them valuable insights into the ways their students were thinking (Miller, 1992). They gave students five minutes during each lesson to respond to prompts related to the subject matter they were studying such as:

Explain why $\frac{0}{5} = 0$ and why $\frac{5}{0}$ is undefined.

Explain why x and y represent the same number in the expressions: $4x = 28$ and $4y = 28$.

The responses these teachers received from their students sometimes surprised them and prompted them to reconsider assumptions they had been making about what the students understood.

It is important to remember, however, that many people (adults as well as children) find it very hard to express their ideas fully in writing. One of the big problems for many is the need to imagine how your audience is likely to understand and respond to what you are writing. When interacting face-to-face, we can generally tell whether the person we are talking to is following what we are saying or is bored or frustrated because we are giving too much unnecessary detail, and we adjust what we are saying in order to match the needs and expectations of our audience. Judging this is much harder in writing, even when you know your reader well. This means that teachers have to remember that written answers that include too little information or too much irrelevant detail may arise from students' difficulty with the process of communication rather than with the mathematics.

The more complex and substantial the task is, the greater the number of judgements that have to be made about what to include in a written solution or report. Knowing the criteria by which a piece of work is to be judged is likely to help students to produce writing that shows the required skills, knowledge and understanding, but there may also be

THINK POINT

(a) Estimate the value of 326 ÷ 18

Answer: 17

(b) Explain how you got your answer

Answer: In my head

hidden assumptions on the part of both teacher and students that make assessment of the students' writing less valid. For example, Ann MacNamara and Tom Roper report overhearing a group of students discussing a finding they had come across during an investigative task, and deciding not to include it in their written report because another group had already found the same result (MacNamara and Roper, 1992). Relying only on what students write is likely to underestimate what they are capable of, but, as has been discussed above, we cannot hope to 'overhear' everything that every student does and says during a lesson.

Problems with the interpretation and assessment of written work do not necessarily just arise from weaknesses in the students' writing, but may also come from the assumptions a teacher makes about what they are reading. A study of experienced mathematics teachers assessing GCSE coursework found that, of the three teachers assessing the same student's piece of work, one teacher came to the conclusion that the student was demonstrating a good understanding of the relationship he had noticed in his data, another was of the opinion that he had achieved his result by luck or intuition, while a third credited him only with 'trying' rather than with achieving a correct result (Morgan and Watson, 2002). Such difficulties in interpreting and evaluating seem most likely to arise when students' mathematical work is unusual or creative. This is sometimes taken as an argument for restricting methods of assessment, especially summative and high-stakes assessment, to more 'objective' tests – that is, methods where it is straightforward to determine whether answers are right or wrong, with no room for interpretation on the part of the assessor. We believe that such restriction would be a mistake for two main reasons: first, we would gain only a very partial picture of students' mathematical capabilities and achievements; second, we would be giving out a strong message to students, their parents and other 'users' of assessment information that only those parts of mathematics that can be assessed in this simple way are to be valued.

Discussion with students can help to fill in some of the parts that are missing from our picture of their achievement, as two-way oral inter-actions allow us to continue to ask for more clarification and explana-tion. It is still important to remember, however, that many students, especially those from working-class families and from homes where English is not the first language, may be disadvantaged because the forms of language they are expected to use in school are different from those used at home. In particular, the expected kinds of responses to demands such as 'Explain how you did . . .' involve forms of speech rarely used outside school. This means that, on the one hand, teachers need to listen carefully and sensitively to students' attempts to communicate their understanding while, on the other hand, they also need to help students to develop the forms of language needed to express these kinds of mathematical meanings.

Gathering a range of information

As we have suggested already, if you want to gain useful knowledge about your students that will enable you to plan appropriately and give them helpful feedback, it is likely that you will need to use more than one approach to assessment. Tests give very limited information, although carefully designed diagnostic questions can reveal common errors. Both written and oral responses can be misleading if you do not look at them critically.

It is also important to think about what sort of information you want and what sort of use you intend to make of it. Do you want informa-tion about their current understanding to inform your immediate planning? Do you want to evaluate the teaching and learning of the topic you have just taught? Or do you want to sum up what students can recall over a longer period?

Current understanding: tasks like 'Make up an example which shows someone else what you understand and can do in this topic' reveal what the student thinks is going on. The teacher can record what is necessary for her lesson planning, or who needs extra help or a special challenge. This sort of question can feed into plenary discussion at the end of a lesson to help students share their understandings with each other as well as with you. Diagnostic testing can also be used, in which no mark is given but answers to certain questions indicate the kinds of difficulties students have and these inform future teaching.

Knowledge of what has recently been taught: a post-topic test can be given, perhaps using questions the students have devised, covering the main points of the topic and perhaps linking with other areas of mathematics. Turning such a test into numbers, marks or grades may not be as helpful as recording which questions each student found too hard. An alternative method is to ask small groups of students to make a poster to show what they have learnt, or to write a page about it to an imaginary pen friend, including worked examples of any techniques learnt. These alternatives are useful for learning as well as for assessment, as they require that students reflect on and organise their knowledge in order to communicate it.

Accumulated knowledge: this is typically tested with questions that span a wide range of mathematics and require the recall of facts, techniques and skills. Such tests generally also require students to choose which facts, techniques and skills are relevant to each question. High-stakes tests (discussed below) are mostly of this kind. Part of the challenge of preparing students for this kind of assessment is helping them to identify what mathematics to use for each question. They can be trained to respond to cues, for example: always divide when the question asks 'How many?'; always differentiate when a question says 'Find the maximum'. Of course, although these rules-of-thumb do work quite often, they are not the correct things to do in every context, so students do better if they read the question carefully and have meaningful knowledge to draw on, rather than simply using examination techniques. Research has shown that those whose knowledge of mathematics is a connected network are more able to be flexible with unfamiliar questions (Boaler, 1997).

The type of mathematical knowledge, understanding or skill being assessed will also have an effect on the methods you may use to gather information.

Facts, skills and techniques: in secondary mathematics, most of the techniques and facts that have to be learnt keep reappearing in later topics, and each time this happens students can become more fluent in their use. Regular reviews help the memory, and the teacher can also use such reviews to check that students recall what they might need for the next piece of work. For instance, if working on straight line functions, they can be asked to play a game involving using coordinates (such as

'Battleships') as a warm-up, and the students can check for themselves that they remember how to use them. Where facts are concerned, rather than asking closed questions such as 'What is the name for a five-sided polygon?', giving a more open instruction such as 'Make up a sentence with the words "pentagon" and "symmetry" used mathematically' should result in more information about what is remembered and how it might be connected to other ideas. Many teachers use such review activities as a regular feature of their teaching, often having a brief 'starter' at the beginning of each lesson to review, refresh the students' memories and prepare for the day's topic, as well as to settle the students and get them in the right frame of mind for thinking mathematically.

Speed and accuracy: secondary mathematics frequently demands fluency of some skills in order to achieve more complex ends. For example, algebraic manipulation is central to much further work and multiplication facts are important when factorising quadratics. Speed and accuracy are important so that the student does not have to cope with unnecessary obstacles; thus they need to be worked on explicitly in lessons. One obvious way to do this is through timed tests, but testing does not, in itself, lead to improvement, and the need for speed in tests can confuse some people, making them panic. An alternative is to use activities that engage students themselves in the development of fluency. For example, students who know that they need to get faster usually quite enjoy games that encourage them to do that.

Using and applying mathematics: in some schools, 'Using and applying mathematics' is seen as a separate topic and is addressed once a term by getting students to do an assessed 'investigation'. Apart from the absurdity of separating the idea of the application of mathematics and mathematical reasoning from the learning of mathematical facts and techniques, it does not make sense to assess any area of mathematical activity without relating it to teaching and learning. Extended tasks are needed to provide opportunities for students to develop planning and problem-solving skills, but mathematical reasoning and communication can be developed and assessed as part of the regular activity in the classroom. For example, whatever topic your class is working on, you can ask students to explain and justify their answers and to evaluate each other's explanations.

In discussing these different aspects of mathematics, we have not distinguished clearly between the types of task that might be used to help students develop their knowledge, understanding and skills, and the types of task that might be used for assessment purposes. This is because we believe that good assessment tasks are also good learning tasks. To get detailed information, a teacher needs to be clear about what exactly she hopes students will learn. To return to solving linear equations, if she hopes they will learn to think of this as an 'undoing' procedure, she needs to imagine what might go wrong and offer examples of situations in which 'undoing' is hard to enact, such as $16 - x = 9$. In this example, the answer is obvious without needing a formal method, so is it an appropriate one to consider? Also, the 'subtract from' is a self-inverse operation. (Self-inverse operations were discussed in the context of functions in Chapter 3.) So she has to decide whether to deal with this kind of example explicitly, or whether to leave it for students to figure out on their own or in pairs, and how she will use the information she gets from setting this as an exercise.

EXAMPLE

Nick, a new teacher, was taking a lesson on proportional reasoning in which he posed the question: 'What is the cost of 10 bags of flour at £2.00 per bag?' Students all knew the answer and he asked how they had worked it out. Most said 'doubling'. He then asked what the cost would be if the bags cost £2.50 each. Again, many found the answer and reported methods like doubling, halving and adding. The third variation was that the bags cost £2.30. This took considerably longer. Nick had constructed this sequence of questions deliberately because he had realised that the earlier questions could be solved by ad hoc methods, and that he needed to 'force' them to think about multiplication. The first example did not need a multiplication method; the last signalled that there was a need for a method that could be used in all cases, even if one could choose easier methods for particular numbers. The middle question 'drew out' the doubling and halving methods so that they could be discussed in public.

You might like to think about how Nick's approach of publicly exposing the limitations of ad hoc methods could be used with the self-inverse operation above. What further examples might you use to help students shift from just 'seeing' the answer to needing a method?

In these examples the teacher can gain assessment information, observing who is successful and what methods they use, but there is also structured teaching in which students gradually have to abandon simple methods which have limited value. Good assessment practices are very similar to good teaching practices and, indeed, the two are totally intertwined.

ASSESSMENT FOR EXTRINSIC PURPOSES

In this section we will look at those aspects of assessment that, while clearly impinging on the experiences of teachers and students in the mathematics classroom, are not so directly related to teaching and learning as those we have discussed so far. Assessment of various kinds is used to classify students by making decisions about:

- which mathematics set they could be in;
- which curriculum track they could follow (for example, academic or vocational, Foundation or Higher);
- which examination they could be entered for;
- even which school they could attend.

These decisions affect the type of curriculum that will be offered to students and the kinds of expectations they and their teachers are likely to have about their future learning. Towards the end of their school careers, assessment in the form of examinations is used to provide students with qualifications which are used by employers and further and higher education institutions to select individuals for jobs and for continuing educational opportunities. These uses of assessment are often called 'high-stakes' assessment because of the importance of their consequences for the future life chances of the individual students involved.

This importance can motivate some students to work towards better results or towards a specific grade that they know they need for the job or course they want to enter. On the other hand, some students who know they are unlikely to achieve a high grade may be difficult to motivate to learn because they see no reason to strive towards what they consider to be a pointless qualification. It is also probably unrealistic to expect most young students in the early years of the secondary school to be highly motivated by an appeal to what they might want to do in four or five years' time. Motivation that is exclusively directed towards examination results can also make effective teaching and learning more difficult when students ask 'Why should I be interested in this if it's not going to be on the exam?' or complain: 'I don't want to understand – just tell me how to do it.' Other forms of motivation, related more intrinsically to learning mathematics, were discussed in Chapter 5.

The results of external assessments such as the GCSE and Advanced level examinations and the National Curriculum tests at the end of Key Stages 1, 2 and 3 are also used to monitor the performance of schools and, through the publication of 'league tables', to allow comparisons to be made between them. In many schools they are also used to monitor and set targets for departments and even individual teachers. This use of results is controversial, but we do not intend to address the validity and ethical dimensions of such uses of assessment here (see, for example, Wiliam, 2001). It is enough to note that these ways of using assessment results make such examinations and tests 'high-stakes' for teachers and schools, as well as for students.

ASSESSMENT, THE CURRICULUM AND TEACHING APPROACHES

Assessment is intimately bound up with teaching, learning, classroom dynamics, and teachers' and students' beliefs about what the knowledge of mathematics entails. If we hope that students will be able to discuss possible reasons behind mathematical properties but only ever assess them on a recall of facts, they will not recognise the value we put on reasoning, nor develop the skills that are necessary to show their reasoning in assessable forms. If we value the ability to solve mathematical problems but only ever assess students on 'right answer' responses, they will not recognise the value of developing thinking skills. If we see it as valuable for students to remember the similar properties of certain different classes of mathematical objects but only assess exploratory work, they will not recognise the value of memory.

Through all aspects of their school experience, from the ways books are marked to the responses teachers give in lessons, and certainly the tests they are given and the ways the results are used, students come to know what is valued. Unfortunately, if high-stakes tests dominate as a form of assessment, students and teachers will come to value only what is tested – and this is likely to be only the timed, pressured, performance aspects of mathematics. To compensate for this, you need to ensure that you communicate the value you place on the other important aspects of mathematics by the tasks you select, the formative assessment techniques you use and the forms of feedback you give to your students.

Teachers rightly regard high-stakes assessments as important because of their significance for students' life chances. There are, however, different views about how to prepare students for such events. Some teachers devote a lot of time to giving students practice in appropriate techniques, information about how to answer questions similar to those on the test and experience of 'mock' examinations. Others place more emphasis on secure learning and the practical application of mathematics, so that taking the test is just one part of a broader experience among a range of ways of expressing mathematical progress. Jo Boaler's study of two schools in which the teachers used these contrasting approaches showed that both could be equally successful in helping students to achieve examination grades, but that students in the school which did not 'teach to the test' had much better attitudes towards learning and doing mathematics, and saw it as something that was useful to them in their lives (Boaler, 1997).

The inclusion of teacher-assessed coursework in some high-stakes examinations is one of the ways that curriculum planners have attempted to ensure that preparation for assessment involves more than learning examination techniques. The form of GCSE coursework has changed several times since it was introduced in 1988; at the time of writing it involves all students in investigating a situation mathematically and in undertaking a statistical project. Both of these involve planning and carrying out extended tasks, and communicating the results. The reasons given for using this type of assessment task at GCSE and for having a teacher-assessed component in National Curriculum assessment, in addition to examinations, include the following:

- they assess the application of knowledge in a context that is more relevant to life and work than reproducing it in an examination;
- they assess students' performance in longer, more complex tasks than can be assessed in traditional tests, covering a broader range of mathematical content;

156

- they value communication of mathematics in a variety of forms, rather than limiting it to written answers;
- they value explicitly the processes and dynamics of doing mathematics;
- they alleviate the effects of bias in written tests by providing other assessment environments.[2]

In addition, involving teachers in the assessment process means that it is possible to gain a more valid assessment of students' learning over time and to base assessment not just on a pressured performance of specially prepared skills.

Whatever form high-stakes assessment takes, there is an obligation on the teacher to teach in ways that will allow students to succeed. In other words, the assessment requirements are used as standards for planning the curriculum and how it is taught. 'Teaching to the test' is a rather derogatory way to describe the classroom manifestation of this two-way relationship, but failure to take the nature of the test into account can disadvantage students. There is a fine line to be taken between treating students justly by fully preparing them for the tests they will have to face and ensuring that this does not degenerate into the kind of test training which fails to give them a love for the subject or a foundation on which to build further study. Whatever form the high-stakes assessment has, you need to take it into account somehow, to know about it, to understand its purposes and how evaluation takes place, and to plan accordingly, ensuring at the same time that you do not lose sight of your other, broader objectives for teaching mathematics.

RECORD-KEEPING AND ENSURING FAIRNESS

When teachers keep records the purpose should be clear and they should be fit for their purpose. Some teachers use a three-part system of recording, using small clear symbols: who has 'met' a topic, who understands the basics of it and who understands everything. If these records are merely to give the teacher some indication of how to plan future work, they can be useful, but if they are taken to be summative statements, they ought to be treated with care since the judgements which lead to these symbols being used are likely to have arisen from specific tasks in specific contexts and may also have had to be made quickly in the course of teaching.

Similar care needs to be taken with records of the results of Key Stage tests or standardised tests such as NFER. While these can provide a rough indication of what a child may have achieved, they rely on single measurements taken in stressful conditions and do not provide diagnostic information. Such test results may be most useful as a means of identifying possible anomalies when a student seems to be performing above or below the level suggested by the test. If they are used as a basis for grouping students or deciding what curriculum they should follow, such decisions should be only provisional until more meaningful information has been gathered.

Teachers need to know about learning needs, communication, thinking skills, processes, subject-specific characteristics, general intellectual characteristics, work-related characteristics, personal and social characteristics. None of these features of mathematical work is testable, nor are they easily quantifiable, nor can they be recorded in the way just described. Yet teachers feel they can legitimately make comments about such features. The root problem is the basic expectation that teachers should be able to say something clear and summative about students' mathematics, and about their potential in the subject. In countries such as the UK, where teachers are required by statute to make summative statements, a natural way forward is to work with colleagues so that decisions are made in a critical professional community rather than by individuals.

We would argue that this shared decision-making is crucial for fair decisions and that teachers should think of challenging each other's judgements. It is tempting to interpret as causal what might only be symptoms. For instance, we often hear statements such as: 'This work is level 4; it can't be level 5 because he is in the bottom set.' Yet the student is in the so-called 'bottom set' because of the accumulation of judgements, and now these are being used as if they constitute a basis for a further judgement. Marking according to clear criteria which adequately define standards goes some way towards addressing this kind of fluffy thinking, yet defining mathematical performance is inevitably complex. We know of one Oxbridge mathematics lecturer who misunderstood subtraction with decomposition for several years, not knowing why he could not get the right answer. If he had been subject to current setting and testing policies, he might never have been encouraged to make more progress. In some tests he would have done rather badly!

RE-FOCUSING ON LEARNING

Ultimately, everything teachers do needs to be focused on helping students to learn. This ought to be obvious, but often it gets lost in the complexities of documentation for, and demands on, teachers. It is too easy to focus on fulfilling requirements rather than using students' learning to inform and guide teaching.

What we hope we have done in this chapter is to indicate ways to detach the word 'assessment' from the dominance of written, timed tests and to re-attach it to students' learning. This allows teachers to achieve far more than merely teaching to the test, because teaching becomes a conversation with students about their growth of understanding in the context of the given curriculum.

THINKING ABOUT PRACTICE

- When planning a unit of work, what would it be useful to know about your students' knowledge before, during and after teaching, and how might you find this out?
- How can you help your students to become more aware of their own learning?
- What impact is 'high-stakes' assessment having on your own teaching and on your students' learning?

Part III

Professional values and practice

As well as a love for their subject and a desire to share their knowledge with others, most teachers choose their profession because of a real commitment to helping others and to improving education for all. In this section, we consider the practical implications of this commitment.

The title of Chapter 9, 'Mathematics for all', may sound like an idealistic slogan, but it has serious implications for teachers. Through a small number of detailed case studies of teachers working with classes in different contexts, we consider some of the ways in which students may differ, the implications of such differences for their learning and possible approaches to engaging diverse students, and supporting their various approaches to mathematical learning.

For new teachers, the structures provided by the National Curriculum, the Key Stage 3 Strategy, schemes of work, textbooks and other resources and guidance available in schools provide valuable support as they begin to engage with the question of what to teach and how to teach it. It is important to remember, however, that mathematics teachers are professionals with expertise in their subject and in its teaching. With that expertise comes responsibility to engage critically with the content and form of the curriculum, to participate in debates about what is important in mathematics education, and to play an active role in the professional community. In the final two chapters, we explore the roles that teachers may play in developing mathematics education, first by examining examples of teacher involvement in curriculum development and then by outlining the ways in which mathematics teachers may continue their personal professional development, pursuing different trajectories within a broad community of mathematics education professionals.

Chapter 9

Mathematics for all

KEY QUESTIONS

- How can mathematics teaching be adapted to suit the learning preferences of different groups of students?
- How can a teacher provide for individual students within a whole class setting?

We now shift our focus to consider one of the most challenging aspects of teaching and one that you, as teacher in your own classroom, are in a unique position to carry out, monitor and evaluate. We refer to the aim of including all students in actively learning mathematics, and we will address some of the issues related to this goal. It seems to us that successful teachers are acutely aware of the extent to which their lessons are inclusive and have at least two strategic strands in mind as they plan, teach and evaluate their lessons. They attach great importance to the creation and management of an atmosphere that is conducive to learning for all, and they select approaches to topics to suit individuals and groups within each class. Each of these strands gives rise to a myriad of objectives and when teaching is described as an 'art', it is in recognition of the complexity of this endeavour. The design of every lesson involves the construction of an entity that has to be viewed holistically and in all its detail at the same time, because the learning of individual students has to be addressed in the context of a learning environment that evolves during the lesson.

Some responses to teaching are predictable, related either to the specific nature of individual students' ways of learning or to widely shared ways in which students tend to understand particular mathematical concepts. Other responses arise unexpectedly during the lesson.

EXAMPLE

Hassan was teaching his Year 10 class how to do ruler-and-compass constructions. Most of the class were following his instructions successfully and producing constructions that, when checked by measuring, were seen to be reasonably accurate. However, one boy, Danny, was becoming increasingly frustrated as he repeatedly produced messy drawings that were obviously inaccurate. Hassan could see that Danny was having serious physical problems controlling his compasses so, as well as giving him some hints about how to hold his compasses, suggested that he use the dynamic geometry software on the computer at the back of the classroom to produce the same constructions. Danny's attitude and engagement with the work improved dramatically and he was quickly able to convert the instructions for ruler-and-compass constructions into a sequence of actions on the computer. Moreover, during the plenary discussion at the end of the lesson, he contributed positively, showing a good understanding of the principles underpinning the constructions.

Inevitably, such a degree of flexibility has an impact on the course of the lesson and on planning, but time spent addressing difficulties or discussing alternative perceptions is almost always time well spent. An inclusive atmosphere for learning, when strategies for differentiation include opportunities to negotiate how the students think about mathematics, helps to develop self-awareness and responsibility among the students.

EXAMPLE

Maria found early in the year that, while most of her Year 9 class were confident and fluent in mental calculation, a small group was hesitant in responding during 'starter' activities and gained significantly lower scores than the rest of the class in practice oral tests. This was surprising, as these students were generally achieving as well as, or better than, the rest of the class in other aspects of their work. They appeared to have high levels of anxiety about mental calculation that were preventing them from participating or making progress in this area. Maria discussed the problem with the group and, rather than pressurising them to take part in whole class oral activities, negotiated some individual targets to encourage the students to become more confident and fluent with number facts and with specific strategies for mental calculation. She provided them with some games and practice exercises that they could use at home to work towards their targets. Although she avoided insisting on their participation in whole class oral work, Maria regularly asked some questions directly related to the targets that members of the group had set and soon found that some of them began to volunteer responses. As they progressed, individual students came to show Maria what they could do and to renegotiate their targets.

It is an important part of inclusive practice that students should have the opportunity to become aware of their own learning, recognising their needs, and to play a leading part in tackling their own difficulties. Conversely, when some students feel excluded, or exclude themselves, experienced teachers know that the teaching and learning are less than adequate.

There is a body of professional knowledge and experience about how to enable school mathematics to be more inclusive. In England and Wales, much of this has developed over the past thirty years or so, since the time when the minimum school leaving age was raised to sixteen and it became the expectation that the majority of students would be entered for public examinations. School mathematics began to change in order to become more widely accessible and in response to the perceived needs of industry, commerce and higher education. Teachers worked hard not only to include new content, but also to broaden the range of ways in which mathematical topics might be presented to students. Many school departments adopted innovative approaches, and there was a considerable creative input on the part of teachers and local authority advisers. Teaching schemes were designed and published with particular groups of students in mind, and others were written for use with mixed-ability classes. The Cockcroft recommendations (DES, 1982) helped to spread the expectation that students would experience a wide range of activities in mathematics lessons, including investigative work, which

165

was subsequently supported by GCSE coursework components. In the 1980s there was a particular drive to address the underachievement of female students, and more recently there have been more determined efforts to identify and address underachievement among other groups, including, for example, ethnic minority groups, students for whom English is an additional language and working-class boys. At the same time, there has been an ongoing trend, supported by government policy, for higher proportions of students with physical disabilities and learning difficulties to be educated within mainstream schools. This too has required teachers to give more thought to the inclusiveness of their teaching and, by bringing increasing numbers of support staff into mainstream classrooms, has provided many teachers with valuable opportunities to work alongside other adults with specialist knowledge and experience.

It is interesting and important to note that, even where innovative projects have set out to address the needs of specific groups, developments which have focused on enhancing mathematical learning have tended to produce beneficial effects on the learning of much wider groups of students as well. Some of these developments and the ways in which teachers have been involved in them will be described in more detail in the next chapter. We will now introduce some of the issues about 'mathematics for all' through the medium of three case studies derived from our observations of effective, inclusive teaching.

CASE STUDY A
Year 7 Mixed-ability class – angles in 2-D shapes

The students in this Year 7 class have been in secondary school for just over half a term and their teacher, Tim, has worked hard to establish and maintain positive attitudes to mathematics. Lessons so far have seemed busy and constructive, the transition from primary school appears to have gone well and their form tutor reports several cases of very favourable feedback from parents. The students are all from the same mixed-ability tutor group, but one of the boys, Stefan, has been withdrawn to the learning support unit within the school for all his lessons, on grounds of behaviour. Tim has been setting work for him in consultation with the teacher in the unit and it has been agreed that he rejoin the class for this lesson and, perhaps, for the remainder of the sequence of lessons. One of the targets in Stefan's individual education plan (IEP) is that he should concentrate for longer on set tasks, but he is also known to enjoy drawing patterns and scale diagrams, two of which are on display in the mathematics classroom. He has demonstrated an ability to work at level 6 in the area of number and Tim regularly provides him with the extension tasks that are the main activities for two other high-attaining students, Fran and Sunila.

The lesson topic is to be drawn from the section in the Year 7 scheme of work on identifying, estimating and measuring acute and obtuse angles in 2-D shapes. This is intended to consolidate work most of the students should have done in their primary school, while introducing them to the sum of angles at a point, on a straight line and in a triangle. Tim is unsure of the students' prior knowledge and understanding in the area of shape, space and measures. The focus during the first half-term was on number and half the class were working comfortably at the level 4/5 boundary, but there have been indications that some students, including Matthew who is described as dyslexic on the special educational needs register, have difficulty with directions (left/right) or with using rulers. Matthew produces very little written work but sometimes makes surprisingly perceptive points during discussions. Three other students have been working very slowly in most mathematics lessons and are heavily reliant on the teaching assistant, Remi, who is present for two out of the three lessons each week. Tim and Remi have begun to identify particular learning needs among this small group and expect that they will need support and encouragement to talk about angles. Two other students are in the early stages of learning to speak English but are coping very well with calculations involving number. They have support in some other lessons from a school specialist in English as an additional language (EAL). Tim has made an appointment to discuss the scheme of work with the specialist in order to identify particular linguistic demands and to enable her to reinforce mathematical language during sessions with the students. She has also agreed to talk with the newcomers about the mathematics they studied in their primary schools before they came to England.

Tim approaches his planning for the lessons about angles and 2-D shapes with the following priorities in mind:

- keeping the class working on the same mathematical topics, but differentiating to take into account the wide range of prior knowledge and understanding among the students;

- structuring lessons to provide a variety of activities and to include ways of learning which have emerged as preferences among groups of students;
- targeting the support from Remi and incorporating the advice from the EAL specialist.

After discussing with Remi, Tim comes up with the plan outlined below. We will try to make some of the thinking underlying the plan explicit and, in doing so, suggest some general approaches to planning for lessons that will include all members of a class.

Approaches to differentiation

Given the wide range of levels of attainment within this class and the variation in the prior experience of the students coming from different primary schools, ensuring that all the students are able to access the topic and are given opportunities to make progress in their knowledge and understanding is a major challenge for the teacher. At the same time, Tim thinks it is important to maintain the positive attitudes and involvement that he has seen are generated by the students working together as a whole class. There are a number of ways in which he might think about providing tasks for the students that will meet these criteria.

1   All students work on the same task but interpret it at different levels.

As he is not sure at this stage of the year what experience and levels of achievement all the students have in this new topic area, Tim chooses a starter task to which students can respond at a number of different levels. This will enable him to get a better feel for individual achievements and needs in order to target support and challenge better in later parts of the lesson and in subsequent lessons. The plenary discussion at the end of the lesson also encourages responses at various levels and again will allow Tim to evaluate the range of achievement in the class.

2   All students work on the same task, which is accessible to all at the beginning, but progress through it at different rates with only some reaching the more challenging later parts.

The whole class will be introduced to the idea of giving sets of instructions for drawing angles using the computer program Logo. During this lesson it is likely that the students will only make a start at this, but some will compose instructions for drawing more complex shapes when they do their homework. In the next lesson, when the students will work in pairs in a computer room, Tim anticipates that, while some continue to consolidate their understanding of angle as a measure of turn, others will progress to drawing shapes that will bring them to think about the relationships between angles.

3 **All students work on a task that is essentially the same but which may be adapted to make it more accessible or more challenging for some students. Some may be supported by working with peers or with an adult.**

Tim wants all the students to have some practical, physical experience of handling angles and decides to let pairs of students set each other challenges to make angles of specific sizes using hinged plastic strips. He anticipates that some in the class may have difficulty getting started on the task, so he plans how he will group them and how to deploy the additional adult support, and provides a poster with selected angles on it to allow students to check their work independently. The degree of accuracy expected will be higher for some students who are seen to be confident in their understanding of angle measurement.

4 **Students work on different (though related) tasks with varying levels of difficulty. Individuals may be directed to specific tasks or may be allowed to choose their own level of challenge.**

Towards the end of this lesson, Tim knows he will have a better idea of the range of knowledge and understanding of students within the class, so he plans to use a set of tasks, prepared on individual cards, with different levels of difficulty. To encourage students to feel more in control of their own learning, he allows students some degree of choice between the cards.

Providing a variety of approaches to learning

The plan for the lesson is divided into five separate stages, switching between whole class, paired and individual work. Tim intends the variety in the planned activities to help keep all the students involved and to provide as many as possible with tasks that will match their preferences, while also encouraging them to try other approaches to learning. He knows that some students, including Stefan, would find it more difficult to concentrate on a single task for a longer period of time. In a later lesson on this topic, he intends to try to engage the students in more extended work on an investigative task. He hopes that the practical drawing involved in this will help Stefan to maintain his concentration.

Because of the nature of the topic there is a lot of scope for visualisation, but Tim knows that some students will find this hard to cope with in an abstract way, so he plans to support it with an activity that involves getting a feel for angle by handling physical apparatus. Posters around the room will provide visual reminders and examples that students can choose to use when they feel the need. Some of the posters are intended to stimulate interest and imagination by showing photographs of angles occurring in the context of everyday objects, and in art and architecture.

The use of ICT is likely to be appreciated by the students for its own sake, but using Logo has the important characteristic of developing logical mathematical thinking and the use of formal language by insisting on instructions in a specific form and a correct order. The program gives immediate visual feedback and, after this introduction, will provide an environment for students to work independently and creatively during the next lesson in the computer room.

Making use of additional adult support and the advice of specialists

Tim and Remi are accustomed to working together to identify students' particular ways of carrying out mathematical tasks and then discussing how to intervene with individuals or small groups. This Year 7 class benefits enormously from the time set aside by the two adults to predict difficulties and to work through some mathematics together. Before planning, they discuss their observations about students' abilities to measure and estimate length, and their fluency in talking about directions. They make decisions about grouping the students for some tasks and which outcomes they expect from different groups. Remi has also worked with Stefan in the learning support unit and has talked to him about what will be expected of him when he is working with the whole class. This helps Tim and Remi to decide which other students Stefan should be asked to sit with. During the previous half-term it has become clear which other members of the class are most likely to need support during the lesson and Remi will, as usual, keep an eye on these students. Because of the nature of this new topic, Tim suspects that Matthew, the student identified as dyslexic, is likely to have problems with some aspects of the topic and may try to avoid taking part in some tasks; he makes sure that Remi is aware of the critical points in the lesson so that he will be ready to intervene if necessary.

The development of the mathematical vocabulary needed for this topic is an important objective for all the students and will be addressed especially during the whole class parts of the lesson. Tim will model the use of the mathematical language and will encourage students to use it themselves. The two students who have only recently arrived in the country are still at a stage of being hesitant to speak in whole class situations but, following the advice of the EAL specialist, Tim decides to pair them with other members of the class with whom they will feel comfortable to speak during other parts of the lesson. One will be paired with a bilingual student who can communicate with him both in English and in his home language, while the other will be paired with a girl with whom she has developed a close friendship. The cards with individual tasks are written in simple language, including the key mathematical vocabulary for the topic. These were developed by the mathematics department in conjunction with the EAL specialist the previous year.

Tim's plan

The plan we show in Table 9.1 is just one possibility. We have tried to indicate some of the ways in which a teacher might plan to address the sort of diversity and the individual needs described in this example. Of course, our description of the class can be only partial and Tim's lesson, however inclusive in its intentions, is not guaranteed to be successful. Importantly, the decisions that Tim made are not the only ones possible. A different teacher would probably make different choices and design a very different lesson. As we have said earlier, teaching can be thought of as an art, in which teachers choose and combine components in varying quantities to produce an overall desired effect.

171

Table 9.1 *Tim's lesson plan*

Teacher and student activities	Key issues/support/ assessment
Remember last lesson we measured the door frame. Now, imagine looking down on the door and the door frame from above. Imagine how what you see changes as the door is opened. Now make some sketches of what you see when the door is just a little bit open, half open, wide open.	Key words will be 'arms', 'vertex', 'acute angle', 'right angle', '90°', '45°', '0°', 'protractor' Remi: help those who can't get started on visualising and sketching.
Ask students to repeat their sketches on the overhead projector. Discuss sketches.	Stress idea that 'angle' is a measurement of how much one line turns away from another when the lines are joined together at a point. Identify who already seems secure with angle measurement.
Give out pairs of hinged plastic strips – two different sizes of strip. Hold up a right angle – an acute angle – an obtuse angle – an angle bigger/ smaller than this one. (Target those who used measurement language earlier.) Estimate the size of your angle in degrees.	Watch out for confusion between the size of angle and lengths of arms.
Work with a partner. Take turns to tell your partner what angle to make and check whether they are right. (Accuracy to nearest 10°.)	
Stefan to work with A (usually capable and even-tempered). Rashid to work with B (a bilingual student who shares his first language). Madalena to work with C (a girl with whom she has become quite friendly). Matthew to work with D, at the same table as Fran and Sunila.	Pairs to settle disputes by comparing with guide angles displayed on poster. Remi: check that Matthew does not avoid the practical work. Keep an eye on E, F, G, and if
Extension (for those finding it easy): measure the angles with a protractor (to the nearest degree).	

Table 9.1 *Tim's lesson plan* (continued)

Teacher and student activities	Key issues/support/ assessment
Challenge partner to make a second angle so that the two angles together make a straight line.	necessary put them with partners who will help them get started. Watch out for problems with dexterity; focus on turning; talk about the tasks.
Logo on interactive whiteboard (Remi operating computer.) Tell Mr R how far you want the arrow to move and then how much you want it to turn. Draw one acute angle, right angle, obtuse angle. Copy the instructions into notebooks – to be used next lesson in the computer room.	Target questions to involve everyone.
Homework: Write three more sets of instructions to draw different angles.	Make sure homework is noted in planners.
Has anyone used Logo before? What did you do with it? Bring any examples you have to show us next lesson.	
Distribute two task cards each. (Each card includes: sketch and measure a given angle; give the computer instructions for drawing an angle. Harder cards: find missing angles to make a straight line; instruct the computer to draw a triangle.) Encourage those who have found today's work easy to choose cards that ask them to draw triangles.	Check that students are working on appropriate cards. Computer instructions will be tried out next lesson – or students can try them out at lunch time using the computers in the library.
Plenary	
Look around the room. Where is an angle of 45°? Where is a shape with exactly 2 right angles? Describe this . . . Which is the biggest angle you can see? Estimate . . . Give me instructions to draw . . . etc. Bring in any photographs you have with interesting angles in them so that we can make a display.	Posters around the room include 2-D representations of 3-D objects, and one photographic enlargement of an open door.

CASE STUDY B
Year 8 class in a selective school – algebraic expression of linear relationships

This class is the second set out of three in a partially selective mixed school which has an entrance examination in mathematics and English, and a certain number of places reserved for students with a marked ability in music. Students are set in mathematics from the beginning of Year 7 on the basis of information from their primary schools and their results in the entrance examination, and re-set at the beginning of Year 8 following school examinations. Earlier in the unit of work on algebra, the teacher, Fazila, observed some common errors in multiplying brackets when negative numbers are involved and difficulties in re-writing linear equations in the form $y = mx + c$. When drawing graphs, many of the students are taking a long time to draw up tables of values of x and y, and then insist on plotting many points rather than the recommended three.

Despite the need for the students to become skilful at carrying out several procedures before the end-of-topic test, Fazila has decided to revisit some of the basic ideas that underpin an understanding of linear relationships. Although this is a 'setted' class and the textbook matches the National Curriculum levels that the students achieved six months ago, the approach to straight-line graphs does not seem to be enabling more than a few students to appreciate the power of equations and graphs to represent relationships between variables. The textbook concentrates on constructing graphs from linear equations and, although it provides lots of practice in drawing up tables of values from equations and plotting points, there are few opportunities for students to think about the meanings of the equations and graphs, or the contexts within which they might arise, or to make decisions about how to approach the set questions. This may be why some of them follow procedures so ponderously and why they make 'silly' mistakes. Fazila has observed the students' enthusiasm and creativity in some other subjects and during musical activities, and has real concerns that her mathematics lessons are unsuited to the learning styles of a significant number of the students. She feels that a more holistic approach in which there are seen to be several ways of representing relationships – giving an element of choice and opening up opportunities for discussion – will make the mathematics more accessible to the range of students in the class. Her priority in planning the next section of the unit of work on algebra is therefore to provide the students with a range of ways of thinking about, representing and working with linear relationships.

Alternative perspectives on algebraic relationships

Fazila decides to plan a 'lesson' extending over two forty-five minute lessons and the homework time in between them. The extension of a single structured plan over this period of time is intended to enable reflection, discussion about alternatives, time to practise and consolidate, and satisfactory displays of outcomes. The mathematical tasks will retain a focus on different ways of representing relationships: using visual patterns; in words; by means of algebraic equations in various forms; and graphically. The use of negative numbers and the technicalities of drawing graphs will, for the meantime, be secondary objectives – a natural part of the 'bigger picture'. For this case study, we will not give a detailed lesson plan, but will instead discuss the tasks used in different phases of the lesson and the ways in which they address Fazila's aim to develop a richer understanding of algebraic relationships in a way that is accessible to all the students, tapping into their creativity and enthusiasm.

1 From pattern-making to symbolising relationships

Fazila chooses to start the lesson with whole class discussion around a question about tiles around square ponds (see Figure 9.1). She knows the students met a similar problem in this context in Year 7 and believes that building on this will provide a smooth transition from the practical situation (placing tiles around squares on the overhead projector) to identifying the two variables, discussing the relationship between them in words, deciding on symbols for the variables and suggesting forms of algebraic equation.

The coherence between the forms of representation should become a lot clearer during a whole class discussion which is allowed to run its course – back and forward from one representation to another with plenty of thinking time and choice. It is likely that different students will perceive the physical situation in different ways and will suggest alternative algebraic expressions for the relationship between the length of the side of the pond and the number of tiles required (see Figure 9.2 for some examples). This will provide a useful opportunity for reinforcing

175

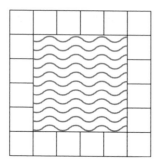

How many tiles would be
needed to go round a
square pond of side ...?

Figure 9.1 *The tile problem*

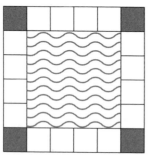

The number of tiles needed is 4 times the
length of the side, plus 4 for the corners.

$n = 4l + 4$

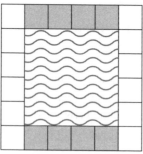

The number of tiles needed is 2 times the
length of the side, plus 2 times two more
than the length of the side.

$n = 2l + 2(l + 2)$

Figure 9.2 *Alternative ways of seeing and representing the tile problem*

students' skills in manipulating algebraic expressions, as well as emphasising the idea of equivalence, and enabling students to recognise and
value their own ways of understanding.

Eventually, Fazila hopes that the students will perceive an equation
such as $n = 4l + 4$ as a neat way of expressing the relationship, an

algebraic form which has emerged from a particular situation and which can be adapted to other situations. The class will also work together on constructing graphs from the equations, with volunteers plotting points on prepared axes on the overhead projector.

2 Making connections between representations

Fazila has made laminated cards that give verbal descriptions of situations involving different types of relationships between variables, not all linear. Working in groups, the students will be asked to interpret and discuss three of the contrasting situations, decide which quantities are the variables, draw up a table of values, write an equation and sketch a possible graph. This will all be recorded informally and the main outcome will be to decide which relationships are linear and which are non-linear. Fazila anticipates that, by working in groups, most of the problems the students were having with graphing will sort themselves out as members of the group discuss and correct each other; if sketching graphs continues to be a serious problem for any group, she plans to give them a graphical calculator to support their work. When she visits the groups Fazila may ask questions about other aspects, such as negative numbers, slope, intercepts, changing the subject and extending the graphs beyond the given domain, but the focus will remain firmly on the main objective of understanding the connection between different representations of relationships between variables.

The homework period will involve the students in creative, individual extensions to this theme. Each student from every group will take responsibility for one question similar to those worked on in class. They will work on it at home and bring in an account of the mathematics to explain to the group at the start of the next lesson. Each student will also be expected to design another situation that is similar mathematically to the one they are working on. Peer assessment is likely to demand some degree of creativity and clarity!

During the second lesson each group of students will be expected to prepare a poster to display the three types of relationships they have been studying and to be able to explain their work to the class if selected to do so. When the presentations are complete, Fazila will initiate discussion of the different kinds of relationship, encouraging the students to express generalisations and to think and talk about the shapes of graphs holistically rather than on a point-by-point basis. She will use a demonstration graphical calculator to display some of the equations and their graphs, and will invite students to suggest other equations that might have similar graphs. In a future lesson, the students will use graphical calculators themselves to explore the properties of graphs.

3 Focus on understanding as well as skills

Although the objectives given in the school's scheme of work emphasise the skills the students should acquire, Fazila's plan does not take the development and practice of these skills as its main focus. By providing opportunities for all the students to explore and develop meaning for different representations of relationships between variables, she anticipates that they will improve their ability to monitor their performance of the required skills, noticing for themselves when answers do not make sense. Of course, she will also take the opportunity during the various stages of the lesson to draw students' attention to critical skills where these are relevant.

The extensive use of whole class discussion and small group work, coupled with the opportunities for students to use their imagination creatively, match Fazila's observations of ways of working that the students have engaged in with enthusiasm in other subject areas. She hopes that, by matching her teaching more to their learning styles, the students will be more likely to engage with the mathematical content of the lessons and less likely to be prepared to follow procedures without thinking or to accept answers that fail to make sense.

CASE STUDY C
Year 10 Lower intermediate set – ratio and similarity

This is the third set out of four drawn from one band of a mixed comprehensive school. The sets were selected largely on the basis of the results of the Key Stage 3 tests taken the previous summer. From their experience in previous years with students who gained similar levels at Key Stage 3, the mathematics department anticipates that only a few of the students in this class are likely to gain more than a grade D in their GCSE examinations the next year and have designed a scheme of work accordingly, aiming to cover the material needed for the Intermediate GCSE syllabus, while concentrating on consolidating the more basic topics. The students have come from two different Year 9 classes and their mathematics teacher, Stella, is aware of resentment from the students from one of these classes. These students feel they were at a disadvantage in the Key Stage 3 tests as they were taught by a succession of supply teachers after their regular teacher resigned halfway through the year. They resent being put into a lower set than they think they deserve and, although some were achieving more in mathematics during Years 7 and 8, their attitudes now seem to be preventing them from making progress. Stella has already fielded comments such as 'We've done this before', 'There's no point in working if I'm only going to get a low grade' and 'What's the use of this after I've left school?' Stella realises that she will need to provide for a range of levels and also to try to promote more positive attitudes to the subject among the significant vocal minority. If young people disengage from mathematics at this point in their education, it can become a major barrier to further development of the problem-solving and mathematical reasoning skills that they will need in the future. The students are approaching adulthood, and Stella thinks they may respond to more mature ways of working and to the presentation of topics in extended forms. As she plans a sequence of lessons on ratio and similarity, she decides to break away from the step-by-step approach often used in the school with such groups and to structure the unit of work as an extended project focusing on the following objectives:

- making explicit links with some areas of working life;
- helping the students to develop greater awareness of their progress towards GCSE and of their own needs to understand and apply mathematics.

Making links with working life

Stella plans the unit of work as a two-week project, starting with an out-of-school visit to a workplace. The students will visit the Town Hall where they will hear about alternative plans for a new leisure centre. Mathematical themes will be introduced in the contexts of scale modelling, financial planning and environmental considerations. Stella has talked with the council officers who will be giving the presentations and has explained her goal that the students should get a flavour of how mathematics and its application through the use of technology is an essential component of the work of the Planning Department. The officers are dynamic and committed young adults and are drawn from a cross-section of ethnic groups in the town. Stella thinks that they should provide positive role models for the students.

Stella's aim of encouraging the students to see their GCSE mathematics as a foundation for developing and applying their knowledge in the future will, however, only be realised if the students perceive links between topics studied in school and what they might be expected to do at work. They will need to be able to imagine themselves in the working environment and to anticipate that they will be comfortable there. Only then will many students develop the commitment to learn and to control their own learning. Following the visit, she designs a series of lessons, including homework, in which students will work in groups on projects set in the context of planning in the local community. The tasks involved in these projects will focus on essential aspects of ratio and similarity through working with scale models and enlargement. Students will be able to use relevant ICT packages at various points in their projects and Stella consults with her colleagues in the geography, science and art departments to enable students to use materials and knowledge from these subject areas during their project work.

Helping students develop awareness of their progress and learning needs

At the end of each lesson some of the groups report briefly on their progress and respond to questioning from other groups and from Stella. This is intended to help them to evaluate and monitor their work, and to take responsibility for the progress of their projects.

As well as working in groups on their projects, the students are regularly given individual homework sheets focusing on the mathematical content with straightforward practice questions and questions similar to those they are likely to encounter in the GCSE examination. This homework is reviewed in class and students are helped to identify those areas of the topic with which they are having difficulty, and to set themselves realistic challenges and targets. In the longer term, Stella plans to continue this approach to consolidation and self-monitoring when she works with this class on other topics. In particular, she intends to start helping some of the students to see what they would need to do in order to achieve a higher GCSE grade at the end of the next year.

PATHWAYS AND BARRIERS TO INCLUSION

The case studies we have presented draw attention to some of the implications of having inclusive aims for mathematics education within and beyond the school curriculum. They demonstrate some of the challenges and suggest how rewarding such teaching can be. Of course, these few examples have not allowed us to address the full range of circumstances faced by mathematics teachers and learners. Barriers to learning come in various forms and they are unevenly distributed between schools. Substantial consideration of inequalities within the educational system as a whole is outside the scope of this book, but their effects on students' learning and the professional development of teachers are likely to be apparent from examples such as those we have chosen. We shall briefly address three such factors, each of which may have had an impact on the students and teachers involved in the cases studies.

The availability and deployment of support staff

We saw in Case Study A the benefits that can accrue from working with other adults both at the planning stage and in the classroom. Tim is fortunate to have the support of Remi and to have been able to make use of the experience and knowledge of an EAL specialist. His school has systems and resources to support the learning of a wide range of students. Importantly, however, Tim himself has realised the importance of making use of the specialist knowledge and experience offered by support staff and specialists, and has made time to consult and plan together. Through working with Remi to support a dyslexic student, he has learnt more about this condition and is better prepared to support other such students in the future. Similarly, his discussion with an EAL specialist and collaboration at departmental level have helped him to distinguish between the language and mathematical needs of the two students in the early stages of learning English and to know some strategies for providing appropriately for them. Classroom support is very limited in most schools, and dependent on the ways that restricted resources for learning support are distributed within the school; this makes dialogue between mathematics teachers and support staff all the more important.

The extent of the inclusion of students with emotional and behavioural difficulties, and school policies and procedures for supporting them and their teachers

One of the significant differences between schools is the proportion of students described as having emotional and behavioural difficulties (EBD). It is also one of the main issues in the debate about the extent to which schools should be inclusive and one of the unintended outcomes of the diversity of educational provision overall. We have provided the merest glimpse of the way that School A provides for the learning of a boy whose behaviour had led to his temporary exclusion from the mainstream classroom. We have seen that Tim and Remi have strategies for integrating Stefan, but these are dependent on him responding positively to the chosen approaches to the mathematical topic and conforming to the expectations which have been made clear to him. Other students may have more difficulty integrating into mainstream classes in ways that are positive for their own learning and for that of other students.

Selection between and within schools

It is sometimes suggested that students will learn better and that teachers will find it easier to teach in classes, or even in schools, in which students are selected according to some measure of attainment. The problems of inclusion will be less, it is argued, if students at similar levels of attainment are put to learn together. This argument does not, however, take into account the many individual ways in which students learn what appears to be similar mathematics in order to achieve these levels. We have seen in Case Study B how Fazila was concerned that her students, apparently selected within a narrow band of attainment, needed a wider range of ways of thinking about relationships between variables than that provided by the textbook aimed at their level. No class, however selective, is entirely homogeneous and there is always a need to be aware of individual understandings, motivations and approaches to learning. It is also important to remember that, while it is often claimed that mathematics is a hierarchical subject that can be defined, as it is in the National

Curriculum, as a sequence of levels, students do not necessarily learn in the same hierarchical way. An individual who appears to be achieving generally at, say, Level 5 in the 'Number' part of the curriculum may also have significant gaps or strengths in their knowledge and understanding of number, while their achievement in other parts of the curriculum may be entirely different.

While selective schools (all or a proportion of whose students are high attainers across subjects or in a specialist area) and 'top sets' in non-selective schools (classes whose students are selected according to some measure of mathematical attainment) may appear to provide atmospheres that are conducive to learning, the evidence that they produce better results is weak (see, for example, Venkatakrishnan and Wiliam, 2003). At the same time, those with behavioural or learning difficulties are likely to be concentrated in the other schools and classes, amplifying the problems faced by teachers. We saw in Case Study C how selection, possibly founded on uncertain grounds, can contribute to disaffection; this is true not only for relatively low-attaining students, but also for those in higher sets who find that their preferred learning styles do not match the teaching provided (Boaler *et al.*, 2000).

Whatever the policy on selection in your school, it is important to be aware of the consequences that it may have for students and of possible inequities that may arise. Although all students in England and Wales have an entitlement to be taught the National Curriculum, the extent to which they have access to the higher levels of the curriculum depends on the teaching and other resources provided for them. This becomes particularly critical at Key Stage 4, when the National Curriculum itself is divided into 'Foundation' and 'Higher' programmes of study. The Foundation Programme of Study is intended to provide appropriately for those students who have not achieved Level 5 securely by the end of Key Stage 3 but, by restricting the mathematical topics that such students have the opportunity to study, it limits their opportunities to progress to higher levels. However successful they may be, the restricted curriculum is likely to form a barrier to entry to Intermediate or Higher level GCSE examinations and hence will prevent students from achieving the crucial 'C' grade.

Throughout this chapter we have used a broad definition of 'inclusion', focusing on the aim of enabling all students to engage with mathematics in ways that allow them to understand what they are doing

183

and to use mathematics in meaningful ways. In order to achieve this for all students it is necessary to recognise the ways in which their existing understandings, motivations and approaches to learning may differ. This may seem an impossible task when you contemplate the thirty or so individuals in each of your classes. It is clear that you cannot be expected to plan separately for each one. In some cases, individual students will have specific requirements that do need to be taken into account so that they can access the curriculum at all. We saw some examples of this in Case Study A where the teaching team made concrete plans to support individuals with learning and behavioural difficulties, and in the early stages of learning English. In other cases, such as those exemplified in Case Studies B and C, a more general knowledge of the class and awareness of the variation in approaches to learning and in motivation is likely to be sufficient. The detailed planning and preparation of resources that we have described in each of the case studies is clearly time-consuming. However, as thinking inclusively becomes an automatic part of a teacher's planning process, the time required reduces; successful strategies for inclusion become part of their repertoire and they build up a set of resources and approaches to teaching particular topics from which they select to suit their classes.

The examples that we have looked at have not specifically addressed the underachievement of certain social groupings. This is not because of a lack of concern for the possible exclusion from learning mathematics of, say, working-class students or students of Afro-Caribbean background. A full discussion of the ways in which the culture of mainstream schools may disadvantage students in these groups is beyond the scope of this book. However, we have attempted throughout not only this chapter but also other chapters to illustrate how mathematics teachers can plan to engage all their students in meaningful mathematics by recognising and taking into account a wide variety of motivations and approaches to learning. We have also tried to communicate an image of mathematics itself that is broad and inclusive: mathematics may be rigorous, certain, game-like, aesthetically pleasing, and at the same time embedded in culture and connected to real human endeavour. Communicating this view of the breadth of mathematics is an important way of enabling all students to recognise that they can participate in doing mathematics and that the subject has something to offer them.

THINKING ABOUT PRACTICE

- How can the specialist knowledge and expertise of support staff be used to best effect in the busy life of the school?
- When planning a sequence of activities, what types of learning preferences are being met and which are being neglected?
- How may grouping students (within the school, in an individual class, or even for a particular activity) affect the opportunities that individual students have for effective learning?

Chapter 10

Teachers and mathematics curriculum development

KEY QUESTIONS

■ Is the job of teaching mathematics always going to be the same?
■ How might you be able to use your knowledge of mathematics in a changing world to influence changes on a variety of levels?

Mathematics teaching is currently informed and framed by detailed descriptions of what to teach, and when and how to teach it. For new teachers it sometimes appears that the curriculum is outside their control, imposed by the authority of the government, examination syllabus or textbook. It is a common experience to feel that their own mathematical knowledge is not valued and their own ideas about how to teach are not respected. Yet others are grateful for the level of support provided by documentation and happily fit into its structures and adopt its suggestions.

In this chapter we are going to describe several ways of working professionally with given curricula, using the recent UK context as an example. We start by discussing the genesis and associated issues concerning the given curriculum, then we describe some ways in which teachers can contribute to its development, including those that are inevitable in their own reflective practice.

THE GENESIS OF THE NATIONAL CURRICULUM

The UK mathematics curriculum has a statutory, legal framework which describes what state-funded schools must teach as a minimum requirement. This National Curriculum (NC) was established after the Education Reform Act of 1988. Originally, it was intended to be a document showing what students were entitled to be taught, and the committee putting it together produced hierarchies of mathematical content under fourteen different headings, graded according to ten levels. This created 140 cells of curriculum content. Most of these were similar to the previously existing curricula, conforming and leading up to what was normally examined at age 16+.

The form and content of the NC was greatly informed by the Cockcroft (DES, 1982) report in which mathematicians, teachers, educators, industrialists, trainers and politicians had agreed that both the content and the teaching style of school mathematics should more closely resemble what would be needed for future economic and academic activity. The introduction of 'Using and Applying' as a named feature of NC mathematics changed the demands of mathematics teaching so that it was no longer acceptable for students to be taught only how to do certain techniques – they had also to be taught how to explore mathematics and how to use mathematics to work on contextual problems. The statutory nature of the NC also made it the legal right of all students to be taught arithmetic, algebra, geometry and statistics, whereas it had been common practice to teach a minority of weaker students only 'everyday' or 'domestic' arithmetic.

Emphasis on the use, application and development of mathematical thinking, along with the increased emphasis on data handling, meant that some other aspects of mathematics had to be reduced. The most obvious omissions were algebraic manipulation for its own sake, such as handling algebraic fractions, and formal geometric proofs. Geometry was called 'shape and space' and consisted largely of knowledge about shapes and their properties, and a transformational approach to reasoning about them. The place of geometry in the school curriculum has been under discussion for decades. Before the 1960s, the geometry curriculum consisted almost totally of Euclidean theorems, proofs and riders, and while for some this was an enriching experience which laid the foundations of mathematical argument, others had to reproduce and apply rote-learnt proofs with little idea of what they meant. The foundation of the Association of Teachers of Mathematics (ATM) was partly a response to the knowledge that there were more interesting ways – transformational ways, for example – to work with spatial mathematics. Gradually, proof fell out of the school curriculum before A-level. More recently, geometrical proof has been reintroduced, due in part to pressure from university mathematicians, and some new teachers currently find themselves teaching it without having ever studied it as learners.

Similarly, some teachers had to learn from scratch about probability and harder statistical concepts, having never studied them before. In fact, the probability requirements of the early NC turned out to underestimate the difficulty of the concepts, and this was one topic which eventually disappeared from primary schools, to the great relief of some primary teachers who had found it hard to teach and some secondary teachers who felt its early introduction had done more harm than good! It would be good to be able to report that this change came about through consultation with teachers, but in fact such consultation was a long time coming, and there was much frustration at the start of the NC, particularly among primary teachers, at a lack of consultation and the sense of being overwhelmed with imposed innovations. At the time of writing this sense has not subsided; there have been changes in the secondary mathematics curriculum in every year since 1988! Some have been generally welcomed by teachers, like the reduction of the NC from fourteen to five, and then to four, attainment targets, thus making the whole structure simpler. Also of interest to teachers was the reduction in the detail of what is prescribed at the higher levels, in contrast to the introduction of much more prescription for teaching at Key Stage 3 (discussed in the next section).

This brief outline slides over much that was controversial in the design and development of the NC. What started as a slow consultative process of development became a rapid, politically motivated imposed change. This is described in detail by Brown (1996) and marked the beginning of an era in which mathematics teaching has continued to be politicised, with direction often given by those outside mathematics education and even, on occasion, by those outside mathematics.

It is worth remembering that the NC is a *minimum* requirement; schools can teach more mathematics to some or all students if they choose, and individual teachers can step outside the NC whenever they like, so long as they teach the legal minimum to everyone. We want to emphasise this to *everyone*, because within schools it is not clear that this is always followed. Students in lower mathematics sets sometimes are not taught everything in the NC, and this decision may be made by individual teachers or by the head of department on the basis of beliefs that certain students 'cannot cope'. After Key Stage 3, when students are

14 years old, this decision can be made legitimately through differential curriculum tracking, but before that stage limitations on what is taught are generally in conflict with the statutory guidelines.

In practice, most schools *only* teach what is in the NC. The positive side of this decision is that they can focus on covering what they legally have to do and thus be accountable in their use of public money. Additionally, it means that there is a common language with which teachers from different schools can communicate, and common assumptions make it easier for students and teachers who change schools. The negative side of this is that there is constant time-pressure on the way teachers organise their subject matter, and any deviation from plans can make teachers, departments and schools feel vulnerable under inspection. Also, little time may be made to explore topical or challenging aspects of the subject, or to use the particular knowledge of expert teachers to devise more holistic approaches to the subject.

For example, it is possible to devise an approach to teaching students about graphs which integrates real-life contexts, functions (including sinusoidal and exponential curves), rates of change, algebraic and pre-calculus concepts to, say, average 13-year-olds supported by the use of ICT and curriculum materials such as those produced by Shell (Joint Matriculation Board and Shell Centre for Mathematical Education, 1985). However, very few teachers would do this, because calculus appears nowhere in the NC and extended time is needed to consolidate and make deeply connected sense of this holistic experience. Similarly, it would be valuable to spend a long time with Year 7 students establishing the habits of enquiry and generalisation that characterise better learners of mathematics throughout secondary school. However, very few teachers do this because there is so much content to 'cover' in the time available, particularly in the schemes of work offered by the National Mathematics Framework.

In Chapter 8, we mentioned the statutory testing regime overlaid on to the NC. While this has the effect of forcing teachers and schools to do what is statutorily required, it also skews the treatment of the curriculum towards what is to be tested. Thus, while the approaches described in the previous paragraph could be justified in terms of mathematical learning, they cannot be justified in terms of covering the syllabus for national tests. Interestingly, there is research which shows that covering the curriculum is not the only, or necessarily the best, way to do well in tests – but we shall return to this later (and see Boaler, 1997; Schoenfeld, 2002).

189

THE NATIONAL FRAMEWORK

While it is not statutory, the mathematics curriculum in lower secondary schools is currently dominated by the Key Stage 3 Strategy and its National Framework for Teaching Mathematics. This is classified as guidance for teaching the NC, but it is often treated as a statutory document in its own right by government, schools and inspectors. This is not surprising as the documents make it very clear that teachers are expected to use it 'or be able to justify not doing so by reference to what they are doing' (DfES, 2001: 2). Its aims are to support the raising of expectations and achievement in lower secondary mathematics through provision of yearly teaching programmes, planning charts, key objectives, examples of lesson plans, advice on teaching and so on. Much of this advice is excellent and based on research or on 'drawing on the best practice in secondary schools'. But in its desire to provide all teachers with the raw materials for good teaching, it presents as almost statutory teaching practices which, while better than having students working silently through textbooks or following a lonely pathway through programmed worksheets, are not the only good ways to teach.

For example, the claim that all lessons *should* have clear objectives known by students from the start outlaws teaching which generates surprise results. The claim that a high proportion of lesson time *should* be used for demonstration, illustration, instruction and dialogue, effectively outlaws teaching that develops students' personal enquiry and exploratory habits. The yearly programmes, which, for example, suggest five chunks of roughly six hours each for algebra, effectively outlaw extended work on developing algebraic thinking and may indeed encourage the kind of fragmentary, technique-focused approaches which failed students in the past. All these items of guidance have been given to avoid what might be worse, but may restrict what could be better.

Since these ideas did not arise from the desk of a civil servant, but came from existing good practice, we want to consider how such good practice developed in the first place. The way forward for trained, specialist mathematics teachers may be to accept what is currently statutory, to treat guidelines as merely guidelines, and to look for ways to further develop practice so that they become a source of ideas for 'best' practice in the future. For non-specialist teachers, the materials and guidelines may be crucial to supporting their work in ensuring high expectations of all students.

The alternative is to accept guidelines as instructions, but this perception can lead to teaching that follows routine patterns, allowing little space for professional creativity, for critical engagement with alternative content and teaching methods, or for positive consideration of the local conditions within which you will work. The tediously repetitive lessons which many students had to suffer in the past, in which the pattern was to watch what the teacher did and then do some similar exercises until they became stuck (two-part lessons), or to work through pages of textbooks without any overall sense of mathematical development (one-part lessons), may be replaced by lessons which are always in three parts and hence just as repetitive, predictable and likely to lead to stereotypical behaviour as any other repeated pattern (see Askew and Brown, 2001, for evidence of this in the primary sector).

For the time being, of course, you have to establish yourself within the practices of the school in which you are working and in relation to the practices of your departmental colleagues – it may seem as if you are destined always to be told what to teach and how and when to teach it. There is, however, a long tradition of active teacher involvement in mathematics curriculum development at national and local level, as well as in individual departments and classrooms. The team that produced the Cockcroft report included several teachers, as have most teams initiating major innovations since. You do not have to wait to be invited to join a major project in order to make changes in the curriculum.

The rest of this chapter will outline some of the ways in which teachers learn from, inform and support each other about such developments.

PROFESSIONAL ASSOCIATION

Some teachers belong to professional subject associations. The Association of Teachers of Mathematics and the Mathematical Association[1] are the appropriate bodies for mathematics teachers and both publish journals that offer ideas and debates about relevant issues. In some other countries, membership of such associations is huge, and the attendance numbers at conferences are several thousand; in this country combined attendance numbers at conferences are only a few hundred. In Sweden, Portugal and New Zealand attendance numbers are over ten times as high, for the population, as they are in the UK. It is hard to identify reasons for this; some suggest that having two associations is confusing, but the reason is more likely to be found in the history of how mathematics has traditionally been taught and beliefs about learning.

Until recently, secondary mathematics teaching was dominated by textbooks, and schools would generally adopt a particular series and use that as a major resource. Thus, there seemed to be no need to think further about the curriculum or teaching methods beyond what was provided and assumed by the publishers. The fact that production of the most dominant textbook series involved the active participation of practising teachers meant that users could believe that any problems had been ironed out somewhere else. The fact that the series contained multi-tracking structures and its own national examination gave teachers the feeling that, by using the series, they did indeed belong to some professional club with an agreed language, aims and standards.

The dominant view of learning mathematics was that a few would be very good, most would be average and there would be a trail of those who found it too hard – and there was little you could do to change this. No one had challenged this by suggesting that the job of educators was to help *everyone* to reach an acceptable minimum level of mathematical knowledge, and it is this challenge (which, unfortunately for the profession, came from politicians outside the field rather than from within) that has led to imposed curricula, targets and methods.

So what is professional association and what does it enable teachers to do? At its most basic, working with colleagues to ensure you do the best you can, sharing ideas and supporting each other are things that all teachers can do within school structures. Many departmental meetings are dominated by discussions about administration, but there are exceptions. One head of department deals with administration on paper and by email so that meetings are free for discussions of how colleagues teach certain topics or how they structure their planning. Another confesses himself to be unable to do paperwork, so the only option open to him is to use meetings to report back to colleagues about what he is thinking about on his current professional development course. A third includes in meetings mathematical puzzles for colleagues to work on and discuss. Another sees it as his job to sort out the administration so that staff can spend meetings sharing ideas about teaching techniques. These represent professional association with a small 'p' and show that, in a non-threatening environment, learning from each other is an acceptable and enriching way to work.

In Japan this practice is expected of teachers. They meet and plan together, use, evaluate and refine each other's plans, and many are published in journals. In France, this work is less widespread, but several groups exist to work in this way with professional researchers to support the work. It is sometimes described as 'didactic engineering', thus bringing to mind the typical engineering development process of trial and adjustment. These approaches contrast strongly with the implication in the Framework and on many websites that lesson plans and teaching methods can be picked up without modification and used successfully by any teacher.

At a local level, the national associations have branch meetings at which people can discuss their work in similar ways, or they may have input from invited outsiders who show resources, promote discussion, or offer help or support with new ideas. This is refreshingly different from the top-down model of training associated with imposed change, in which teachers are told what to do by trainers in whom they may have little confidence.

At a national level, as well as promulgating development through the publication of professional journals, members of the associations form interest and working groups to develop ideas and practices, which may then be published in some form. There are numerous examples of these and several of them have, over the years, contributed to what is now regarded as 'best practice'. In addition, many widely known ways of teaching certain topics started life as ideas in such working groups. Here, then, is one answer to the question 'How did good practice develop before we were all told what to do?'

There are many outstanding examples of teaching strategies, now central to the school curriculum, which were at one time developed and published by associations. Here are a few:

- getting students to investigate mathematics for themselves;
- recognising the power of students' own methods;
- emphasising the development of mathematical thinking;
- using paper-folding and cutting to explore geometric properties;
- involving students in activity, rather than assuming passive learning.

In each case, professional associations provided the forum in which ideas could be worked on and developed among colleagues.

PROFESSIONAL DEVELOPMENT

The fact that learning to teach does not stop when formal training ends is recognised in the provision of professional development courses of a variety of kinds. Some are short courses during which teachers are taught to use new software or are introduced to new guidelines; others are extended courses run by higher education institutions, leading to diplomas or higher degrees. These vary in type, some involving a significant amount of teaching, while others are based more on supporting action research. In each kind, there is usually an extended dissertation related to the teacher's own practice. It is possible to use these courses to do individual curriculum development work, although it is also usual for mathematics teachers to study generic aspects of teaching. We are going to report on a case in which a potentially significant contribution to curriculum change was a result of individual professional development work.

EXAMPLE

Jackie Fairchild pursued a diploma course in which she could choose to develop an aspect of her practice with the support of a higher education tutor and access to libraries and other research facilities. She had developed a belief that some of her Year 7 students might be better able to understand the role of the unknown in linear expressions and equations if she could offer them a diagrammatic representation so they could visualise its meaning. She found through guided, focused reading that similar ideas had been explored by researchers and, indeed, had ancient historical roots (e.g. Fauvel and Gray, 1987). Thus she was able to build her ideas on the foundations of previous work done by others and was sure she was not 're-inventing the wheel'. The ideas are slightly too complex to introduce here, but a general idea can be achieved by imagining a rectangle in which one side is the unknown x and the other is a known value, say, 4. Thus the area of the rectangle is $4x$. Keeping the same length for x, another expression can be built, $2x + 6$, by having a rectangle and 6 extra unit squares. Knowing that these are equal, i.e. $4x = 2x + 6$, is the same as knowing that their areas are equal, so that students can play around with the shapes on the right-hand side to make a complete rectangle, thus showing that x is 3. (See Figure 10.1.)

194

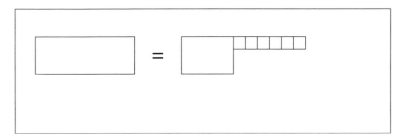

Figure 10.1 $4x = 2x + 6$

The discipline of the diploma course and her own self-doubt led Jackie to test her approach with other classes, used by other teachers, against control groups taught in more traditional, symbolic ways. Her own classes and those of other teachers using the approach did much better in post-tests than the control classes.

Even allowing for important doubts about whether the control groups were appropriate matches for the experimental groups, this project has created wide interest. In addition, the study has an interesting feature in that the ideas of one teacher were also successful when others used them. This is not always the case, since anyone's good ideas are necessarily a product of their own situation and beliefs, and what works with one teacher may not work with another. In this study, however, there was time to work together and discuss issues as they arose. Thus, what started as the professional development of one teacher extended to become a professional dialogue with colleagues, leading to effective curriculum development.

TEACHERS' ACTION RESEARCH

Jackie's work had benefited from her association with an institution that provided research facilities and support. A particularly powerful form of involvement in curriculum development is through engaging in research, because the work can be supported by literature, evaluated in valid ways and discussed with others who have a more theoretical perspective than immediate colleagues. Teacher-researchers address issues that are relevant in their own contexts, generating new knowledge about teaching and learning to inform their own professional development, as well as contributing to the knowledge and decision-making of the wider professional community. This mechanism for development is recognised by the provision of funding to individuals and groups of teachers to carry out supported projects in their own schools. An example of this is the use Jim Noble and Rob Shadbolt made of Best Practice Research Scholarships (BPRS). They worked in the same school and thus were able to create their own critical collegial research community. They chose to use the money to fund the development of curriculum materials using the context of 'food' to frame extended mathematical exploration which, while it contained several opportunities for students to engage with the mathematics of the statutory curriculum, also enabled them to raise their own questions and lines of investigation, thus embedding mathematics in socially meaningful practices and improving motivation for arithmetic and data-handling.

A group of three teachers attached to the University of Birmingham also worked together, supported by BPRS awards, and similarly found themselves seeking to extend the duration of tasks they offered students. Contrary to the model suggested by the Framework, they found that they could get their weakest students to question, explore and respond to complex, mysterious, mathematical situations. Thus, what started as a desire to improve their teaching became a move towards developing extended tasks. This kind of focusing is a typical result of action research, as teacher-researchers systematically plan to act in certain ways, evaluate the results of their actions and use their analysis to identify more specific features on which they wish to work to get certain effects. Of course, the initial choice of focus, and the way results are interpreted, will depend on the teacher's beliefs about teaching and learning. Ideally, these will be informed by reading research about similar situations.

In one case the teacher had such faith in the action-research process that she failed to cover all the topics that were expected by the NC, but her students significantly surpassed expectations in their national tests, some of them apparently leaping two levels in one year! Here is an example of the phenomenon described earlier, that curriculum coverage is not necessarily the best or only way to improve attainment in tests. This teacher's results have not yet been published, but similar phenomena have been reported elsewhere.

CURRICULUM DEVELOPMENT PROJECTS

In Boaler's (1997) study, students at one of two contrasting research schools performed similarly to the matched school in procedural test questions, but did significantly better in questions that required them to use mathematical knowledge. This was also true in a pilot study with another pair of schools. What was happening in the schools whose students did better? Amazingly, the students in those schools were not covering the curriculum completely or in great detail; instead, they were exploring mathematical situations and focusing on thinking and reasoning. In particular, they had not had the full drilling and test preparation that students in the comparison schools had; they had not been taught everything they needed to apply in the tests; and they had very little experience of practising procedures and techniques. What they had was excellent preparation for working with unfamiliar mathematical situations, so that is what they did in the examination! There were ways in which they could have done even better in the tests, and the weaknesses of the school's approach are made clear in Boaler's book, but the basic message is echoed in a paper by Schoenfeld (2002) in which similar results were found in Pittsburgh. Again, the emphasis of the teaching had been on the development of mathematical problem-solving rather than on the building of a knowledge bank; again, students did as well as anyone else on procedural questions and far better on less straightforward questions.

The reason for writing about these two professional research projects here is that they both act as evaluations for the curriculum development projects which inspired the teachers to take this approach to teaching. There are two main models for this kind of work: in one, the outsiders ask the teachers to use materials or methods so that these can be tested before wider dissemination; in the other, teachers are themselves intimately involved in the development work from the beginning.

In the 1970s, the Inner London Education Authority funded the creation of the SMILE (Secondary Mathematics Individualised Learning Experience) project to produce curriculum materials that could be used in secondary schools to support mathematics teaching. This was driven by a vision of teaching that would:

- allow individuals to progress at their own pace;
- provide interesting and varied kinds of task;
- respond to individual strengths and needs;

- allow mixed ability teaching;
- allow full integration of students from all cultural and language backgrounds into mainstream classes; and, incidentally,
- provide access to mathematics for those whose teachers might not be very well qualified.

Teachers were recruited to run the project and most materials were designed primarily by teachers, and then tested and developed by others in the project. Regular reviews and rewritings took place to ensure that the users' experiences and ideas had priority in the development of the scheme. The project, which still exists in a slightly different form, held frequent meetings and conferences at which teachers could discuss their daily, local knowledge of teaching in their very diverse classrooms. The scheme has occasionally been used in an unacceptable way as a sort of robotic teacher, but the positive long-term effects of the heyday of SMILE still exist in the rich bank of materials produced, the professionalism of the teachers who have been involved with the scheme, the fundamental beliefs about access to mathematics for all, and the model of teachers who are able to make central, effective and valid curriculum decisions.

In the late 1980s, the Association of Teachers of Mathematics convened a group of teachers representing several schools to develop ways of teaching and assessing mathematics through activity and extended tasks, rather than by learning mathematics as a collection of techniques assessed by timed, written tests. The aim was to explore ways in which authentic mathematical activity could be the main teaching mode. Students would be assessed on a wide range of mathematical behaviour, such as:

- mathematical communication
- reasoning
- interpretation
- mathematical attitude
- knowledge
- the application and creation of knowledge, etc.

The project had to ensure that through this approach students would learn meaningful, recognisable mathematics and achieve standards that were comparable, or beyond, those who were learning in other ways.

198

Teachers ran the project themselves, and much of the development work involved discussing ideas for mathematical exploration and evaluating the work that students produced as a result. Each participating school created a curriculum which went far beyond a list of topics to be 'covered', both in its expectations of students and in the complexity of the mathematics explored. For example, it was not unusual to find Year 9 or 10 students categorising the effects of 2-by-2 matrix transformations on two-dimensional shapes, or articulating for themselves why the gradient of a function was zero at its maximum value. Examples of this teaching approach can be found in Ollerton and Watson (2001) and Ollerton (2002). Although the project was effectively stopped by legislation introduced by the Conservative government in 1994, its long-term effects can still be found in the breadth of the criteria used for assessing mathematical coursework at GCSE level and in the international interest shown in Boaler's research study (see above).

A more recent scheme is that produced by CAME (Cognitive Acceleration in Mathematics Education), using a top-down model to introduce ways of thinking mathematically into mathematics lessons (see Adhami, 2001). By 'top-down' we mean that model lesson plans and tasks are produced by the team and offered to teachers who try them out in their own classrooms. Several of the ideas and approaches used in CAME are developed from earlier projects which involved teachers as co-developers, and the introduction of CAME into schools is sometimes a two-way process, with ideas coming from teachers as well as centrally. For example, several teachers have commented that they find themselves using typical CAME approaches in all their teaching, as if the lesson plans provided in the published materials have taken a 'cork out of the bottle' of their own imaginations. Ideally, of course, all lessons would necessarily include some interesting, thought-provoking challenges, but after over a decade of being told what to do, and with a shortage of well-qualified mathematicians entering teaching, it is not surprising that some teachers feel they need help finding a way out of getting bogged down in 'covering the curriculum'. CAME offers ways to structure whole class interaction about well-known open tasks, and also ways to open up closed tasks by identifying a network of progression through the concepts involved. Some teachers found it easier to engage with the social aspects of classroom organisation and management of interaction than the cognitive principles on which CAME is based. This illustrates a common feature of curriculum projects, that the principles which have

199

contributed to design may not be understood or seen as essential by the teachers who use it – hence the importance of teachers being actively involved in curriculum innovation as, indeed, CAME has tried to promote.

Finally, recent innovation from ground level has led to some schools reorganising their curriculum so that mathematics is taught in conjunction with science and technology. In Kingshurst City Technology College, a team approach has been developed in which cross-curricular projects (concerned with energy, structures, toys, etc.) are pursued for a significant proportion of the available time instead of separate subject teaching. The initiative was very much led and developed by teachers, but with strong support from managers and higher education advisers. Teaching and learning styles have widened, students are involved in self- and peer assessment, and are reported to be more confident and more likely to develop deep understanding. At St John's School in Wiltshire, the focus for all subjects is now 'how to learn' and mathematics teachers teach in teams to create an integrated curriculum, overlapping subject boundaries. The loss of time to concentrate on mathematical content is offset by increased time to work mathematically in broader domains, and test results have risen.

The Advisory Committee on Mathematics Education (ACME) (http://www.acme-uk.org/), which includes a practising teacher as well as mathematicians and mathematics educators involved in working with teachers, has published a report on the continuing professional development of mathematics teachers proposing the creation of a National Academy for Teachers of Mathematics. The proposal recognises that the most powerful changes are those that arise in practice, through practice, enabling individual teachers to improve their teaching with support from educators, researchers and others. As we write, there are plans to take this forward in some form, which will make the initiatives described above the norm rather than the exception. Even if this does not happen, we have shown that development and change are possible, even within a regime of prescribed content.

From the start of your career, you are involved in curriculum development every time you evaluate a lesson and change your future plans as a result. You plan your own track from a given scheme of work, using your own theories and ideas, as well as those gained from other sources, such as colleagues or publications. For instance, you might decide to approach algebra as a way to express structure throughout all your teaching, where your colleagues may teach it as generalised arithmetic or as a sequence of rules of procedure. Talking about this and comparing students' learning is a form of micro-curriculum development. This development work spreads outwards from you when you discuss ideas with colleagues, and share worksheets and activities. Further afield, you may find yourself sharing ideas on the Internet with other teachers, perhaps even from other countries. Your decisions result in your students experiencing a slightly different curriculum from that experienced by other students; you are unique and therefore have something special to offer others.

QUESTIONING THE IMPOSED CURRICULUM

Ultimately, however, we see it as a professional responsibility not just to find ways to teach very well within an imposed curriculum, but also to question the assumptions that lie behind it. Thus, in the 1960s teachers questioned the domination of academic mathematics in secondary curricula and developed their own alternative projects and examination syllabuses to provide a more holistic, meaningful experience for all students. These projects and experiments informed the Cockcroft committee and, eventually, influenced the current National Curriculum. Politicians viewed the introduction of a broad and complex system of mathematics for all with some scepticism. Early attempts to retain a sense of the complexity of the subject, rather than reduce it to a list of so-called 'basic' skills, were described as 'elaborate nonsense' by one politician (a non-mathematician) (Broadfoot and Gipps, 1996), and Margaret Thatcher objected to mathematics teachers' attempts to use their subject as a context for empowering disadvantaged students by ridiculing the phrase 'anti-racist mathematics'. In the 1990s there was a further backlash as the nation realised that it was short of mathematicians and expected to repair this by reintroducing a more formal element to the subject. Meanwhile, school students' test results at the age of 14 became a political performance indicator and several cohorts were subjected to well-funded cramming treatments, bearing little relationship to the 'using and applying' philosophy of the NC and more to the 'performance' philosophy that had preceded it. The high status of such tests inevitably reduces the range of what is taught to what can be tested. As we write, there are signs of rebellion about national testing among politicians, mental health professionals, religious leaders, parents and teachers, but there are also signs that the kinds of questions asked in the tests are becoming more and more designed to demonstrate understanding rather than merely credit performance.

In addition, there are growing numbers of teachers deciding to choose what they will teach from overfull curricula in order to ensure deeper understanding of key ideas rather than superficial coverage of many ideas. John, head of mathematics in an Australian school, decided he would teach only 60 per cent of an examination syllabus in order to create time for exploration and confidence-building. He chose the 60 per cent limit so that every student still had a very good chance of passing the exam. By doing this, he managed to persuade more girls and the less-confident boys who had previously been daunted by the speed at which difficult concepts had to be understood, to opt for further study in mathematics.

A similar tension exists in official documentation describing good teaching, which on the one hand suggests that each lesson should have a clearly stated objective, but on the other suggests that each student should develop the responsibility for independent learning. In an enquiring classroom, independent thinkers and learners can easily alter the direction of the lesson. Is the teacher supposed to ignore their ideas and continue to aim for the original objective, even when something more interesting emerges for the students? New teachers are often criticised for not following their lesson plans or alternatively for not being flexible enough! As well as observing how experienced teachers handle this tension, new teachers should be clear about what they hope students will learn during a sequence of lessons, but should also be prepared to listen and respond in individual lessons. Lessons should not be dominated by the concerns of a few students, but obviously exciting ideas can be pursued either when they arise, so long as this includes other students, or in a subsequent lesson after the teacher has had a chance to re-think the sequence, otherwise students may well give up trying to be interested or independent.

The central questions about the curriculum remain stable as answers to them fly about.

What are the aims of mathematics teaching in school? The teachers who developed 'anti-racist' approaches to mathematics clearly saw the subject as a tool to develop social and critical numerate awareness, among other things.

What mathematics is it appropriate to teach? Some see mathematics as a tool for numerate and spatially informed living, and hence would exclude aspects that are purely of intrinsic mathematical interest.

To whom should mathematics be taught? Some see proof as an example of the highest levels of thinking that mathematics can offer, and therefore it should be available to everyone to learn about it as a right. Others believe that only a few have the potential to understand it and therefore it should be kept for those who can do something with it.

We will leave these questions, as old textbook writers used to say, for the reader.

THINKING ABOUT PRACTICE

■ In the schools with which you are familiar, who decides what mathematics should be taught?

■ What opportunities for curriculum development are available in your school or area?

■ There are likely to be curriculum changes in progress as you read this book. Can these be enacted merely as changes in content, or do they challenge teaching methods at a more fundamental level?

Chapter 11

Looking forward: aspects of professional development for mathematics teachers

---

KEY QUESTIONS

- What forms can professional development take at various points in the career of a mathematics teacher?
- How is individual professional development related to the development of the mathematics curriculum and of the profession as a whole?

In the course of our professional lives, all of us continue to gain new experiences and, as we do so, we need to make sense of them and to incorporate them into our ways of thinking about teaching and learning. At some points in our lives, we will actively seek out such new experiences in order to overcome specific problems or to gain the satisfaction of facing new challenges. At other times, we will be presented with new ideas, demands and challenges by our students and colleagues or by changes in the curriculum or in government education policies. Whether we see such changes as positive opportunities or as impositions, they inevitably involve changes in our working environment and in the ways we understand our own practice. As the authors of this book, we see professional development as something that continues throughout a teacher's career. In our vision, it encompasses the development of the knowledge and skills of an individual teacher, the individual's trajectory along a path of career advancement and the development of the profession through the activities of teachers within their departments, schools and professional associations. As we will try to show, these aspects are intimately connected.

There are many paths that careers in education can take, including movement into areas that take teachers away from their subject specialism. For example, some mathematics teachers become interested in the pastoral side of teaching and follow paths that take them into counselling or responsibility for a year group. Others will make use of their management and administrative skills by taking on whole school responsibilities for timetabling, staff development or organising external examinations. Choosing to develop your career in such directions can be very fulfilling and rewarding, and clearly allows you to fulfil important functions within your school, but it is also likely to mean that you have less time to focus on mathematics. In this book, we are concerned primarily with the teaching and learning of mathematics. In this chapter, therefore, we will concentrate on those professional development opportunities and career paths that build upon your subject knowledge and expertise as a teacher of your subject. The opportunities and trajectories we will discuss should all involve deepening teachers' understanding of the processes of learning and teaching mathematics and of mathematics itself, and developing their ambition and vision to improve the learning experience for students of mathematics. For many, it will also lead to career enhancement, taking the opportunity to lead a mathematics department, to support the development of new mathematics teachers, or to develop some aspect of the mathematics curriculum within a school or as part of a local or national project.

PROFESSIONAL DEVELOPMENT OPPORTUNITIES

Opportunities for professional development occur in various different forms at all stages of a teacher's career. They include formally organised courses, and school and departmental initiatives, but they also include informal discussion and collaboration with colleagues and individual reflection, reading and experimentation. In this section, we present some examples of particular case studies of professional development and provide a commentary on each example in which we attempt to draw out the features of the case study that we feel are most important in contributing to successful professional development, both for the individuals involved and for the profession as a whole.

EXAMPLE 1: Supporting the newly qualified teacher

Anna, a newly qualified teacher (NQT), is released from school to attend a course for mathematics NQTs run by the local education authority (LEA), together with the local higher education institution (HEI). It is a welcome relief from teaching Year 8 on Wednesday afternoon! She meets and chats with the other NQTs on the course, sharing the problems and triumphs of the past weeks and finding that they are facing many of the same issues that she is. The afternoon's session focuses on strategies for teaching low-attaining students in the upper years of the secondary school. Anna, like several other teachers on the course, is facing difficulty motivating these students and coping with challenging behaviour from some of them. The adviser/tutor guides discussion of the experiences of the teachers in the group, focusing their attention on analysing why the strategies they have tried worked or did not work. The group then looks at a number of mathematical tasks that are relevant to the curriculum for this group of students, some brought by members of the group and some suggested by the adviser/tutor. They work together to consider how students might respond and adapt the tasks to make them more motivating and to take account of the need to manage student behaviour. During the following two weeks, Anna tries some of these adapted tasks with her Year 10 class. At the next meeting of the course, the session starts with a review and evaluation of this experience and those of the other course members. During the rest of the year, Anna continues to develop her strategies for working with this group. She keeps a diary, describing the strategies and reflecting on their outcomes, making connections with the discussions in the course sessions and with the reading she has done that relates to this area. This reflective diary is submitted to the HEI at the end of the year and Anna is awarded credit towards an Advanced Professional Diploma or Masters degree.

Commentary

The opportunity to share experiences is a central part, both of individual development and of the development of the communities of teachers. For a teacher like Anna, early in her career, it is perhaps even more important because of the reassurance it provides that she is not alone in the difficulties she is encountering (and the mistakes she is making). Recognising that others have similar problems and are making similar mistakes makes it possible to think more dispassionately and analytically about the situations within which they arise and about possible solution strategies, rather than feeling that the difficulties are a personal failure.

The sharing, design and evaluation of tasks for the classroom provides Anna with a wider repertoire of resources to try out with her class, but also, through the analytic discussion about the principles for adapting tasks, provides her with general strategies to apply to developing further resources. At the same time, the collaborative way in which this group of new teachers works with a more experienced member of the profession contributes to the development of shared professional values and language. The course members are being inducted into a professional community in which they not only learn from more experienced colleagues, but also play an active role in contributing to the development of mathematics teaching.

In her school department, Anna shares some of the tasks that she finds help to motivate her Year 10 students with a colleague who takes a similar class. This not only widens the potential impact of the development of mathematics teaching, but also serves to enhance Anna's position as a full participant within her department with a positive contribution to make, rather than as a dependent newcomer with 'problems'.

Anna finds it difficult to maintain a reflective diary and read what others have written about both the theoretical and practical aspects of teaching this group of students alongside her day-to-day commitments in school. As the year progresses, however, she finds that her diary provides reassuring evidence of her personal professional growth and that her reading enhances her sense of self-worth and of the teaching profession as a whole. She recognises that teaching is not just a practical activity, but one that also involves substantial intellectual engagement – not just anyone can do it! The academic credit that Anna gains at the end of the year provides an important recognition of the value of her work, as well as serving as a first step towards a qualification that may help her to gain promotion.

EXAMPLE 2: Expanding horizons for experienced teachers

Barry has been teaching mathematics for five years and has just moved to be second in department in a new school. This school has recently fitted all of its classrooms with interactive whiteboards, which none of the mathematics department have much expertise with. They have all learnt the basics of how to operate the equipment, but have few ideas about how they might be used to make a real difference to their teaching. As part of his role as second in department, Barry agrees to take on responsibility for learning more about how interactive whiteboards can be used in teaching and learning mathematics and disseminating this to other members of the department. Together with his head of department and the senior teacher in charge of continuing professional development for the whole school, Barry draws up a plan that includes attending a one-day course at a local teachers' centre. At this course he is introduced to a range of concrete ideas about how interactive whiteboards can enhance teaching and learning in a number of areas of the mathematics curriculum, using several types of software. He becomes particularly enthusiastic about the potential that the medium has for developing students' visualisation and communication skills, aspects that he is aware are underdeveloped in his own teaching. On returning to school, he decides to focus on just one of these ideas initially, using dynamic geometry to develop students' ability to form and test conjectures. He works on this with several of his classes until he feels confident, then shares it with his colleagues at a departmental meeting, demonstrating the way he has used the equipment, talking about what he was pleased with and what went wrong, and distributing copies of his lesson plans, help sheets and other resources he used with his classes. Following this meeting, Barry arranges to team teach with each of the other mathematics teachers, starting with the head of department, to help them to get started. With his own classes, he starts to use some of the other ideas offered on the course and to develop new ideas of his own. As a result of contacts with other local teachers and the LEA mathematics adviser at the teachers' centre, he joins a group of teachers from several schools, developing, trialling and evaluating activities, using interactive whiteboards across the mathematics curriculum.

Commentary

In this example, we see Barry having the opportunity to develop in several different areas. At one level, he is enhancing his personal repertoire as a classroom teacher, learning how to use a new form of technology and simultaneously working on his teaching of mathematical visualisation and communication. While the new technology was identified as a priority by his school, he was able to choose for himself the area of mathematics to apply it to, thus making the process more relevant to him and more likely to be effective in the long term.

The need to disseminate what he has learnt within his department gives Barry an opportunity for professional development at another level. He has to find ways of communicating with his new colleagues that will make them feel positive about trying out the ideas he is suggesting, as well as providing them with information and skills. The involvement of the head of department is important in this, smoothing Barry's path by demonstrating to the rest of the department that even the most experienced teacher can take on board new ways of teaching and can learn from a more junior colleague. Through this experience, Barry has a chance to develop his leadership skills and his ability to share his expertise with others, skills that will be fundamental to his further career progression, whether he chooses to take on further management responsibilities or to seek Advanced Skills Teacher status.

Involvement with a group of colleagues from different schools has important benefits not only for Barry and the other individual teachers and schools involved, but also for the development of knowledge about teaching mathematics in the profession as a whole. The dissemination and evaluation of new ideas is enhanced among the members of the local group, but there are also significant opportunities for the activities developed by the group to be shared more widely through, for example, presentations at local or national meetings of professional associations; articles describing their work published in a professional journal; the publication of a collection of resources on a website or in a pamphlet or book through the LEA, a professional association or a commercial publisher; and the provision of professional development sessions to mathematics departments in other schools or at a teachers' centre. Thus we see the strong connection between individual teacher professional development and the development of the curriculum as discussed in Chapter 10.

EXAMPLE 3: Departmental development

At Crosshill High School, prompted by the recent arrival of a significant number of students for whom English is an additional language, there is a whole school initiative to focus on developing language across the curriculum. The head of mathematics is asked to produce a departmental policy on language in mathematics, compatible with the whole school policy, and an action plan for putting this policy into practice. A whole school training day provides a number of general ideas about the support that can be provided for learners and about useful teaching approaches, but none of the examples provided are directly related to mathematics. During the afternoon of the training day, there is an opportunity for members of the mathematics department to meet together to discuss the implications and identify priorities in their subject area. They agree to focus initially on two areas: providing subject-specific support for students with English as an additional language and increasing all learners' use of mathematical language.

Before the next departmental meeting, the head of department drafts a policy and an action plan, which are discussed, amended and agreed by the department. The action plan indicates the need for time for teachers to work together and to produce resources, and for support for the department from the language support team. The school senior management team approves the plan and agrees to fund the time and support required. Work on the two development areas then progresses:

1   Providing subject-specific support for students with English as an additional language. Two of the language support team already provide some in-class support. One member of the mathematics department agrees to liaise with them and, in the first instance, to look with their help at the written materials used with Year 7 students, to identify where these students are likely to encounter difficulties and to consider strategies for addressing these. She then meets with the other five members of the department who teach Year 7 classes to share out the work of developing a pack of materials and guidance for teachers to supplement the existing scheme of work. At the end of each unit of work during the year these teachers get together with the two language support staff to review and revise what they have produced. As the year progresses, the mathematics teachers begin to be more able to identify potential problem areas independently and to plan in similar ways for their other classes, as well as for Year 7.

2   Increasing learners' use of mathematical language. All members of the department are already identifying mathematical key words in their planning and these are displayed in classrooms, but the teachers are aware that many of the students do not always use this vocabulary appropriately, either when speaking or when writing. Finding ways to encourage students to use mathematical language themselves is thus identified as one of the targets for the

department. A newly qualified member of the department had worked on this issue the previous year as part of the assessed work for his initial training course. He shares some of the practical ideas he had researched with the rest of the department. Members of the department pair up to observe each other teaching. After each observed lesson, the pair discuss the opportunities provided for learners to speak and write mathematically, and to identify ways in which these could be increased and supported. The ideas arising from these peer observations are shared at departmental meetings.

Commentary

Although this example looks as if it is about whole school development, the way in which this is organised and supported within the mathematics department and by the management of the school means that each individual teacher also has the opportunity to think about language in mathematics and to develop their teaching practice. Responsibilities are delegated among members of the department and even the most junior member of the team is seen to have something useful to offer. Another important feature of this example is the use made of the expertise of non-mathematics specialists. Establishing a dialogue between subject specialists and support staff is likely to enhance the skills of both and the experiences offered to learners. Some practical illustrations of such collaborations are given in the book *Talking Maths, Talking Languages* (ATM, 1993).

Working together with other members of the department is a central part of the development as the teachers engage in the cycle of development, trialling and evaluation of new resources, and in peer observation and discussion of each other's lessons. We see how devoting time to one aspect of the curriculum or teaching methods can have a wider effect as teachers incorporate new developments into other parts of their timetable. Opportunities for teachers to share their experiences in these ways can open their eyes to alternative ways of thinking about and teaching, and can help individuals to evaluate their own practice more effectively.

ADDRESSING SPECIFIC NEEDS AND INTERESTS

The case studies described above cannot, of course, cover all the opportunities for professional development that may be available and relevant for you at some point in your career. Many courses are offered by local education authorities or national projects, by schools that have led curriculum developments, by independent consultants, examination boards and higher education institutions. These may be suitable for individual teachers or for whole departments, and may range from as little as an evening or half a day, to two or three years of part-time study. We cannot hope to provide a full list of what may be available, but we will just mention here two areas of professional development that may be particularly relevant to many teachers at an early stage of their career or after an interruption.

Developing advanced mathematical subject knowledge. Many mathematics teachers start their first jobs inadequately prepared to teach at Advanced level, partly because there are few practical opportunities to work on this during the initial training period, but also because of gaps in their own mathematical education or a lack of confidence with some advanced topics. Indeed, very few teachers are fully prepared to teach all aspects of the curriculum at this level. As the curriculum changes, even experienced teachers may need help to top up their subject knowledge. In recent years, 'Discrete or Decision Mathematics' has been introduced into Advanced level syllabuses, and it has been found that, although this area is a popular choice for students (being of direct relevance to further studies in computer science and economics), there is a shortage of teachers who have studied it as part of their own secondary or university education. You will find that examination boards may offer support that is relevant to their own syllabuses, and some HEI also offer short courses focusing on teaching at Advanced level. Another alternative, to be followed as much because you enjoy studying mathematics as because it will enhance your ability to teach, is to enrol for courses in the mathematics department of an HEI, perhaps leading to a Masters level qualification in mathematics.

Coming to terms with changing contexts. One of the most attractive, but also most challenging, aspects of teaching is that the job does not stay the same for very long and is not the same everywhere. Whenever you move between schools you will find that you need an initial period of adaptation to re-learn some of the aspects of the job that you took for granted in your previous school. Even more learning is likely to be required, however experienced you may be, if you have taken a break from teaching for any reason or if you are coming from overseas to teach in the UK. In these cases, many LEAs and HEIs organise 'returners' courses or courses for overseas trained teachers to help you update your knowledge of the curriculum and assessment arrangements, and to become familiar with current expectations of teachers and learners.

The examples that we have provided above clearly do not encompass all the possible forms of professional development opportunity. What we have attempted to do is to indicate some of the different ways in which individual teachers may encounter and take advantage of the opportunities for development at various points in their careers. We have also tried to highlight the intimate relationship between the development of an individual teacher and the development of groups of mathematics teachers, of the profession more widely and of the quality of mathematics teaching. Teaching can sometimes feel a lonely profession, each teacher isolated in his or her own classroom. The key to personal professional development and the satisfaction that comes with this is working with fellow teachers and other professionals both within the walls of the classroom and the school, and outside the school as part of the broader community of mathematics teachers.

PROFESSIONAL TRAJECTORIES

On entering teaching, just surviving in the classroom may seem the most realistic goal. As soon as you begin to find your feet in your first appointment, however, it is likely that various opportunities will arise within your department or school to take on additional responsibilities. Alternatively, you may begin thinking about moving schools in order to gain a greater breadth of experience, to face new challenges or to gain promotion. Or you may consider starting a course to enhance your academic qualifications. It is important that you should consider these opportunities carefully, not only in order to avoid becoming overburdened, but also to think about how they might help your development along a career path that you will find personally rewarding. In this section, we consider the nature of various career paths, the skills required and challenges posed, and the satisfactions and frustrations that may be encountered. The routes we have identified are not mutually exclusive. Indeed, many teachers will have experience of some aspect of several of these areas at some point during their professional life, and some job descriptions will involve several areas at once. At various times, we, the authors of this book, have between us taken on all these roles, often being involved in more than one at the same time.

Team leadership: managing a mathematics department

Becoming head of a mathematics department is perhaps the most obvious career path for a mathematics teacher who wishes to maintain their commitment to the subject. At the time of writing, a shortage of well-qualified mathematics teachers and an aging workforce, with many nearing retirement, mean that promotion can come very quickly for new entrants to the profession. We know of talented beginning teachers who have taken on responsibility as second in department during their second year of teaching and have gained a head of department post just two years later. Other teachers will take longer before they feel ready to take on these responsibilities. In most cases, it is likely that you would be expected to take on responsibilities within the department before applying for a head of department job by, for example, developing the mathematics curriculum for low-attaining or gifted and talented students; overseeing the conduct and organisation of GCSE coursework; ordering and monitoring the use of resources; leading developments at Key Stage 3.

An important part of a head of department's role is to represent their subject within the school as a whole. This involves making a case for a share of the resources (money, staff, ICT facilities, teaching time, training, etc.) that are available centrally. It also involves participating in whole school initiatives and making sure that other members of the school community (senior management, governors, heads of other curriculum areas, etc.) are aware of and understand the role the mathematics department plays in the school, the issues faced and the resources needed. Non-mathematicians often labour under misapprehensions about teaching and learning mathematics, such as: using ICT is not a problem for mathematics teachers because they all know about computers; students aren't taught (fractions/equations/ . . .) properly nowadays because they can't do it when they come to their (science/geography/ . . .) lesson; mathematics teachers don't have to worry about (literacy/citizenship/ . . .) because all they have to teach is skills; motivating students to study mathematics is not a problem because they know they have to do it up to GCSE level.

There are, of course, administrative responsibilities that are under-taken by a head of department, but the other important part of the role that we will describe here is providing leadership and support to more junior colleagues within the department. It is impossible to list every-thing that you might do, but the job will include at least:

- keeping up to date with developments in the curriculum, both those which are imposed by changes in the National Curriculum and examinations syllabuses or by other government initiatives, and those which are being discussed and tried out by innovative mathematics teachers, and helping other members of the department to keep up to date also;
- leading development within the department, ensuring that all members of the team understand the aims and practical implications of any innovations, showing by example that change is possible and encouraging collegiality within the department;
- identifying the strengths and weaknesses of the department as a whole and of individuals within it, and working to build on the strengths and address the weaknesses;
- supporting the professional development of other members of the department, helping them to identify developmental needs and the means to address them, providing them with opportunities and encouragement to enhance their own careers.

Sharing excellent practice: curriculum support; advanced skills teaching; advisory teaching

Some teachers with a deep interest in teaching and learning are not inter-ested in or suited to the sort of management role required of a head of department. If they have good communication skills as well as successful classroom practice, there are career paths that enable them to share their expertise with other teachers. Developing the curriculum and assessment materials, schemes of work and recommended teaching approaches for a group of students with specific needs or for an aspect of the curriculum is one way in which such a teacher is likely to start making an impact within their own school. While this may be a first step towards promotion to head of department, it can also lead to advancement that is more focused on classroom practice. An advanced skills teacher is a successful classroom teacher who works alongside colleagues in her own school and in neighbouring schools to demonstrate good approaches to teaching and to help her colleagues to develop their own teaching skills. Of course, the sharing of practice is likely to happen in both directions; there is always something to be learnt from moving into new contexts and looking at your own practice from a colleague's perspective.

Advisory teachers are generally employed by an LEA to work with teachers and departments in the local area. They may work in similar ways to those used by an advanced skills teacher, but they will also act as consultants for schools, run courses for local teachers and play a leading role in disseminating and supporting new curriculum initiatives. An attractive and challenging part of this role is the opportunity it provides to work in and learn about a range of different contexts. On the other hand, some miss the responsibilities and rewards of seeing the progress made by their 'own' classes.

Innovating, developing and researching the curriculum and teaching methods

Throughout this chapter and Chapter 10 there have been examples of teachers involved in curriculum development, research and improving teaching at various different levels. Indeed, we would argue that this is something that most teachers will be involved in throughout their careers. For some, however, this can become a more substantial focus of their work. The careers described above involve practical engagement with colleagues in their classrooms, but there is also the need for people to write materials and guidance for teachers, and to trial and evaluate developments formally. Participating in these ways in curriculum development can be done alongside your classroom teaching, perhaps in collaboration with a group of colleagues under the aegis of one of the professional associations. It may involve temporary secondment from your school, perhaps funded by a research and development project based at an HEI. There are also opportunities for experienced teachers to leave the classroom to work for a project or for an organisation such as the QCA or an examination board.

You can get involved in research into mathematics education in collaboration with an HEI through school-based projects, as described in the previous chapter, or as part of a higher degree course. Some teachers find the process of research so fascinating that they seek to make this a more substantial part of their work by moving to work in an HEI, often combining research with teaching in initial teacher education and continuing professional development courses.

Looking to the future of the profession: initial teacher education

Most teachers are involved in working with new entrants to the profession at some point in their career. At the most basic level, this can mean allowing a beginning teacher to take some measure of responsibility for one of the classes on your timetable. At times, particularly if the beginning teacher is struggling, this can seem like an extra burden. Most of the time, however, it provides a valuable opportunity for your own professional development, as well as passing on your expertise to a new teacher. Helping a new colleague with their planning, observing them teaching and giving feedback afterwards all require you to articulate what you consider to be good practice and, in doing so, to reflect on what you are doing yourself, as well as on what you see. Many teachers report that they learn a lot and develop their own practice as a result of working with beginning teachers.

Taking on the role of mentor for a beginning teacher within your department has additional challenges and satisfactions. As well as coordinating with your colleagues to provide an appropriate programme for the beginning teacher, you will find an even greater need to be analytical in your thinking about teaching as you advise and induct your new colleague. When your beginning teacher has difficulties with a class, how can you help them to identify the one thing they are doing wrong or the one thing they should do to put it right? When the beginning teacher is doing well, how can you advise and help them to extend their experience and to address challenging yet manageable targets? Seeing a beginning teacher responding to your help, achieving the targets you set and developing under your guidance into a promising new colleague brings with it a real sense of achievement.

Of course, being a skilful practitioner yourself is not the same as being skilful at passing on your expertise. If your school is in partnership for initial teacher education with a higher education institution, then it is probable that the HEI provides training and support for mentors. There are also likely to be opportunities to become involved in planning and course development, and in interviewing candidates for initial teacher education (ITE) courses. For those who enjoy and are successful at this work, there is the possibility of playing a role in the HEI side of initial teacher education.

WHO CAN HELP?

Within your school

All newly qualified teachers should have a mentor within their school, part of whose job is to help identify where professional development is required and to ensure that support is provided in the form of time and appropriate forms of training. This mentor may not be a mathematics specialist so, while they should be aware of sources of generic support and training, they may not know about all the relevant opportunities for mathematics-specific development. They are also unlikely to be fully aware of subject-specific issues for a new teacher of mathematics. For guidance on these aspects, the beginning teacher and their mentor will need to turn to experienced members of the mathematics department.

For all teachers, a major source of support and development is their colleagues in their subject department. At the most basic level, everyday conversations about what happened with Year 8 today can involve: confirmation that the 'silly mistake' that half the class made is a common error, known to experienced teachers; practical suggestions of approaches to teaching the topic that have worked for others; the sharing of resources and ideas.

In many mathematics departments, an important aspect of interaction among members of the department will be enjoyment in doing mathematics; working together to find a more efficient or elegant solution to an Advanced level problem; sharing alternative approaches to the investigative task set for GCSE students; debating which student's response to this week's challenge deserves the top prize; trying to find a solution to a problem posed in one of the professional journals. Most often this is something that happens informally between colleagues, although we know of mathematics departments where doing some mathematics together is on the agenda of every departmental meeting. As well as directly supporting classroom teaching by deepening your knowledge of specific problems your students may be working on, doing mathematics with your colleagues helps to reinforce your identity as a teacher of *mathematics*. Refreshing the experience of struggling with a new problem or wondering over someone else's solution are important reminders of what learning and doing mathematics should be like for students. Maintaining your own enthusiasm for doing mathematics is vital to communicating enthusiasm to your students.

More formal types of professional development within your school department include the use of designated training days for the whole department to work together on some aspect of their practice – for example, to develop their ICT skills or to prepare for the introduction of a change to the curriculum. Whether this is led by a member of the department or by an invited outsider, it is most likely to be effective if there is some concrete action for all members to take to follow it up in practice.

It is important to remember that schools have budgets for professional development. Like other parts of school budgets, these are usually not big enough to meet all the demands made on them. However, you should be entitled to ask for financial support in the form of course fees or supply cover to help you gain the professional development you need. You will need to make a case that shows how your school will benefit, as well as how you will benefit personally. We hope that the discussion in this chapter can provide you with some of the arguments to help you make your case.

Advisory services, teachers' centres, discussion groups – real and virtual

Although provision is not uniform across the country, there are advisory services and teachers' centres in many areas, usually run by local education authorities, that provide support for individuals and departments in the form of courses, resources, guidance and advisory teachers who may work in schools alongside teachers and departments to develop specific aspects of the curriculum or of the teaching practice within the school. There are also private consultants who offer similar services.

More recent developments are Internet-based resources and discussion groups. There are some rich sources of ideas and resources, although it can be time-consuming to find them and sort out which of them are worthwhile. 'Conferences' or discussion groups such as those located at the Virtual Teachers' Centre (http://vtc.ngfl.gov.uk/, part of the government-run National Grid for Learning) provide opportunities to ask for help and to share ideas with colleagues across the country. At the time of writing, these facilities are not widely used. It seems likely, however, that various kinds of Internet sites will become an increasingly important resource for teachers.

Many beginning teachers in initial teacher education courses have found that one of the best sources of support is their fellow beginning teachers. Peer support groups, whether they are set up formally as part of a course or informally by a group of friends, whether they are organised as an Internet discussion group or as a weekly social get-together after school, are one of the most important sources of reassurance, new ideas and critical but supportive evaluation.

Higher education institutions

As well as providing initial teacher education courses in partnership with schools, HEIs offer many opportunities for continuing professional development. These include support for LEAs and school departments in the form of local courses and consultancy, as well as short courses and more substantial courses with academic credit for individual teachers. Advanced Professional Diploma and Masters level courses in education are widely available and usually combine opportunities to work on developing your own professional practice, to widen your knowledge about teaching and learning through reading and discussion, and to engage in deeper research in an area of your own choosing. As well as traditional full-time and part-time courses, HEIs are increasingly offering courses that are more flexible, using distance learning, Internet-based learning and mixed modes of attendance to make it easier for busy professionals to fit study into their lives.

Professional associations

The two main professional associations for mathematics teachers are the Association of Teachers of Mathematics (ATM) and the Mathematical Association (MA). These associations facilitate the sharing and dissemination of innovative practices and resources for teaching and learning through their journals and other publications and through their meetings.

 220

At times, they also offer specific professional development support and they have been influential in shaping the direction of curriculum reforms. Both associations hold annual national conferences during the school holiday period at which you can meet with a wide range of teachers to hear about innovative approaches to teaching, to discuss current issues, to do mathematics together and generally to think about teaching and learning mathematics in a relaxed but stimulating setting. In many areas, these associations also have local groups that meet more frequently. In addition, the ATM and the MA support working groups, bringing together small groups of teachers, mathematicians and teacher educators to work on issues of current importance to mathematics teaching. These groups may undertake some research, design curriculum resources, produce a discussion paper for wider dissemination, collect and publish ideas for lessons, and so on.

LOOKING FORWARD TO MAKING A DIFFERENCE

In this chapter we have tried to share our vision of the inextricable relationship between the development of individual teachers and the development of the curriculum, teaching and learning in mathematics departments, local areas and in the profession as a whole. Even the most basic, everyday discussion with your colleagues about what happened in today's Year 8 lesson or what to do with Year 10 tomorrow afternoon involves the sharing of experiences, knowledge about learning, insights into mathematics, ideas about teaching approaches and evaluation of all of these. This forms the bedrock of your personal development as a mathematics teacher and as a member of the community of mathematics educators. There will, however, be times in your career when your needs, interests and ambitions, those of your department or those of the wider professional community demand a more structured or supported development, focused on more specific objectives or designed to widen your perspective. We have indicated above at least some of the range of possibilities for professional development that are available to you as a teacher of mathematics and the ways in which these may interact with the development of the profession. At each stage in your career you will need to reflect on your own priorities (in relation to those of your colleagues), identify the opportunities available to you, and seek advice and support to help you achieve your goals.

Schools, their mathematics departments and classrooms, and the teachers and students within them are not isolated from society – a society whose citizens face rapidly changing conditions and challenges. Teachers entering the profession now are likely during their careers to see many changes in the curriculum and in accepted ideas about teaching and learning, as well as changes in the expectations and knowledge of the young people in their classes. Just surviving as a teacher will involve coming to terms with such changes. We hope, however, that you will want to do more than just survive. In order to do more, you have to realise that you, as an individual and as a member of the community of teachers of mathematics, can make a difference. Many teachers are motivated to enter the profession by the desire to make a difference to the lives of young people. Helping young people to learn and to be well prepared for the future is always a central part of the role of all professionals involved in education. But you can also have a wider influence, beyond the learners in your own classroom, by enhancing the quality of teaching and learning in your school or sharing this with other local teachers; supporting the initial steps of new members of the profession; raising the profile of mathematics within your school or more widely; researching and adding to what we know about teaching and learning, and disseminating this knowledge among other teachers and researchers; producing materials and guidance to help others develop their teaching; helping to influence future changes to the curriculum and to policies related to teaching and learning.

THINKING ABOUT PRACTICE

- What aspects of your professional practice and knowledge do you want to develop in the short term (this year), the medium term (the next two or three years) and the long term (the course of your career as a mathematics teacher)?
- What contribution do you envisage making to the development of the profession of mathematics teaching, within your own school and more widely?
- What sources of support (people, funding, courses) do you know are available to you now and what do you anticipate you will need in the future?

Notes

Chapter 2 Why teach mathematics? Why learn mathematics?

1 As we write, a national inquiry into mathematics at this level is considering these matters.

2 Since 2001, this project has been renamed CountOn. Its website http://www. counton.org/ is a useful source of mathematical activities and links to other sites.

3 Details of the specifications of current qualifications are available from the examination boards or from the Qualifications and Curriculum Authority http://www.qca.org.uk/.

Chapter 3 From university to school mathematics

1 Mathematicians argued that set theory was a necessary (mathematical) foundation for the number system. The study of set theory was inserted into the primary and secondary school curriculum, but it did not prove to be a good way of providing a sound basis for *learning* about the number system (especially as many teachers did not understand or believe in the philosophy behind the change). For further discussion, see Moon (1986).

2 The idea of 'accommodation' as one of the fundamental processes of learning originated in the work of the psychologist Jean Piaget. An accessible introduction to his work and to other theories of learning that are relevant to mathematics education can be found in Bloomfield and Harries, undated.

Chapter 5 Understanding learning

1 Pizzas (or cakes) sliced into equal pieces, are frequently used by teachers and textbooks as metaphors for fractions (see Chapter 4 for a discussion of metaphors as tools for learning). This may be a useful way of thinking about some aspects of fractions, but is less applicable for others and can be confusing. For example, 2 pizzas divided between 8 people may provide

meaningful imagery for the calculation $2 \div 8$, but it is not so easy to use similar imagery for the apparently similar calculation $2 \div \frac{1}{4}$.

Chapter 7 More themes in mathematics lessons: usefulness, sense and learning

1 Many charities produce educational packs that would help with this kind of work.

2 There are various commercial toys that provide similar equipment; drinking straws with pipe-cleaner joints or with rubber bands running through them can be used; 'Geostrips', available from educational suppliers, are best.

3 Of course, there are also situations in which mathematics gives accurate predictions (such as the use of formulae to predict graphical values).

4 BODMAS is an algorithm that prioritises the order of operations and is used internationally.

Chapter 8 Why assess and what to assess

1 The term 'formative' means that the assessment is part of ongoing work, informing both the student and teacher about progress. In contrast, 'summative' assessment is a summing up of what the student has learnt and can do at a particular point (usually at the end of a course or a stage of education), often providing a grade or level to describe this.

2 There has been extensive research on the systemic unfairness of timed written tests, showing that they discriminate against girls and students working in a second language (Gipps and Murphy, 1994), and that certain types of question discriminate against working-class students (Cooper and Dunne, 1998). Tests cannot take everything the student knows into account and students can be trained to take them without gaining a deep understanding of the subject.

Chapter 10 Teachers and mathematics curriculum development

1 The associations can be contacted via their websites: Association of Teachers of Mathematics: http://www.atm.org.uk/; Mathematical Association: http://www.m-a.org.uk/

References

Adhami, M. (2001) 'Responsive questioning in a mixed-ability group', *Support for Learning*, 16(1): 28–34.

Anderson, J., Goulding, M., Hatch, G., Love, E., Morgan, C., Rodd, M. and Shiu, C. (2000) 'I went to university to learn mathematics . . .', *Mathematics Teaching*, 173: 50–5.

Askew, M. and Brown, M. (eds) (2001) *Teaching and Learning Primary Numeracy: Policy, Practice and Effectiveness*, Nottingham: British Educational Research Association.

ATM (1993) *Talking Maths, Talking Languages*, Derby: Association of Teachers of Mathematics.

Barnard, T. (1995) 'The impact of meaning on students' ability to negate statements', *Proceedings of the 19th Conference of the International Group for the Psychology of Mathematics Education*, 2: 3–10, Recife, Brazil.

Black, P., Harrison, C., Lee, C., Marshall, B. and Wiliam, D. (2002) *Working Inside the Black Box*, London: Department of Education and Professional Studies, King's College London.

Blease, D. (1983) 'Teacher expectations and the self-fulfilling prophesy', *Educational Studies*, 9(1): 123–35.

Bloomfield, A. and Harries, T. (undated) 'An introduction to theories about learning in mathematics', in A. Bloomfield and T. Harries (eds) *Teaching, Learning and Mathematics: Challenging Beliefs*, Derby: Association of Teachers of Mathematics, pp. 1–22.

Boaler, J. (1997) *Experiencing School Mathematics: Teaching Styles, Sex and Setting*, Buckingham: Open University Press.

Boaler, J., Wiliam, D. and Brown, M. (2000) 'Experiences of ability grouping – disaffection, polarisation and the construction of failure', *British Educational Research Journal*, 26(5): 631–48.

Boye, A. (2002) *Some elements of history of the negative numbers*. Online. Available http://nti.educa.rcanaria.es/penelope/uk_confboye.htm (accessed 18 November 2003).

Broadfoot, P. and Gipps, C. (1996) 'Assessment developments in England and Wales: The triumph of tradition', in A. Little and A. Wolf (eds) *Assessment in Transition: Learning, Monitoring and Selection in International Perspective*, Oxford: Pergamon, pp. 134–53.

Brown, M. (1996) 'The context for research – the evolution of the National Curriculum', in D. C. Johnson and A. Millett (eds) *Implementing the Mathematics National Curriculum: Policy, Politics and Practice*, London: Paul Chapman, pp. 1–28.

Bynner, J. and Parsons, S. (2000) 'The impact of poor numeracy on employment and career progression', in C. Tikly and A. Wolf (eds) *The Maths We Need Now: Demands, Deficits and Remedies*, London: Institute of Education, pp. 26–51.

Capewell, D., Comyns, M., Flinton, G., Fowler, G., Grewal-Joy, K., Huby, D., Johnson, P., Jones, P., Kranat, J., Molyneux, I., Mullarkey, P. and Patel, N. (2002) *Framework Maths 7C*, Oxford: Oxford University Press.

Clayton, M. (1999) 'Industrial applied mathematics is changing as technology advances: What skills does mathematics education need to provide?', in C. Hoyles, C. Morgan and G. Woodhouse (eds) *Rethinking the Mathematics Curriculum*, London: Falmer Press.

Cooper, B. and Dunne, M. (1998) 'Social class, gender, equity and National Curriculum tests in mathematics', in P. Gates (ed.) *Proceedings of the First International Mathematics Education and Society Conference*, Nottingham: Centre for the Study of Mathematics Education, Nottingham University: 132–47.

Cooper, B. and Dunne, M. (2000) *Assessing Children's Mathematical Knowledge: Social Class, Sex and Problem-Solving*, Buckingham: Open University Press.

Daniels, H. (2001) *Vygotsky and Pedagogy*, London: RoutledgeFalmer.

Denvir, B. and Brown, M. (1986) 'Understanding of number concepts in low attaining 7–9 year olds: Part II. The teaching studies', *Educational Studies in Mathematics*, 17(2): 143–64.

DES (1982) *Mathematics Counts: Report of the committee of inquiry into the teaching of mathematics in schools under the chairmanship of Dr W. H. Cockcroft*, London: HMSO.

DfEE (1999) *Mathematics: The National Curriculum for England*, London: Department for Education and Employment.

DfES (2001) *Key Stage 3 National Strategy – Framework for Teaching Mathematics: Years 7, 8 and 9*, London: Department for Education and Skills.

DfES (2002) *Qualifying to Teach: Professional Standards for Qualified Teacher Status and Requirements for Initial Teacher Training*, London: Teacher Training Agency.

Dolton, P. J. and Vignoles, A. F. (2000) 'The pay-off to mathematics A level', in C. Tikly and A. Wolf (eds) *The Mathematics We Need Now: Demands, Deficits and Remedies*, London: Institute of Education, pp. 52–73.

Dweck, C. (2000) *Self-Theories: Their Role in Motivation, Personality, and Development*, Philadelphia, PA: Psychology Press.

Edexcel (2001) *Coursework Guide – Using and Applying Mathematics*, London: Edexcel.

Fauvel, J. and Gray, J. (eds) (1987) *The History of Mathematics: A Reader*, London: Macmillan.

Flannery, S. (2002) *In Code: A Mathematical Journey*, London: Profile Books.

Gardner, H. (1999) *The Disciplined Mind: What All Students Should Understand*, Cambridge, MA: Simon and Schuster.

Gerdes, P. (1988) 'On culture, geometrical thinking and mathematics education', *Educational Studies in Mathematics*, 19(2): 137–62.

Gipps, C., and Murphy, P. (1994) *A Fair Test? Assessment, Achievement and Equity*, Buckingham: Open University Press.

Hart, K. M. (ed.) (1981) *Children's Understanding of Mathematics: 11–16*, London: John Murray.

Houssart, J. (2001) 'Rival classroom discourses and inquiry mathematics: The "whisperers"', *For the Learning of Mathematics*, 21(3): 2–8.

Hoyles, C., Noss, R. and Pozzi, S. (2002) 'Proportional reasoning in nursing practice', *Journal for Research in Mathematics Education*, 32(1): 4–27.

Johnston-Wilder, S., Johnston-Wilder, P., Pimm, D. and Westwell, J. (eds) (1999) *Learning to Teach Mathematics in the Secondary School*, London: Routledge.

Joint Matriculation Board and Shell Centre for Mathematical Education (1985) *The Language of Functions and Graphs*, Nottingham: University of Nottingham.

Joseph, G. G. (1991) *The Crest of the Peacock: Non-European Roots of Mathematics*, London: Penguin.

Knijnik, G. (2000) 'O político, o social e o cultural no ato de educar matematicamente as novas gerações', in E. Fernandes and J. F. Matos (eds) *Actas do ProfMat 2000*, Funchal, Madeira: Associação de Professores de Matemática, pp. 48–58.

Lave, J. and Wenger, E. (1991) *Situated Learning: Legitimate Peripheral Participation*, Cambridge: Cambridge University Press.

MacNamara, A. and Roper, T. (1992) 'Unrecorded, unobserved and suppressed attainment: Can our pupils do more than we know?', *Mathematics in School*, 21(5): 12–13.

Marton, F. and Saljo, R. (1984) 'Approaches to learning', in F. Marton, D. Hounsell and N. Entwistle (eds) *The Experience of Learning*, Edinburgh: Scottish Academic Press.

Mason, K. and Ruddock, G. (1986) *Decimals: Assessment at Age 11 and 15*, Windsor: NFER-Nelson.

Metz, M. (1991) 'Islamic design', in L. Jones (ed.) *Mathematics and Art*, Cheltenham: Stanley Thornes, pp. 97–112.

Miller, L. D. (1992) 'Teacher benefits from using impromptu writing prompts in algebra classes', *Journal for Research in Mathematics Education*, 23(4): 329–40.

Moon, B. (1986) *The 'New Maths' Curriculum Controversy: An International Story*, Lewes: Falmer.

227

REFERENCES

Morgan, C. and Watson, A. (2002) 'The interpretative nature of teachers' assessment of pupils' mathematics: Issues for equity', *Journal for Research in Mathematics Education*, 33(2): 78–110.

Nesher, P. and Teubal, E. (1975) 'Verbal cues as an interfering factor in verbal problem solving', *Educational Studies in Mathematics*, 6: 41–51.

Nickson, M. (2000) *Teaching and Learning Mathematics: A Teacher's Guide to Recent Research and its Application*, London: Cassell Education.

Noss, R. and Hoyles, C. (1996) *Windows on Mathematical Meanings: Learning Cultures and Computers*, Dordrecht: Kluwer.

Noss, R., Hoyles, C. and Pozzi, S. (2002) 'Abstraction in expertise: A study of nurses' conceptions of concentration', *Journal for Research in Mathematics Education*, 33(3): 204–29.

Nunes, T., Schliemann, A. D. and Carraher, D. W. (1993) *Street Mathematics and School Mathematics*, Cambridge: Cambridge University Press.

Ollerton, M. (2002) *Learning Mathematics Without a Textbook*, Derby: Association of Teachers of Mathematics.

Ollerton, M. and Watson, A. (2001) *Inclusive Mathematics 11–18*, London: Continuum.

Pask, G. (1976) 'Styles and strategies of learning', *British Journal of Educational Psychology*, 46: 128–48.

Perks, P. and Prestage, S. (2002) 'Does the software change the maths? Part 2', *Micromath*, 18(2): 37–41.

Perks, P., Prestage, S. and Hewitt, D. (2002) 'Does the software change the maths? Part 1', *Micromath*, 18(1): 28–31.

Prestage, S. and Perks, P. (2001) *Adapting and Extending Secondary Mathematics Activities: New Tasks for Old*, London: David Fulton.

Schoenfeld, A. (2002) 'Making mathematics work for all children: Issues of standards, testing and equity', *Educational Researcher*, 31(1): 12–25.

Skemp, R. (1976) 'Relational and instrumental understanding', *Mathematics Teaching*, 77: 20–6.

Skovsmose, O. (1994) *Towards a Philosophy of Critical Mathematics Education*, Dordrecht: Kluwer Academic Publishers.

Tanner, H. and Jones, S. (1994) 'Using peer and self-assessment to develop modelling skills with students aged 11 to 16: A socio-constructivist view', *Educational Studies in Mathematics*, 27(4): 413–31.

Thurston, W. (1995) 'On proof and progress in mathematics', *For the Learning of Mathematics*, 15(1): 29–37.

Venkatakrishnan, H. and Wiliam, D. (2003) 'Tracking and mixed-ability grouping in secondary school mathematics classrooms: A case study', *British Educational Research Journal*, 29(2): 189–204.

von Glasersfeld, E. (1995) *Radical Constructivism: A Way of Knowing and Learning*, London: Falmer.

Vygotsky, L. (1986) *Thought and Language*, trans. A. Kozulin, Cambridge, MA: MIT Press.

Watson, A. (1997) 'Coming to know pupils: A study of informal teacher assessment of mathematics', in E. Pehkonen (ed.) *Proceedings of the 21st*

Conference of the International Group for the Psychology of Mathematics Education: Volume 4, Lahti: University of Helsinki, Lahti Research and Training Centre: 270–77.

Wiliam, D. (2001) *Level Best: Levels of Attainment in National Curriculum Assessment*, London: Association of Teachers and Lecturers.

Williams, J. S., Wake, G. D. and Boreham, N. C. (2001) 'School or college mathematics and workplace practice: An activity theory perspective', in C. Morgan and K. Jones (eds) *Research in Mathematics Education: Volume 3*, London: British Society for Research into Learning Mathematics, pp. 69–83.

Wood, D. (1998) *How Children Think and Learn*, Oxford: Blackwell.

Index